42 of my poems here

LIGHT FROM THE EAST is the first comprehensive collection of literature from the five major culture areas of the East—China, Japan, Korea, Vietnam, and India. Covering twenty centuries of Asian writing in more than two hundred selections, it places special emphasis on the modern literary contributions of these cultures and provides an invaluable understanding of what the peoples of the other side of the world think, feel, and believe today.

WILLIAM McNAUGHTON received his Ph.D. in Chinese Language and Literature from Yale in 1965. He was Assistant Professor of Chinese at Oberlin College from 1965 to 1970, and at present is Visiting Lecturer in Chinese. His books include *The Taoist Vision* (1971); *The Book of Songs* (1971); with Lenore Mayhew, *A Gold Orchid* (1972) and *As Though Dreaming* (1977); *Chinese Literature: An Anthology* (1974); *The Confucian Vision* (1974); and *Reading and Writing Chinese* (1977).

OTHER LAUREL BOOKS OF RELATED INTEREST:

THE CHINESE MACHIAVELLI
by Dennis and Ching Ping Bloodworth

800,000,000: THE REAL CHINA
by Ross Terrill

DELTA BOOKS OF RELATED INTEREST:

POEMS OF MAO TSE-TUNG
Hua-ling Nieh Engle and Paul Engle, Trs.

JAPAN: From Prehistory to Modern Times
by John Whitney Hall

THE MIND OF CHINA
by Ben-Ami Scharfstein

LIFE AND DEATH OF YUKIO MISHIMA
by Henry Scott-Stokes

LIGHT FROM the EAST

An Anthology of Asian Literature: China, Japan, Korea, Vietnam, and India

William McNaughton

A LAUREL EDITION
Published by
Dell Publishing Co., Inc.
1 Dag Hammarskjold Plaza
New York, New York 10017

ISBN: 0-440-34712-2

Printed in the United States of America

First Laurel printing—August 1978

ACKNOWLEDGMENTS

"Rats" and "Lily Bud": Reprinted by permission of the publishers from Ezra Pound, THE CLASSIC ANTHOLOGY DEFINED BY CONFUCIUS, Cambridge, Mass.: Harvard University Press, © 1954 by the President and Fellows of Harvard College.

"The Beautiful Toilet": From Ezra Pound, PERSONAE. Copyright 1926 by Ezra Pound. Reprinted by permission of New Directions Publishing Corporation.

"Moving House" by T'ao Ch'ien: From TRANSLATIONS FROM THE CHINESE by Arthur Waley. Copyright 1919 and renewed 1947 by Arthur Waley. Copyright 1941 and renewed 1969 by Alfred A. Knopf, Inc. Reprinted by permission of the publisher. Reprinted from 170 CHINESE POEMS by Arthur Waley by permission of Constable Publishers.

"The Tzu Yeh Songs": Reprinted by permission of Charles E. Tuttle Co., Inc.

"Beside Lake Yi" and "A Portrait of Ts'ui Hsing-tsung" by Wang Wei: Reprinted from POEMS OF WANG WEI by permission of the Charles E. Tuttle Co., Inc.

"A Poetic Dialogue: Wang Wei and P'ei Ti—The Creek by the Luan House" by Wang Wei: Reprinted by permission of the translator, Robert Bly.

"Old Poem" and "The Girls of Yueh" by Li Po: Copyright © 1978 by Lenore Mayhew. Used by permission of the translator.

"The River-Merchant's Wife: A Letter" by Li Po: From Ezra Pound, PERSONAE. Copyright 1926 by Ezra Pound. Reprinted by permission of New Directions Publishing Corporation.

"Another Poem on the River-Merchant's Wife" by Li Po: Copyright © 1978 by Lenore Mayhew. Used by permission of the translator.

"April" by Pak Mogwol: Reprinted by permission of Unesco from ANTHOLOGY OF KOREAN POETRY, Unesco Collection of Representative Works, English translation © Unesco 1964. Used by permission of the translator, Peter H. Lee.

"Women" by Nguyen Khuyen: Copyright © 1978 by Bill Faber. Used by permission of the translator.

"Water Ration," "Country Prison" and "Exercise Time—Permission to Walk in the Prison Yard" by Ho Chi Minh: Copyright © 1978 by Bill Faber. Used by permission of the translator.

"Story 5: Heron and Crab" and "Story 6: Lion and Hare": Reprinted from THE PANCHATANTRA translated by Franklin Egerton by permission of A. S. Barnes & Company, Inc. Reprinted by permission of Unesco. © Unesco 1965.

"Subha" by Rabindranath Tagore: Reprinted with permission of Macmillan Publishing Co., Inc., from MASHI AND OTHER STORIES by Rabindranath Tagore. Copyright 1918 by Macmillan Publishing Co., Inc., renewed 1946 by Rabindranath Tagore. Used by permission of the Trustees of the Tagore Estate and Macmillan, London and Basingstoke.

"The Barber's Trade Union" by Mulk Raj Anand: Reprinted from BARBER'S TRADE UNION AND OTHER STORIES by permission of the author.

"Karma" by Khushwant Singh: Used by permission of the author.

"Rama and Ravana in Battle" by Valmiki: From THE RAMAYANA by R. K. Narayan. Copyright © 1972 by R. K. Narayan. Reprinted by permission of the Viking Press, and the William Morris Agency, Inc.

"My Lover Is Lord of Hill Country" by Devakulathar: Copyright © 1978 by Lenore Mayhew. Used by permission of the translator.

"The Big Conch Shells are Silent" by Mangudi Marudhanar: Copyright © 1978 by Lenore Mayhew. Used by permission of the translator.

CONTENTS

PART FIVE: INDIA

INTRODUCTION

Material in this anthology is drawn from five centers of Asian civilization: China, Japan, India, Vietnam, and Korea. Reading the literature of Asians should help us understand Asian values: the way Asians think, feel, and believe; and the ways they are likely to act in varying situations. Such is the power of imaginative literature. Of course no one volume can elucidate Asia completely. But Lao-tzu, 2500 years ago, said, "The longest journey begins with a single step."

One of our Western ideals, since Homer characterized Odysseus, has been "to see many men's cities and learn their manners." A reading of Asian literature can help us fulfill this ideal. The Chinese sage Mencius said, "The scholar never steps outside his gate, yet he knows about events in the farthest corner of the world."

Marshall McLuhan interprets the great events of recent history as "dissonances" and "perturbations" created by the contact of East with West, and he describes contemporary intellectual history as "the East westernizing, and the West easternizing." If Professor McLuhan is right, it will soon be impossible to understand what is happening in our own culture without knowing something about Asia. (Indeed, I believe that time is already here.) Film has been ahead of the other arts in bringing the East to us: a number of the films most enjoyed in the West, during the past few years, have been from and about Asia, and most of them have been based on classics and masterpieces of Asian literature: *Pather Panchali, Rashomon, Ugetsu, Gate of Hell.*

Western man has for some time believed the saying: *ex oriente lux,* spiritual light comes from the East, and the current spiritual crisis of Western man has intensified that belief. The intellectual and spiritual life of the United States has been enriched and changed by light from the East for over a hundred years. Whitman, Emerson, and Thoreau all knew Oriental literary and religious classics and made use of them in their work. Many writers of modern Western literature have turned to the East for the same enlightenment. Herman Hesse and J. D. Salinger tried to put Eastern spiritual messages in an idiom contemporary Westerners could understand. e. e. cummings repudiated the mechanical world, which he so much despised, by saying it was not "in Tao."[1] T. S. Eliot's "The Wasteland" reaches its climax in a series of quotations and paraphrases from the Buddha's "Fire Sermon" and Ezra Pound based his modern epic *The Cantos* on Confucius. An interest in Asian literature is not mere exoticism.

In choosing among Asian literary works, I have been guided primarily by the question, what works are most essential to an understanding of Asian civilization? And I have tried particularly to pick works that help explain *modern* Asia. Roughly forty percent of the material included is modern. The rest, if I have succeeded, should help the reader understand the roots of modern Asia and, therefore, its future direction. The modern Chinese poem "The Bamboos" contains the lines:

> Taking up our ancestors' dreams
> again, you dismantled
> the old society.

This doesn't make much sense unless you have some idea of what the "ancestors' dreams" were. And this idea the premodern material should supply.

With this in mind, I have paid careful attention to what Asians themselves are reading now (or what their leaders are trying to get them to read). To take a single case: the Chinese literary tradition includes a number of first-rank novels. Two of them—*A Saga of the Marshes* and *A Tale of Three Kingdoms*[2]—were among Mao Tse-tung's favorite

[1] "Tao:" a central idea in the Chinese philosophy Taoism. See pp. 35–36.

[2] A reader interested in the other works can find excerpts from them in William McNaughton, ed., *Chinese Literature: An Anthology* (Rutland and Tokyo: Charles E. Tuttle Co., 1974).

works and are now being read more than ever in China. Since they help us to understand modern China better than would other novels of equal literary merit, I have chosen excerpts from them.

I have also included works that seem to me to be of special interest for some particular virtue of form. For example, as Western literature *(Ulysses, The Cantos)* tends to become more cinematographic, such Asian literary works and models as the poetic sequence, linked-verse poems, and the poetry/prose travel diary, become more important as well as more attractive to Western readers.

In making my selections I also have had in mind certain social and philosophical issues of which we have become more conscious in the last years. The Communist women's movement had as its slogan "One-half China," and few observers would deny that one of the major achievements of the present Peking government has been to advance the status of women in Chinese society and to recognize the contribution women have made to Chinese culture. The importance of that contribution—not only in China, but throughout Asia—became evident to me as I watched this collection grow and noticed both the number and quality of the work by women it included. During one period in Japanese literary history, men—who got a formal education not available to women—wrote in Chinese. It was the women, who, sticking to their own language, produced almost all of the literature worth reading now. Besides the preeminent figure of Lady Murasaki—there may not be her equal in all Japanese literature—the reader will find, in various literatures represented below, works by such women writers as Hwang Jin-i, Yosano Akiko, Mo Yun-suk, and Yi Byong-bok.[1] Any one of them is entitled to occupy a place in world literature with Jane Austen, and some, perhaps, with Sappho.

[1] Other women writers included are: the anonymous author of the Tzu Yeh songs, an anonymous woman poet of the Ming dynasty, Hu P'in-ch'ing, Lady Ise, the anonymous author of the *ko-uta* "Song," Akiko Yanagiwara, anonymous author of "The Bakery," Hong Nang, Dieu Nhan, Ho Xuan Huong, and Khirti Chaudhari. One of Yosano Akiko's poems ("The Day": see p. 241), written more than thirty years ago, has been taken up by the Women's Movement. (Many of the translations in this anthology are also done by women.)

Although there are great differences among the five Asian nations represented in this anthology, all of them are bound together by several shared religious visions and philosophical points of view. Most important of these binding forces are Confucianism, Taoism, Buddhism, and Zen Buddhism. Let us look briefly at each of them. (Hinduism, the ancient religion of India, is relevant to only one of our five countries, and therefore, will be discussed separately in a later chapter.)

CONFUCIANISM

Confucius (551–479 B.C.), called the founder of Confucianism, said: "I'm a transmitter, not an inventor." Confucius did in fact transmit the values of several generations of Chinese before him, and the vitality of Confucianism in China most probably comes from these deep roots. Confucius, or if not he, his school, also put together several literary works, including a record of Confucius's conversations, called the *Analects,* which later generations, and eventually the government itself, found useful. In time, any candidate for a prestigious and remunerative post in China's civil service, or mandarinate, had to pass a series of difficult examinations on Confucianism. Because the Chinese civil service system was imitated in Japan, Vietnam, and Korea, the examinations became both an effect and a cause of the spread of Confucianism throughout the Far East.

Confucianism is organized around what Westerners call ancestor worship, an exalted sense of family and clan. Each home has an altar on which the small ancestral tablets of dead parents are kept and honored by means of incense, prayers, etc. According to the Confucian classic, *The Book of Documents,* "The ruler is the father and mother of the common people"; the entire nation is, therefore, a great family. The ruler was supposed to "treat the common people like relatives," maintaining religious ceremonies, enforcing conservation and agricultural laws and practices, and rewarding virtue and honest talent. He was also to hold in balance cosmological forces—heavenly, earthly, and human.

Confucius once said that *shu* (usually defined by Westerners as reciprocity) was the core of his teaching. To him *shu* meant, "What you yourself do not want, do not do to the other man," and he tried to get his students to live up to the ideal of the *chün-tzu* (gentleman, superior man). The *chün-tzu* was supposed to be frank and straightforward, to be committed to the common good; to be loyal to his friends and those who had helped him; to have human feelings for others; to be trustworthy; to know the culture, and to respect social and religious forms.

The four foundations of a stable social order, as given by the Confucian philosopher Mencius (372–289 B.C.), are: 1) natural human feeling for others, graded according to one's relationship to them; 2) commitment to the common good; 3) respect for social and religious forms; and 4) a liberal education. The social order is held together by five relations: those between prince and minister; those between father and son; those between older and younger brother; those between husband and wife; and those between friend and friend. A final important point is the Confucian belief in *T'ien-ming,* or Heaven's mandate: a ruler rules because he has Heaven's mandate to rule; and if he doesn't rule well, the mandate will pass to someone else, a reflection of Heaven's will that one dynasty succeed the other. A little thought will reveal that this idea is a general justification of revolution.

TAOISM

The founder of Taoism is generally taken to be Lao-tzu (?570–? B.C.), though some scholars now believe there was no such person. But whether or not the man existed, there *is* a book, the *Tao Te Ching,* and in it, and in the writings of Chuang-tzu (365–290 B.C.), is presented a powerful and sophisticated view of life.

The trouble begins when you try to talk about that view. "If you know," said Lao-tzu, "you don't talk about it; if you talk about it, you don't know." The Taoists believe that "everything flows"; that in every situation you should watch the natural directions of that flow, and that any action you take should be in harmony with those directions. This respect for the natural directions of things tends to make the Taoists patient, and both patience and respect are combined in the Taoist concept of *wu-wei.* Many Western scholars define *wu-wei* as non-action, but I prefer to define it as anti-action —action in accord with the natural qualities of a situation.

The Taoists also talk about the Tao, which generally means (insofar as definition is possible) something like natural process. They also talk about selflike, a primary virtue for them. Other important subjects are *Te,* the effect of anti-action, or *wu-wei;* and *hsu,* or emptiness. (Chinese paintings that are mostly empty space exemplify *hsu.*) The Taoists prize such childlike qualities as naturalness and spontaneity, and such "feminine" qualities as flexibility and gentleness. This may explain their great influence on art and literature in the Far East. They are also alive to and enjoy the spontaneities of nature. Lao-tzu says, "The ten thousand things interact, and so I watch for the rebound." I suppose that that might serve, too, as a definition of one corner of *wu-wei.*

In addition to the philosophy which, against the advice of its founder, I have tried to discuss above, there is another point of view called Taoism. In order to keep them apart, we can refer to Lao-tzu's and Chuang-tzu's view as "philosophical Taoism" and to the other view as "Cultistic Taoism." "Cultistic Taoism" is much less important as philosophy; it is briefly discussed on pp. 124–125.

BUDDHISM

The religious vision known to us as Buddhism is based on the teachings of Gautama Buddha (563–483 B.C.). Buddhism was born in India, but after a comparatively short time it gave way almost completely to the older Indian religion, Hinduism; and it played its greatest role in the spiritual life of the countries into which it was transplanted, among them China, Japan, and Vietnam.

According to the Buddhist view, every physical thing, including living things, is an aggregation. Further, Buddhists believe that in time all aggregations come apart, so that no living being or physical thing has any permanence or lasting identity. To think it has, say the Buddhists, is to be the victim of illusion. All victims of this illusion are subject to the Great Chain of Causation: through birth, death, and rebirth they go on forming new aggregates in the physical universe that will, in time, come apart again. Escape from illusion, and so from the Chain of Causation, is called Nirvana, which literally means "a blowing-out," as of a candle. Though there are sectarian differences among Buddhists about the proper means to Nirvana, all of them believe that Nirvana can be achieved through the perception that the illusion *is* illusion and through moral conduct, concentration and meditation, as prescribed by the Buddha and by various Buddhist texts. The Buddha's own basic teaching is summarized in "The Four Noble Truths" and "The Eightfold Path," both of which appear here in Chapter 17. The "Five Precepts" of Buddhism enjoin the believer not to take life, including animal and insect life; not to take "what isn't given"; not to take illegal sexual pleasure; not to lie; and not to drink intoxicants.

Early Buddhism identifies three kinds of "perfected beings": Buddhas, who see the Truth and teach it; private Buddhas, who see the Truth and do not teach it; and Arhats, who learn the Truth from others (rather than see it for themselves) and teach it. Later Buddhism proposes another ideal instead of the Arhat: the Bodhisattva. A Bodhisattva is a being that has reached the threshold of Nirvana but does not step across because it wants to help others achieve Nirvana. In effect, then, the Bodhisattva is a goddess or god of mercy. This difference between Arhat and Bodhisattva is the main one between the older, or "Hinayana," Buddhism and the newer, or "Mahayana," Buddhism.

ZEN BUDDHISM

Buddhism was probably first introduced to China around A.D. 64. In the second century a number of Buddhist sutras were translated into Chinese, and late in the fourth century, ninety-eight more Buddhist scriptures were translated. In A.D. 645, the Buddhist monk Hsuan-tsang traveled to India and brought back many more scriptures. The new religion was bound to feel the influence of indigenous Chinese belief, and in fact a good rough definition of Ch'an (Japanese: "Zen") Buddhism is: Buddhism greatly influenced by Taoism. In fact Zen seems to me to be something so startling and different that I feel it requires separate treatment.

The adherents of Zen say that their doctrine is a doctrine of no words; no explanations, no instruction, and no knowledge. The aim of Zen is awakening, or enlightenment. This in itself is not so different from ordinary Buddhism. The Zen-believers, however, feel that no one can help you achieve this awakening, and their teaching is therefore directed primarily toward getting the student to achieve it for himself. D. T. Suzuki explains:

> Zen aims at the opening of satori, or at acquiring a new point of view as regards life and the universe. The Zen masters . . . are always found trying to avail themselves of every apparently trivial incident of life in order to make the disciples' minds flow into a channel hitherto altogether unperceived. It is like picking a hidden lock; the flood of new experiences gushes forth from the opening. It is again like the clock's striking the hours; when the appointed time comes it clicks, and the whole percussion of sounds is released. The mind seems to have something of this mechanism; when a certain moment is reached, a hitherto closed screen is lifted, an entirely new vista opens up, and the tone of one's whole life thereafter changes. This mental clicking or opening is called satori by the Zen masters and is insisted upon as the main object of their discipline.[1]

Throughout the history of Zen, the founders, patriarchs, and Zen masters have done or said things to which special importance has become attached, perhaps because these things illustrate the "lifting of the screen" to which Dr. Suzuki refers; or perhaps because it was felt that anecdotes about these events might induce the screen to lift in others. These anecdotes are often called *mondo*, literally "question and answer"; and in fact they are often in question-answer format, as the reader will discover in Chapter 4. Mondo may be used as part of the formal instruction of the Zen novice. In more formal use they are sometimes called "koans." "Koan" literally means "public-case." When the new monk comes to a monastery of the Rinzai sect, for example, his study usually begins when the teacher poses

[1] D. T. Suzuki, *Essays in Zen Buddhism,* First Series (New York: Harper and Brothers, 1949), p. 235.

for him one of three classic koans: (1) Chao-chou's "Moo!" (p. 141), (2) Hui-neng's "original face" (p. 138); or (3) Hakuin Zenji's (1685–1768) "What is the sound of one hand clapping?"

Some Zen students classify koans into five separate categories. In some of the formal instruction of the Rinzai sect these five categories are used as a curriculum, the koans of the first category being sort of prerequisite for koans of the second category, and so on. The first category is *hosshin* koans, the study of which is supposed to deepen the student's insight into "this, our original home" and to get the student constantly to live in it. An example is:

> Empty-handed, he holds a hoe;
> Walking, he rides a water-buffalo.[1]

The second category is *kikan* koans, through the study of which the student should come to share in "the patriarchs' marvelous realm of differentiation."[2] A famous example of *kikan* koan is Chao-chou's "cypress-tree in the front yard" (p. 142). After *hosshin* koans and *kikan* koans, the student is supposed to move on to *gonsen* koans. *Gonsen* means "the study and investigation of words." The fourth category is *nanto* koans. *Nanto* means "difficult to pass through." Wu-tsu Fa-yen's "water-buffalo" (p. 149) is a *nanto* koan. After *nanto* koans comes the fifth and final category: *goi* koans or "Five Ranks koans." The "Five Ranks koans" are seen as the culmination of the formal study of Zen. They have been called "*the* philosophy of Zen."

To some readers all these categories, hierarchies, prerequisites, and ranks may seem a bit scholastic. What would the founder of Rinzai Zen (Lin-chi) himself have thought of it all as a means of enlightenment? I wonder.

THE TRANSLATIONS

I have tried to make this an anthology of the best Asian literature, and of Asian literature in the best translation,

[1] *Cf.* Isshu Miura and Ruth Fuller Sasaki, *The Zen Koan, Its History and Use in Rinzai Zen* (New York: Harcourt, Brace and World, 1965), pp. 48–49.

[2] Miura and Sasaki, *op. cit.*, p. 49.

which means to me translations that have at least some of the beauty of the original. Among the authors represented are two Nobel Prize-winners—Yasunari Kawabata and Rabindranath Tagore—and some of the most famous figures in literary history—Li Po, Chuang-tzu, Kabir, Lady Murasaki. The translators include several National Book Award winners (some for their translations, some for their own original work), among them Robert Bly, Burton Watson, and Edward Seidensticker; one Bollingen poetry prizewinner, Ezra Pound; one Pulitzer Prize-winner, Gary Snyder; and one Nobel prizewinner, William Butler Yeats. Also among the translators are such distinguished modern writers and translators as Thomas Merton, Denise Levertov, Arthur Waley, Sir Richard Burton, Josephine Miles, L. E. Nathan, Chang Yin-nan, Lewis Walmsley, Lenore Mayhew, Vincent McHugh, C. H. Kwock, Wai-lim Yip, David Young, and Cid Corman.

I am also pleased to be able to introduce to the reader a number of gifted new translators—John Levy, R. Steve Jackson, Cynthia Hogue, Suzanne Olton, Richard Kent, and Margrit von Braun. Among this group, several are quite young, and it seems to me to bode well for our future understanding of Asia that so many talented members of the new generation have taken an interest in Asian literature and culture.

Where there has been no English translation, or no suitable modern one, for a work which I felt was essential to this anthology, I have made translations or versions myself. For example, I have translated a good bit of material from modern China, including some of Mao Tse-tung's poems; I have made my own versions of a number of important Vietnamese poems, classical and modern. Incidentally, several of the Vietnamese poems included here are by men whom contemporary Americans know better in other guises—Le Duc Tho, Xuan Thuy, Ho Chi Minh. Their work is represented because of its value in helping us understand modern Asia.

Some of the best translations from Asian literature in this century have been made by men who did not know the original language, or who did not know very much of it, but who learned how to find their way about in one or more of the principal Asian literatures. William Butler Yeats, knowing no Indian languages, worked on the Upanishads with Shree Purohit Swami. Some of Pound's finest translations of Chinese poems were done before he knew any Chinese. The poet Robert Bly, who is not a specialist in Hindi, Bengali, Chinese, or Japanese, has given us beautiful and accurate versions of Kabir, Tagore, Wang Wei, and Issa, who wrote respectively in those languages.

The anthology also includes some material that has never previously been published in English: a number of Taoist tales; war stories from the Chinese histories; anecdotes about the Zen master Lin-chi (Japanese "Rinzai"); Korean poems; Indian poems; a Vietnamese tale. In fact, the reader should find, mixed in with "classics" in the translation of Asian literature, a significant amount of completely new material.

If I have any conclusion to draw from my work, it is, to quote a famous line from the Chinese novel *A Saga of the Marshes:*

ssu hai chih nei, chieh hsiung-ti yeh

"All men are brothers."

W. McN.
Oberlin, 1977

PART ONE: CHINA

Chapter 1
CHINESE STORIES

Storytelling has flourished in China in a variety of guises—stories told by public storytellers in the marketplaces, shadow-plays, drum-songs, puppet shows. Artistic fiction, so far as we know, originated in the T'ang dynasty (A.D. 618–907), when men of letters, poets, and scholars produced a large number of excellent and powerful tales called *ch'uan ch'i,* or strange legends. But the *ch'uan ch'i* were written in classical Chinese, not in the spoken language. As a consequence their audience was limited, and their tradition was not dynamic.

The dynamic tradition in Chinese stories belonged to the public storytellers. They used the speech of the day: they had to if they wanted to attract a crowd in the marketplace. In the Sung dynasty (A.D. 960–1279), as the commercial revolution brought leisure and some education to an increasing number of people outside the government bureaucracy, the texts that the public storytellers had been using began to have a market as books, printed, published, and preserved in versions that clearly reveal their origin. In fact the Chinese name for this kind of fiction is *hua-pen,* which means promptbook, and that is exactly what they were—the texts the public storyteller used to prompt him as he worked.

A promptbook story begins with an introduction only very loosely related to the main story. The introduction may be a poem or poems; a little speech on the moral of the story-to-come; two or three other stories that are related to the main story in some way, perhaps in having the same moral; the introduction may even be in the form of a discussion of several poems. The public storyteller needed the introduction to attract his audience and to give it a chance to settle down before he began the main story. The promptbook stories also are full of storyteller phrases—

remarks made directly to the audience: "Now keep your ears clean, I have something important to say," or, "How would you say he was dressed?" The storytellers also liked to introduce poems, sometimes by well-known poets, into the story for various artistic purposes of delay, intensification, and the like.

Besides being a good example of the *hua-pen* form, "The Story of a Braggart" introduces the reader to the Amazon, or heroic woman, a type popular in Chinese lore. The theaters in Taiwan are filled with swordsman films, and the heroes of over half of them (by rough estimate) are women.

In modern times Chinese stories have been much influenced by Western fiction. The first literary productions of Lu Hsun (1881–1936), considered by many to be China's greatest modern writer, were translations of Western fiction.

There are also in this chapter some revolutionary memoirs by Chang Chin-hsi. This material sits on the borderline—often a very thin line in Chinese literature—between history and fiction. One of the main publishing efforts of the present Chinese government has been to produce a history of the Chinese revolution as recalled by the ordinary men and women who lived through it. Behind this is the belief that "the collective memory is valid as history."[1] In the mid-fifties the China Youth Press invited the general public to submit revolutionary memoirs, stories of the revolution and of their experience in it. The material selected by the press was published in sixteen volumes between 1957 and 1961, under the title *The Red Flag Waves*. It is from this work that Chang Chin-hsi's recollections are taken. None of this material has, to my knowledge, appeared in English before.

The materials in *The Red Flag Waves* are valuable not only as history, but also as ways of learning about the contemporary Chinese state of mind. They are as valuable for this, I believe, as any imaginative literature. Though memoirs, these materials in certain ways resemble imaginative literature by including conversations of twenty-five years

[1] See Robert Rinden and Roxane Witke, *The Red Flag Waves: A Guide to the Hung-ch'i p'iao-p'iao Collection* (Berkeley: Center for Chinese Studies, 1968), p. 9.

ago, tiny incidents, insignificant facts reconstructed in detail, without notes or other aids to the memory. These materials, conceived by an official publishing house as an object of study and as a surrogate for real revolutionary experience, broke the professional historian's monopoly on history. The only professional influence was in the interaction of editor with writer.

Ling Meng-ch'u

(1580–1644)

THE STORY OF A BRAGGART

'Tis not a creature's size alone
That makes it weak or strong;
A centipede can kill a snake,
Although it is not long.

Since no creature in the world is without a rival, none should boast of its size or strength. In South China there are huge pythons, hundreds of feet long, which feed on human flesh; so all the natives there keep centipedes, the largest of them over a foot in length. They shut these centipedes up within or beside their hard, hollow pillows; for when a python approaches a centipede will make a harsh, rustling sound and once let out, will arch its back and leap ten feet to grip the great snake's neck like a vise and suck its lifeblood till the python dies. Thus a monster hundreds of feet long and thick as a barrel is killed by a creature one foot long and no thicker than a finger, as witness the ancient saying: A centipede can kill a python.

Or take the following story. In the third year of the Cheng Ho period of the Han Dynasty (90 B.C.), a king of the Massagetae in the west presented Emperor Wu with a wild beast. It had a yellow tail and was something like a two-month-old puppy, being roughly the size of a wildcat. When the envoy carried this animal in to present it, and the emperor saw how puny it looked, he laughed.

"Do you call this a wild beast?" he demanded. "Let me hear it bark."

The envoy raised one finger, whereupon the beast licked its chops, tossed its head and let out a roar like a thunderclap, its eyes flickering lightning. The emperor fell off his golden throne, while his attendants and imperial guards dropped to their knees, all the weapons in their hands clattering to the ground. Very much annoyed, Emperor Wu ordered the beast to be taken to the imperial park and thrown to the tigers; and the warden of the park accordingly carried it there and set it down by the tigers' den. But when the tigers saw it, they shrank back fearfully, then fell on their knees before it; and when the warden reported this, the emperor became angrier than ever and swore to have the beast killed. By the next day, however, both envoy and beast had vanished.

As for men, there is no limit to their strength or skill. A strong man may always meet another stronger than himself. There was once a scholar, whose name and native place I have forgotten, who had remarkable strength, excelled in military arts, and had always championed those in distress. Going to the capital for an examination, he took no servant with him but relied on his own strength and skill, riding alone on a good steed and carrying his dagger, bow, and arrows at his waist. On the way he hunted game to eat with his wine at the taverns where he rested. One day, as he was traveling through Shantung, his horse galloped so fast that he passed the usual stage; and upon reaching a village as night fell, he decided to stop there. Noticing a house with its gate ajar and lamplight shining out, he alighted and led his horse inside to a large courtyard empty but for three or four boulders from Lake Taihu, with three rooms at the far end and another on each side. An old woman was sitting in the middle spinning flax; but she stood up at the sound of a horse's hooves and asked the stranger his business.

"I've lost my way, ma'am," called the scholar. "I want to beg a lodging for the night."

"I don't think I can put you up, sir," she replied. "It's not for me to say."

A note of sadness in her voice puzzled the scholar.

"Where have the men of your house gone, ma'am?" he asked. "Why are you alone here?"

"I'm an old widow, and my only son is a traveling merchant."

"Have you no daughter-in-law?"

A shadow passed over the old woman's face.

"I have a daughter-in-law who is a match for any man and well able to manage a house," she answered. "But she's a great, strapping termagant with a fiery temper. The least little thing will make her fly into a rage, and she can knock me down with one finger. Although I hold my breath and watch my step, she is always finding fault with me and bullying me. That's why, when you asked to stay, I told you I couldn't decide."

When she had said this, her tears fell like rain.

The scholar frowned indignantly.

"Can such a thing be?" he cried. "Where is this shrew? I'll soon rid you of her."

He tethered his horse to a boulder and drew his sword.

"Don't attempt the impossible, sir," said the old woman. "My daughter-in-law is terrible once she's roused. She knows nothing of sewing, but goes out every day after the noonday meal to catch deer or rabbit in the hills with her bare hands, then cures the game she brings back and sells it for a few strings of cash. She often doesn't get home till late at night. If not for the money she brings in, we couldn't make ends meet; so I dare not offend her."

At that the scholar sheathed his sword again.

"All my life I have challenged the strong, championed the weak, and helped those in distress," he declared. "A mere woman should be easy to deal with. But since you depend on her to support you, ma'am, I won't kill her. I'll just give her a sound beating to teach her to mend her ways."

"She will be back soon, sir," said the old woman. "I hope you'll be careful."

The scholar waited in great indignation till a huge shadowy form came through the gate and a heavy load was thrown down in the courtyard.

"Fetch a light, old woman!" someone shouted. "And take this in."

"What fine beast have you caught this time?" quavered the old dame.

She shone her lamp on it, then gave a start; for the dead beast was a huge tiger with beautiful stripes. When the scholar's horse saw the tiger, it reared in terror; and the young woman asked:

"Where does that horse come from?"

Dark as it was, the scholar could see that she was tall and swarthy; and she had carried a tiger home on her back.

"She seems a very powerful woman," he thought with dismay.

So he hastily led his horse to one side and tethered it again, then stepped forward.

"I am a scholar who has lost his way," he said. "After passing the usual stage, I was lucky enough to reach your honorable village; and when I saw your gate was not locked, I made bold to ask for a night's lodging."

"You must excuse my mother-in-law," said the young woman with a laugh. "How could she keep a distinguished guest standing outside so late at night?" Then she pointed to the dead tiger. "I came across this wild cat in the hills today and struggled with it for a long time before I killed it," she explained. "That's why I am late. I have been very remiss as a hostess; but I hope our honorable guest will overlook it."

She spoke so frankly and politely that he thought: "This woman must be amenable to reason."

And aloud he replied: "Not at all, not at all."

The woman went inside and brought out a chair.

"I would ask you in," she said, "but it is not fitting for men and women to mix; so I must ask you to sit in the corridor."

She set a table before him, lit a lamp, and put it on the table, then picked up the dead tiger in the courtyard and carried it to the kitchen. After a short time she reappeared with a pot of warm wine, an enormous dish of steaming tiger meat, another of salted venison, and several plates of pheasant, hare, and other cured game.

"Please don't take offense, sir," she requested him, "at our humble fare."

Impressed by her courtesy, the young man poured himself wine and drank; and presently, when he had finished the meal, he raised clasped hands in salutation.

"Thank you for such a feast," he said.

"You cover us with shame," she replied.

When she brought a tray to clear away the dishes, the scholar seized the opportunity to speak to her.

"How is it," he inquired, "that one as brave and intelligent as yourself is a little lacking in respect to your elders?"

When the young woman heard this, she plumped the tray down and stopped clearing the table.

"What has that old witch been saying to you?" she demanded angrily.

"Nothing, nothing!" the scholar explained hastily. "I just felt your manner to her showed a certain lack of respect, and was not quite what one would expect from a daughter-in-law toward her mother-in-law. And seeing how well you treat your guests and how able and reasonable you appear, I ventured to raise the point."

Seizing the lapel of his coat with one hand and the lamp with the other, the young woman marched him over to the boulders.

"Stand there!" she ordered. "I have something to tell you."

The scholar could not get away, but he promised himself:

"If she fails to justify her attitude, I'll give her a good beating."

Then the young woman patted the rock against which she was leaning.

"Listen to what happened the other day," she said, "and say which of us was in the right."

She described a disagreement she had had with her mother-in-law.

"That's one case," she told him.

Then, as she traced a line with her finger on the boulder, rock splinters flew up and a groove more than one inch deep appeared. She enumerated three incidents and traced three lines, each of them over an inch deep, as if carved out with a chisel. The scholar turned crimson and sweated with fright.

"You were right each time, ma'am," he stammered. "You were right each time."

His brave scheme to correct her had vanished completely. As if doused with a bucket of icy water, he scarcely dared breathe. After the young woman had had her say, she brought out a couch for the scholar and fed his horse, then went in, locked the door of the room she shared with the old woman, put out the light, and slept. But the scholar could not sleep a wink all night.

"What strength!" he marveled. "It's a good thing I didn't come to blows with her. Otherwise that would have been the end of me."

When dawn broke he saddled his horse, thanked his hostess, and left without another word. And never again dared he give himself airs or meddle with other people's affairs, for fear he might be worsted by someone stronger than himself.

I shall tell you now of another man who, because he boasted of his ability, received a bad fright and made a fool of himself.

The tiger lords it in the woods,
And savage beasts before it fall;
But if a lion's roar is heard,
The tiger is no use at all.

During the Chia Ching period (1522–1566), there lived in Chiaoho County, Chihli Province, a man named Liu Tung-shan, a sergeant in the Peking police force who had mastered all military arts and was a fine archer and horseman. Because his arrows always found their mark, he was famed for his bowmanship; and however fierce a bandit might be, Liu would catch him as easily as a turtle in a jar. So he gradually became a man of substance, and after he was thirty he resigned from the police service, of which he was tired, to become a horse-dealer.

Toward the end of that year, having driven a dozen donkeys and horses to the capital and sold them for more than a hundred taels of silver, Liu went to Hsuanwu Gate to hire a donkey to ride home. In the hostelry attached to the stables he met a neighbor named Chang, who had also come to the capital; and they had a meal together.

"Where are you off to?" asked Chang.

"I've come to hire a donkey," replied Liu, after telling Chang of his successful transaction. "I shall spend the night here and start home tomorrow."

"Traveling has been difficult recently," said Chang. "There are highwaymen near Lianghsiang and Chengchow who rob travelers in broad daylight; and you are carrying a good deal of silver and riding alone. You had better be careful."

When Liu heard this he smiled all over his face, clenched his fists and went through the motions of drawing a bow.

"In twenty years I have never met an archer who's a match for me," he declared with a hearty laugh. "I shan't lose any money on this trip, I promise you."

He spoke so loudly that everyone in the tavern turned to look, and some asked his name or murmured their admiration. But Chang, conscious that he had spoken tactlessly, took his leave.

Liu slept till the fifth watch the next morning, when he washed and dressed, bound his silver tightly round his waist under his jacket, slung his bow on his back, girded on a sword, and stowed twenty arrows in his high boots. Then he picked a sturdy mule, leapt on its back, and with a flick of his whip was off. After about a dozen miles he reached Lianghsiang, where he was overtaken by a rider who reined in his horse as soon as he came up with Liu. This horseman was a handsome, well-dressed youth of twenty or thereabouts.

> He was armed with a sword and a bow,
> Had a hat made of felt on his head,
> Had a score of new shafts on his back,
> While his horse wore a tassel of red,
> His fine shirt was of bright yellow silk,
> 'Twas a handsome young horsemen indeed!
> And his mount pawed the ground as it neighed,
> For his beast was a mettlesome steed.

As Liu gazed at him, the young man called out: "Shall we travel together, sir?"

Then he clasped his hands in salute, and added: "May I ask your name?"

"Liu Tung-shan, at your service."

"I have long heard of your great fame, sir; and I am fortunate to have met you. Where are you going?"

"I am going home to Chiaoho."

"What luck for me! I come from a scholar's family in Lingchih, and studied the classics as a boy; but I was so fond of shooting and riding that I gave up book learning.

Three years ago I took some capital to Peking to set up in business, and did not do so badly; so now I am going home to get married. If I can have your company on the road, sir, I shall feel much safer; and we can travel together as far as Hochien. Fate has been kind to me."

Since this youth had a well-lined purse, and was soft of speech, handsome and slight, Liu felt that he could not be a bad character. And he was only too glad to have a companion on the road.

"I shall be delighted to accompany you," he said.

That evening they put up in the same inn, dined together, slept in one room, and felt as close to each other as brothers. As they rode side by side out of Chuochow the next day, the young man said:

"You have a great reputation for capturing bandits, sir. May I ask how many you have caught, and whether you met any brave fellows?"

Liu was just waiting for an opportunity to boast of his skill, so this question proved an irresistible temptation; and, since his companion was young and green, he began to brag.

"With this bow and these two hands I have caught more bandits than I can count," he declared. "But I never met a worthy opponent. Rats like that are nothing to me. Because I'm past my youth now and prefer a quiet life, I've left my old profession; but if we come across any highwaymen on the road, I'll catch a couple to show you how to do it."

The young man gave a faint smile.

"You don't say so," he murmured.

Then, leaning over from his saddle, he stretched out his hand.

"May I have a look at your bow?" he asked.

When Liu passed it over from his mule, the young man took the bow in his left hand and drew it to its full extent with his right, bending it several times in succession as effortlessly as if it were soft string. Liu changed color in amazement, then asked to look at the young man's bow. This bow weighed about twenty pounds, and, though Liu tugged and strained till he was purple in the face, he could not even bend it into the shape of a crescent moon. He thrust out his tongue in dismay.

"What a strong bow!" he cried. "What amazing strength you must have! I cannot begin to compare with you."

"I am not particularly strong," replied the youth. "But your bow is too soft."

Liu was loud in his praise, while the young man modestly disclaimed his compliments.

After lodging in one inn that night they set off together again the next day; but when they were passing Hsiung-hsien and the sun was sinking in the west, the young man suddenly spurred his steed and galloped forward as if he had wings, until Liu could see him no more. The former police sergeant, who had much experience of bandits, was naturally alarmed.

"I'm in for it now," he thought, "if this is a bad man. How can I defend myself against such wonderful strength? I shall never escape with my life."

Although his heart was going pit-a-pat, he had to press on. And after he had ridden another two stages he saw the young man some hundred yards ahead, with an arrow fitted to his bow, which was bent like a full moon.

"You say you have never met your match," cried the youth. "Listen to my arrows now!"

While he was still speaking, arrows started whistling past Liu's ears like little birds skimming by. But not one of them touched him. Then the young man put another arrow to his bow and aimed at Liu's face.

"You are an intelligent man," he said with a laugh. "Hurry up and give me that money for your donkeys and horses before I shoot."

Aware that he was no match for this youth, Liu tumbled down from his saddle in a panic, untied the bag of silver at his waist and went down on his knees to offer it with both hands.

"Take my money," he said, kowtowing. "But spare my life!"

The young man reached down from his horse to take the bag.

"Who wants your life?" he shouted. "Be off with you now! I have business here; so I can't go with you, my little fellow."

He turned his horse's head and made off northward like a streak of smoke. Yellow dust sprang up behind him and soon he was lost from sight. After standing like one stupefied for some time, Liu started beating his breast and stamping his feet.

"I don't mind losing the silver, but how can I hold up my head after this?" he raged. "My reputation will be ruined. Curse it!"

Thoroughly crestfallen, he shambled empty-handed back to his home in Chiaoho, where he told his wife what had happened and she lamented with him. Then they decided to raise enough capital to open a tavern outside the city. Liu stopped going about with bow and arrows and dared not mention his misadventure either, for fear that the story might spread and spoil his good name.

One cold winter day three years later, Liu and his wife were selling wine in their tavern when eleven horsemen stopped at the door. Mounted on fine horses richly caparisoned, they were dressed in doublets and armed with bows, arrows, and swords. Alighting one after another, they unsaddled their steeds and entered the tavern, while Liu took the saddles and led the horses to his stable.

One of the horsemen, a lad of fifteen or sixteen who was over six foot tall, did not dismount.

"I shall go into the house opposite," he told the rest.

"We shall come presently to wait on you," they replied.

When the lad had left, the ten men started drinking; and Liu prepared chicken, pork, beef, and mutton for them. They fell to with appetite, and soon finished nearly seventy pounds of meat and seven jars of wine, then bid Liu send wine and food to the lad in the house opposite. All this food and wine was still too little for them, however; so they opened their leather bags and took out deer trotters, pheasant, roast hare, and other game.

"This is our contribution," they told Liu with a laugh. "Come and join us."

Liu declined, but sat down at their table to watch them. He was glancing at a man with a felt hat hiding his face in the left-hand corner, when the fellow suddenly raised his head. Then Liu, frightened almost out of his wits, moaned in terror. For this was the young man who had robbed him at Hsiunghsien.

"This is the end!" he thought. "How is the little money I've got going to satisfy them? Last time one man proved more than a match for me; and now there are ten of them, no doubt all equally powerful. What can I do?"

His heart thumping, he stared wretchedly into his wine

cup, not daring to say a word. But presently they all stood up and asked him to drink.

"How have you been since last I saw you, Mr. Liu?" called the young man on the left, pushing back his felt hat. "I appreciated your company and help last time we met, and I have never forgotten you."

Turning pale, Liu fell on his knees.

"Spare me!" he cried.

The young man leapt from his seat, raised Liu up and took him by the hand.

"This will never do!" he said. "When we overheard you that day in the tavern by Hsuanwu Gate boasting of your skill and claiming that no one was a match for you, we felt indignant; and my friends told me to play a trick on you. But I broke my promise to go to Hochien with you, and I have often remembered how we traveled together and felt grateful for your kindness. Now I must repay you tenfold."

He took one thousand taels of silver from his bag and put them on the table.

"Please accept this trifle as a token of my esteem."

Sure that he must be dreaming, Liu looked stunned for a moment.

"You are joking," he said at last. "I can't take that."

Seeing his bewilderment, the young man clapped his hands encouragingly.

"How can a gentleman lie?" he demanded. "You are a stout fellow, too—why should you be so timid? Do you think we really need your money? Hurry up and take it."

Hearing this, Liu realized that he was sincere; and, like one waking from a dream, he dared no longer refuse but went in and told his wife, bidding her help him carry the silver inside. This done, he discussed with her what to do.

"These gallants have been so generous that we must treat them well," he said. "Let us slaughter some pigs, open some more jars of wine, and ask them to stay here for a few days."

When Liu returned to the outer room to express his thanks, he conveyed this wish to the young man, who told the rest.

"Since this is an old friend, why not stay?" they said. "But we must ask permission."

Then they went across the road to speak to the lad in the

house opposite. Liu, who accompanied them, noticed that they treated the boy with great deference, while he for his part behaved with great dignity.

"Very well," said the boy, when they had explained that the tavern-keeper wanted to keep them for a few days. "But mind you don't sleep too soundly after feasting, and show due consideration for your host. If I hear the least brawling, the two daggers at my side will taste blood."

"We understand," they replied, although Liu was puzzled.

Returning to his tavern, they fell to drinking heartily again and sent more wine to the house opposite. The ten men did not keep the lad company, however, but left him to eat and drink alone; and he consumed five times more than any of them. Then, smiling, the lad took a silver ladle from his bag, relit the stove and made himself pancakes. After eating about a hundred pancakes he cleared the table and strode out; but where he went Liu did not know. He came back, however, that evening and lodged in the house opposite, without entering the tavern. The other men feasted and enjoyed themselves with Liu; and whenever they went across the street to see the boy, he said very little to them and carried himself haughtily. To satisfy his curiosity, Liu privately questioned the man he had met before.

"Who is your young leader?"

Instead of answering, the young man repeated the question to the others, and they laughed but did not reply. After two days they packed up, mounted their horses, and cantered off, the lad riding in front and the others following behind, leaving Liu as mystified as ever.

Now that he was comfortably off, thanks to the thousand taels of silver, Liu felt insecure in his tavern and moved into the city to set up in business. Later, when he told others his story, some said that the lad was obviously the leader of the band; but judging by his behavior he was afraid lest there might be a plot against them and therefore stayed in the house opposite where he could keep an eye on things. That he did not eat with the others simply showed that he was their superior. And when he went out at night by himself he was obviously on some secret mission; but, of course, there was no way of knowing what it was. After this, Liu, who had always boasted of his strength and skill, stopped talking about military arts and laid aside his bow and arrows to become a respectable citizen, living to a ripe old age.

And the moral of the story is that man should not set too much store by his strength or ability; for his fancied superiority means only that he has not yet met his master.

Yang Hsien-yi and Gladys Yang

Lu Hsun
(1881–1936)

Lu was a member of the editorial board of the influential magazine *New Youth* and in 1930 helped organize the China League of Left-Wing Writers.

IN THE WINE SHOP

During my travels from the North to the Southeast I made a detour to visit my home, then to S——. This town is only about ten miles from my native place, and can be reached in less than half a day by a small boat. I had taught school here for a year. In the depth of winter, after snow, the landscape was chilly. Indolence and nostalgia combined finally made me put up for a short time in Lo Szu Hotel—a hotel which had not been there before. The town was small. I looked for several old colleagues I thought I might find, but not one was there, having long since gone their different ways. And when I passed the gate of the school, that too had changed its name and appearance, making me feel quite a stranger. In less than two hours my enthusiasm had waned, and I rather reproached myself for coming.

The hotel in which I stayed let rooms but did not supply meals; rice and dishes could be ordered from outside, but they were quite unpalatable, tasting like mud. Outside the window was only a stained and spotted wall, covered with withered moss. Above was the slaty sky, dead white without any coloring; moreover a light flurry of snow had begun to fall. I had had a poor lunch to begin with, and had nothing to do to while away the time, so quite naturally I thought of a small wine shop I had known very well in the old days, called "One Barrel House," which, I reckoned, could not be far from the hotel. I immediately locked the door of my room and set out for the wine shop. Actually all I wanted was to escape the boredom of my stay, I did not really want to drink. "One Barrel House" was still there, its narrow, moldering shop front and dilapidated signboard unchanged. But from the accountant down to the waiter there was not a single person I knew—in "One Barrel House" too I had become a complete stranger. Still I walked up the familiar flight of stairs in the corner of the room, and so reached the little upper story. Up here there were still the same five small wooden tables, unchanged. Only the back window, which had originally had a wooden lattice, had been fitted with glass panes.

"A pint of yellow wine. Dishes? Ten slices of fried bean-curd, with plenty of pepper sauce!"

As I gave the order to the waiter who had come up with me, I walked to the back and sat down at the table by the window. This upstairs room was absolutely empty, enabling me to take possession of the best seat from which one could look out onto the deserted courtyard beneath. The courtyard probably did not belong to the wine shop. I had looked out at it many times before in the past, sometimes too in snowy weather. But now, to eyes accustomed to the North, the sight was sufficiently striking: several old plum trees were actually in full blossom to rival the snow, as if entirely oblivious of winter; while beside the crumbling pavilion there was still a camellia with a dozen crimson blossoms standing out against its thick, dark green foliage, blazing in the snow as bright as fire, indignant and arrogant, as if despising the wanderer's wanderlust. And then I suddenly remembered the moistness of the heaped snow here, clinging, glistening and shining, quite unlike the dry northern snow, which, when a high wind blows, will fly up and fill the sky like mist. . . .

"Your wine, sir . . ." said the waiter carelessly, and put down the cup, chopsticks, wine pot and dish. The wine had come. I turned to the table, set right the utensils and filled my cup. I felt that the North was certainly not my home, and yet when I came South I could only count as a stranger. The dry snow up there, which flew like powder, and the soft snow here, which clung lingeringly, both seemed equally alien to me. In a slightly melancholy mood, I took a leisurely sip of wine. The wine was quite pure, the fried beancurd was also excellently cooked. The only pity was that the pepper sauce was too thin but then the people of S—— had never understood pungent flavors.

Probably because it was only afternoon, the place had none of the atmosphere of a wine shop. I had already drunk three cups of wine, but apart from myself there were still only four empty wooden tables in the place. Looking at the deserted courtyard, I began to feel lonely, yet I did not want any other customers to come up. Therefore when now and then I heard the sound of footsteps on the stairs I could not help feeling displeased, and was relieved to find it was only the waiter. And so I drank another two cups of wine.

"This time it must be a customer," I thought, for the footsteps sounded much slower than those of the waiter. When I judged that he must be at the top of the stairs, I raised my head rather apprehensively to look at this unwelcome company, then gave a start and stood up. I could never have guessed that here of all places I should unexpectedly meet a friend—if such he would still allow me to call him. The newcomer was an old classmate who had been my colleague when I was a teacher, and although he had changed a great deal I knew him as soon as I saw him. Only he had become much slower in his movements, very unlike the nimble and active Lu Wei-fu of the old days.

"Ah, Wei-fu, is it you? I never expected to meet you here."

"Oh, it's you? Neither did I ever . . ."

I urged him to join me, but only after some hesitation did he seem willing to sit down. I thought this very strange, and felt rather hurt and displeased. When one looked closely at him he had still the same disorderly hair and pale oblong face, but he was thinner. He looked very quiet, or perhaps dispirited, and his eyes beneath their thick black brows had lost their alertness; but when he looked slowly around in the direction of the deserted courtyard he suddenly flashed out one of those piercing looks which I had seen so often at school.

"Well," I said cheerfully but somewhat awkwardly, "we

have not seen each other now for more than ten years. I heard long ago that you were at Tsinan, but I was so wretchedly lazy I never wrote. . . ."

"I was just the same. I have been at Taiyuan for more than two years now, with my mother. When I came back to fetch her I learned that you had already left, left for good and all."

"What are you doing at Taiyuan?" I asked.

"Teaching in the family of a fellow provincial."

"And before that?"

"Before that?" He took a cigarette from his pocket, lit it and put it in his mouth, watching the smoke he puffed out, then said reflectively, "Simply futile work, equivalent to doing nothing at all."

He also asked what had happened to me since we separated. I gave him a rough idea, at the same time calling the waiter to bring a cup and chopsticks, so that he could first share my wine, after which we would have another two pints heated. We also ordered dishes. In the past we had never stood on ceremony, but now we began to be so formal no one could say which dish was chosen by whom, and finally we fixed on four suggested by the waiter: fried beans, cold meat, fried beancurd, fried fish.

"As soon as I came back I knew I was a fool." Holding his cigarette in one hand and the wine-cup in the other, he spoke with a bitter smile. "When I was young and saw bees or flies stopping in one place, I would find some means to frighten them so that they flew off, but after flying in a small circle they would come back again to stop in the same place; and I thought this really very foolish, and also pathetic. But I didn't think that I would have flown back, too, myself, after only flying in a small circle. And I didn't think you would have come back either. Couldn't you have flown a little further?"

"That's difficult to say. Probably I, too, have simply flown in a small circle." I also spoke with a rather bitter smile. "But why did you fly back?"

"For something quite futile." In one gulp he emptied his cup, then took several pulls at his cigarette, and opened his eyes a little wider. "Futile—but you may as well hear about it."

The waiter brought up the freshly heated wine and dishes, and set them on the table. The upstairs room, warmed with smoke and the fragrance of fried beancurd, seemed to become more cheerful, while outside the snow fell still more thickly.

"Perhaps you knew before," he went on, "I had a little brother who died when he was three, and was buried in the country here. I can't even remember clearly what he looked like, but I have heard my mother say he was a very lovable child, and very fond of me. Even now it brings tears to her eyes to speak of him. This spring an elder cousin wrote to tell us that the ground beside his grave was gradually being swamped, and he was afraid before long it would slip into the river: we should go at once and do something about it. As soon as my mother knew this, she became very upset, and couldn't sleep for several nights—she can read letters herself. But what could I do? I had no money, no time: there was nothing that could be done. Only now, by taking advantage of my New Year's holiday, have I been able to come South to move his grave." He drained another cup of wine, looked out of the window and exclaimed: "Could you find anything like this up North? Flowers in thick snow, and beneath the snow not frozen. So the day before yesterday I bought a small coffin, because I reckoned that the one under the ground must have rotted long ago—I took cotton and bedding, hired four workmen, and went into the country to move his grave. At the time I suddenly felt very happy, eager to dig up the grave, eager to see the body of the little brother who had been so fond of me: this was a new sensation for me. When we reached the grave, sure enough, the river water was encroaching on it and already only about two feet away. The poor grave had not had any earth added to it for two years, and had sunk in. I stood in the snow, firmly pointed it out to the workmen, and said: 'Dig it up!'

"I really am a commonplace fellow. I felt that my voice at this juncture was rather unnatural, and that this order was the greatest I had given in all my life. But the workmen didn't find it at all strange, and simply set to work to dig. When they had reached the enclosure I had a look, and indeed the wood of the coffin had rotted almost completely away, leaving only a heap of splinters and small fragments of wood. My heart beat faster and I set these aside myself very carefully, wanting to see my little brother. However, I was taken by surprise. Bedding, clothes, skeleton, all had gone! I thought: 'These have all rotted away, but I always heard that the most difficult substance to rot is hair; perhaps there is still some hair.' So I bent down and looked carefully in the mud where the pillow should have been, but there was none. Not a trace remained."

I suddenly noticed that the rims of his eyes had become rather red, but realized at once that this was the effect of the wine. He had scarcely touched the dishes, only drinking incessantly, so that he had already drunk more than one pint, and his looks and gestures had all become more vigorous, gradually resembling the Lu Wei-fu I had known. I called the waiter to heat two more pints of wine, then turned back and, taking my wine-cup, face to face with him, I listened in silence.

"Actually it need not really have been moved again; I had only to level the ground, sell the coffin, and that would have been the end of it. Although there would have been something rather singular in my going to sell the coffin, still, if the price were low enough the shop from which I bought it would have taken it, and at least I could have saved a little money for wine. But I didn't do so. I still spread out the bedding, wrapped up in cotton some of the clay where his body had been, covered it up, put it in the new coffin, moved it to the grave where my father is buried, and buried it beside him. And because I used bricks for an enclosure of the coffin I was busy again most of yesterday, supervising the work. But in this way I can count the affair ended, at least enough to deceive my mother and set her mind at rest. Well, well, you look at me like that. Are you blaming me for being too changed? Yes, I still remember the time when we went together to the Tutelary God's Temple to pull off the images' beards, how all day long we used to discuss methods of revolutionizing China until we even came to blows. But now I am like this, fond of appearances, of compromise. Sometimes I think: 'If my old friends were to see me now, probably they would no longer acknowledge me as a friend.' But this is what I am like now."

He took out another cigarette, put it in his mouth and lit it.

"Judging by your expression, you still seem to have hope for me. Naturally I am much more obtuse than before, but there are still some things I realize. This makes me grateful to you, at the same time rather uneasy. I am afraid I am only letting down the old friends who even now still have some hope for me. . . . " He stopped and took a few puffs of smoke. . . .

There was a rustle outside the window, as a pile of snow slipped down from the camellia which it had been bending beneath its weight; then the branches of the tree straightened themselves, showing even more clearly their dark thick foliage and blood-red flowers. The slate color of the sky increased in intensity. Small sparrows chirped, probably because evening was near, and since the ground was covered with snow they could find nothing to eat and all went early to their nests to sleep. . . .

"When I have got through New Year I shall go back to teaching Confucius as before."

"Are you teaching Confucius?" I asked in astonishment.

"Of course. Did you think I was teaching English? First I had two pupils, one studying the *Book of Odes,* the other *Mencius.* Recently I have got another, a girl, who is studying the *Canon for Girls.*[1] I don't even teach mathematics; not that I wouldn't teach it, but they don't want it taught."

"I could really never have guessed that you would be teaching such books."

"Their father wants them to study these. I'm an outsider, so it's all the same to me. Who cares about such futile affairs anyway? There's no need to take them seriously."

His whole face was scarlet as if he were quite drunk, but the gleam in his eyes had died down. I gave a slight sigh, and for a time found nothing to say. There was a clatter on the stairs as several customers came up. The first was short, with a round bloated face; the second was tall with a red nose standing out conspicuously on his face. Behind them were others, and as they walked up the small upper floor shook. I turned to look at Lu Wei-fu, who was just trying to catch my eye; and then I called the waiter to bring the bill.

"Is your salary enough for you to live on?" I asked as I prepared to leave.

[1] A book giving the feudal standard of behavior for girls, and the virtues they should cultivate.

"I have twenty dollars a month, not quite enough to manage on."

"Then what do you mean to do after?"

"After? I don't know. Just think: Has any single thing turned out as we hoped of all we planned in the past? I'm not sure of anything now, not even sure of what I will do tomorrow, not even of the next minute. . . ."

The waiter brought up the bill and gave it to me, and he did not behave so formally as before, just glanced at me, then went on smoking and allowed me to pay the bill.

We went out of the wine shop together. His hotel lay in the opposite direction from mine, so we said good-bye at the door. As I walked alone toward my hotel, cold wind and snow beat against my face, but I felt refreshed. I saw that the sky was already dark, woven together with houses and streets into the white shifting web of thick snow.

Yang Hsien-yi and Gladys Yang

Chang Chin-hsi
(b. *ca.* 1914)

This narrative is based on an oral account.

GROWING UP IN A RED CRADLE

"One foot, cow shit; one foot, mud"—I heard *that* often enough that year. It was 1927, and I had come to town and enrolled in the higher primary school—fifth and sixth grades. The other kids in the school were businessmen's sons, landlords' sons, and sons of wealthy farmers, and my family made ends meet "*tzu-kei tzu-tsu*"—the best we could.

When the other students teased me, "wind by the ears," I said to myself. Once in a while I had a stare-down with one of them. I didn't think they were good for much, hot to eat, hot to "fool around," that was all. I worked on my work and, at examination time, kept my name up among the first five.

There were two teachers at the school I particularly liked, a geography teacher named Liu Hsien-tseng and a language teacher named Sung Po-chou. Mr. Liu and Mr. Sung were both Communist Party members. They saw that I put my back into my work, even that I got some pretty good results, and they noticed that I always played a part in movements for the common good. So in winter that year, they recommended me as a member to the Communist Party's Youth Corps.

Getting into the Youth Corps, for me it was, whap! I had new eyes, whop! I'd gotten a shot of new blood. My life of fighting back had begun. . . .

We Chase Out a Reactionary Principal

In the summer of 1928 I graduated from the Li County Upper Grade School. The organization sent me to the county Normal School to continue my studies and to push the revolution. The Normal School principal at that time was named Chang Chao-i, a reactionary if there ever was one. He worked hand in glove with the district magistrate, the chief of police, and the head of the tax office, and with them he was one of the "four great evil gentry."

This guy, the principal I mean, his private life was corrupt, really rotten. He kept several little "maids" to sleep with. What he did with the school, how he managed it—do I need to tell you how bad it was? As for the school budget, what he took in from public support, what he took in from private tuition didn't go into books, maps, lab equipment; it didn't go into tables, chairs, benches, stools. Principal Chang put it in his own pocket.

By 1928, of course, it already had been several years since the May Fourth Movement.[1] In schools all over the country, they were now teaching vernacular literature. But in our school they were still pushing literature in the classi-

[1] Nationwide reform movement that broke out on May 4, 1919, when students demonstrated against results of the Paris Peace Conference. The movement was accelerated by police brutality. The vernacular literature movement—to get all Chinese writers to use the modern spoken language—was proclaimed about a year earlier.

cal language, and teenage babies that we were supposed to be, they were still having us memorize that Mencius stuff, those "Grammar Aids." And that hardheaded old fool principal would still make a lousy poem and recite it to make fun of the new poetry:

> "Black clouds fill the sky,
> Heavy rain beats down,
> The storm rises . . . the storm falls,
> Rain fills the ditches and moats."

And Principal Chang would say, "What kind of a poem is this? It's not worth a dog's fart!"

All we Communist Youth Corps members in the school really hated the guy. We decided we should try to remove him from his job.

But getting rid of old Chang Chao-i wasn't such an easy business. I don't need to tell you he was an "earth-head snake." He had very close relations with the reactionary government.

I should say that the state of mind of us students was, well, very confused. Like this. There were three groups of students. First, there was a group of Communist Youth Corps members and of revolutionary students "not afraid of Heaven, not afraid of Earth," who with one heart and one purpose wanted to chase our reactionary principal out of office. Second, there were students who had really figured out the difference between right and wrong. The only thing they worried about was how to get the schoolwork done on time. They had never asked themselves any questions about how the school was run. These students were in the majority in our school, were in the middle, and most of them had come from Sung Ridge Elementary School. The third group, of which Liu Ch'ung-shu and Liu Chih-t'ang were representative—this third group believed the old thought was great. They warmly supported "Let the principal run the school." They gathered up information and reported "secrets" to the principal. They thought they would use the power of the puppet county battalion to smash us. This group was small.

At this time I was in charge of public information for the Communist Youth Corps at the County Normal School. I and my comrades talked over the situation. We felt the total situation was too negative; if we depended only on our Youth Corps, we thought, we probably wouldn't succeed.

We asked a Party member higher up to give us a little advice. The Party told us: first, fight to get "the masses"—in our case, that meant fight to bring over the middle group of students—and to isolate the reactionary group; then, when a majority stood on our side, with one move we could drive out the reactionary principal.

There were two student organizations in our school. One was The Fight-for-Freedom Alliance, the other The Anti-Imperialism Alliance. The people who did the work in these two organizations were mostly Communist Party members and Youth Corps members. We talked it over. We decided we should go through these two organizations, The Fight-for-Freedom Alliance and The Anti-Imperialism Alliance.

In the fight to bring over our fellow students, we *liao-t'ienned*—chatted the weather or rapped—with other students, we talked about current events, the news, what was in the news. We sent out propaganda material from time to time, and we gave them pamphlets.

There was a student named Liu Te-han. He came from the original Sung Ridge Elementary School. Te-han was very good in his classwork, he was all by himself in the way other students respected him. We got *him* on our side, and then all the students from Sung Ridge Elementary came over. Now we were a lot stronger.

We asked the Party higher-up who had shown us the way before if it wasn't better to move without delay. A decision was reached that now was the time to throw out our diseased-with-conservatism principal.

On the day we were to chase off the principal, things really were happening at the school. The yard was full of students. We had surrounded the principal's office, and three deep inside, three deep outside, we formed an "iron bucket" all around. A student with a voice that carried stood in front of everybody and led us in chanting slogans:

"Off the reactionary principal!

"Fight corruption! Throw out Chang Chao-i!"

Our Communist Youth Corps members went to the principal's apartment to chase him out. What do you think? The skin on that guy's face was really thick! There he was and wouldn't leave. One of the students, a kid named Ma

("Horse"), was pretty brave, and *t'ung! t'ung! t'ung!* he rushed into the principal's apartment, and "with seven hands and eight legs," Ma took the principal's bags, belongings, and books and set them on the road outside the main school gate.

When the principal looked here, looked there, and saw there was no way he could brazen it through, he glided away gray in the face. After this the school's administrators, teachers, etc.—except one or two who would have preferred that we kept old Chang—well, they all came over to our side.

By 1930 most of the students in the school were Communist Youth Corps members. Later on the Li County Normal School had developed a number of revolutionary cadres for the Party, and they did great work in a couple of uprisings and incidents we had in the area and in the fight against taxes. No wonder people started calling Li County Normal School "The Red Cradle."

The Fight Against Taxes

I suppose the wildest fight I was in, when I was young, was the fight against the tax-per-head on slaughtered animals. It was more than twenty years ago . . . but I look back and think of it now, it seems like yesterday. . . .

At the time our Li County was just like towns and markets run by the Kuomintang—more taxes than a cow has got hairs on its back. It was just about sucking out all the people's blood. But my story is about the tax-per-head on slaughtered animals. It was collected without pity, and there was no rhyme or reason to it.

The Li County Revenue Service contracted with a broker named Ch'en for our tax on slaughtered animals. Ch'en subcontracted the revenues from this northern district to a family named Yen.

Toward the end of 1930, just before the New Year holiday, family after family, household after household, if they were still making it at all, got ready to butcher a pig or a sheep to celebrate. And this time Yen sent a man around, a pouch hanging over his belt, to collect from everybody in the area a special tax—the tax-per-head on slaughtered animals. Anyone who slaughtered a pig or sheep, whether he was going to take it in and sell it in the market, or eat it himself, had to pay the tax.

When the farmers heard *this* news, they fried with rage: "Feed for hogs, you spend your own money for it; hogs, you put the weight on them yourself; for New Year's, you want to butcher it for your own dinner. WHAT IS THIS 'PAY A TAX ON IT'?" In the west end of town there were some well-known gentry like Ho Tzu-jen, and they felt—"They want *more* taxes, like this: it's really not right." And about the County Revenue Service, and about the tax subcontractor Yen—well, they had their opinion.

We did some research. We found out that things were like this all over the area. We decided we should lead everybody in a fight against the tax.

December 12, 1930, was a day everybody came to market in the city. That day all our Communist Youth Corps troops went into action: they went to the market to propagandize and to organize for the fight against the tax. When the farmers heard somebody was going to resist the tax, they all began to whoop. One told ten, ten told a hundred: "Everybody go to the county building and hand in a petition. Swear—resist the tax on slaughtered animals, or die!"

That same day farmers all over the county heard there was going to be tax resistance at the county seat, so they all harnessed up their carts, or rode on cattle, and brought beehive corn bread and wheat cakes to the county seat. By noon at the cattle market inside the south gate, more than ten thousand people had collected in the streets. It was "a mountain of people, an ocean of people." The little cattle market was so crowded there wasn't room for a drop of water.

I spoke first to the crowds:

"Neighbors! These crooks don't want us to celebrate the New Year! We brought our hogs with our own money, didn't we? We didn't steal them, did we? We didn't rustle them from another man's field, did we? We went without this, went without that, to buy feed for the hogs, and fed 'em. The government didn't *send* anybody to help us raise them, did it?

"Now it's New Year's. We want to celebrate. We want to slaughter a fat pig to eat, ourselves, at home. Not to bring to market here and sell. Right? What do they want more tax for? Kill a pig and pay them two dollars! For *what*? What did they do?

"Let's all go together and put the question to the district magistrate."

By this time people had gotten pretty worked up. Everywhere there were shouts: "Let's petition! Let's petition!"

"Fight back against ruinous taxes!"

"Swear to the death: don't pay the tax on slaughtered animals!"

All at once the crowd started to move. Li County Party representative Wang Chih-yuan directed from the back. He led the fight. By now large numbers of people had joined the march. A lot of them originally had just come to town for the market, and now they flowed into the march like a tide. They all wanted to go to the county building to petition. The streets were full of people, the alleys were full of people, the noise and uproar were terrible.

The marchers that were to present the petition reached the county building. They stood out front and terrified the people in the building. The people in the building looked out at the crowd, and each by each their faces turned gray with fear. None of them would open the main gate.

We sent a delegation to invite the district magistrate outside. We asked him to issue an order that the tax-per-head on slaughtered animals was abolished, otherwise we would trash the county building. The district magistrate, Mao P'i-en, seeing how many of us there were, had no choice. District magistrate Mao P'i-en said to the crowd:

"Ladies and gentlemen! Distinguished visitors! We are all neighbors and friends. How could there be a thing we couldn't talk over and negotiate? This tax on slaughtered animals—I think the best thing to do, at the present time, is to remit collection of it. However, this tax was levied at the level of state government, and in order to abolish it once for all, we have to ask the state government for instructions."

We felt we had gotten what we wanted. But we asked a Party representative for advice at this point. Finally we decided to announce that, for the time being, everyone should go home. But before the demonstration had broken up, a farmer shouted from the crowd,

"Suppose they send somebody here to collect the tax? Then what?"

We didn't even have a chance to answer. Everybody shouted together, "We'll kill him!"

The demonstration of more than ten thousand people, satisfied with their day's work, went away "drumming on their tummies," and returned home. The New Year's holiday came and went. Everybody slaughtered his pig and ate it up. When the state chairman himself came to collect the tax, it was too late. The subcontractor, Yen, went about his other business quietly and never mentioned the tax on slaughtered animals again.

William McNaughton

Chapter 2
CHINESE MILITARY WRITING: HISTORY AND FICTION

A MILITARY MACHINE IS LIKE A FIRE:
KEEP ONE AROUND LONG ENOUGH, YOU'LL
GET BURNED BY IT YOURSELF.
—*The Spring and Autumn Annals*

"War," says Dante, "is one of the three great subjects" of the highest literature, for on it depends the safety of the nation and of its citizens. (The other two great subjects, for Dante, were love and righteousness.) In the case of China, particularly modern China, there are other good reasons to study writings on war.

Without understanding war as it has been waged and written about in China, we cannot understand Mao Tse-tung or his thought. Mao Tse-tung, as Professor Stuart Schram has pointed out, "thinks in military metaphors, writes in military metaphors." Of course, military metaphors might come naturally to any Marxist, with all the Marxist rhetoric of class conflict and struggle. But Mao's and the Chinese military way of thinking is related to more than merely consciousness of the historical dialectic. Much of Mao's thought, during long years of his adult life, has been devoted to the solution of military problems: there are a hundred thousand Nationalist soldiers in the county; how do we stay alive tonight? Mao's contribution to Marxist theory is not generally praised, but many find him to be a truly original military thinker.

Without understanding war in China, we cannot understand contemporary China, for contemporary China was born out of a century of war: 1839–42, first Opium War (against England); 1856, second Opium War; 1894–95, first Sino-Japanese War; 1898–1900, Boxer Rebellion, Allied troops occupy Peking; bandit suppression actions against peasant uprisings and against Communists in the late twenties and early thirties; second Sino-Japanese War, 1931–1945; full-scale civil war between Nationalists and Communists, ending in 1949 with Communist victory; the Korean War. Out of this history has come a China whose mythology is primarily heroic and military—resistance and survival, survival and guerrilla war, guerrilla war and full-scale war ending in victory over enemies of superior strength.

The father of modern guerrilla war is not, as some people think, Mao Tse-tung. That honor belongs to a military writer named Sun Tzu, who lived in the 6th century B.C. There is, I hope, enough material from Sun Tzu in this anthology to familiarize the reader with the guerrilla way of thinking, the subtlety and cleverness of which, I believe, can be traced back to Taoism, with its great tolerance of, and delight in, paradox. Mao Tse-tung's thought owes more, for its style and inner movement, to Taoism than to any other influence. There is also historical material, not available before in English, from one of Mao's favorite books—the *T'ung chien Kang-mu,* a comprehensive history of China first compiled in the twelfth century A.D. and updated by later historians. Other material below comes from the *Historical Records* written by Ssu-ma Ch'ien during the Han dynasty (206 B.C.–A.D. 220). Ssu-ma Ch'ien's job as court astrologer gave him use of the imperial library, and, continuing the work begun by his father Ssu-ma T'an, from whom he had inherited his position, he wrote a masterpiece in 130 chapters and over 700,000 characters. According to Edwin O. Reischauer and John K. Fairbank, Ssu-ma Ch'ien "set a standard for historical scholarship in China that was probably not equalled in the West until relatively modern times"; "his succinct prose style also set a literary standard"; "he came as close as any man has" to writing "universal history."[1]

After the history there is material from two great Chinese novels, both of which have historical bases.[2] Mao was thinking of these novels when he said that, as a youth,

[1] Edwin O. Reischauer and John K. Fairbank, *East Asia: The Great Tradition* (Boston: Houghton Mifflin, 1960), pp. 11–12.

[2] Because of the importance of historical incident to this material, whether historical or fictional, I have arranged the material in this chapter according to its historical chronology rather than according to the literary chronology.

he did not enjoy reading the Confucian classics, but that he loved "the romances of old China, and especially stories of rebellions." And it was to one of them, *A Saga of the Marshes,* that he referred when, as a youth counseling his peers on a proper course of revolutionary action, he said, "We must learn to imitate the heroes of Bridge Mountain." Throughout his life he never really changed that counsel.

When the Chinese talk of fiction, they are likely to refer to the four miraculous works: *A Tale of Three Kingdoms*[1] (fourteenth century), *A Saga of the Marshes*[2] (fourteenth century), *The Way West*[3] (sixteenth century), and *The Golden Lotus*[4] (sixteenth century). Our excerpts are from the first two, the ones most popular in China today. A Shanghai publisher recently began to bring them out in serial comic book editions, in a program of mass education and an effort to popularize the mythology of the Revolution.

Sun Tzu
(sixth century B.C.)

THE ART OF WAR

War is the great affair for a nation. It is the ground on which a nation grows or decays, the means by which a nation endures or dissolves. A nation cannot ignore it.

In waging war we have five fundamental things to consider as we work out our plans and tie them in with the special circumstances of the particular case. These five fun-

[1] English translation: C. H. Brewitt-Taylor, *Romance of the Three Kingdoms,* 2 vols. (Rutland, Vt., and Tokyo: Charles E. Tuttle Co., 1959).

[2] English translation: Pearl Buck, *All Men Are Brothers* (New York: John Day, 1968).

[3] English translation: Arthur Waley, *Monkey* (New York: John Day, 1943).

[4] English translation: Clement Egerton, *Golden Lotus* (London: Routledge, 1939).

damental things are called moral influence, sky, earth, leadership, and logistics.

Under moral influence the common people will think like those above them. The common people will die with them or live with them and will not be afraid of any danger.

"Sky" means when it gets dark and when it gets light, when it gets cold and when it warms up, the way in which time is reckoned, the way the seasons change.

"Earth" means: how close is this? How far is that? What ground is dangerous? What ground is safe? Where are there plains? Where are there passes? What land can you live off? What land is wasteland?

A good leader knows what he's doing, you can believe what he says, he is humane and has a sense of humor, is brave and has discipline.

"Logistics" means organization of personnel into units, a book of regulations, a system of promotions, the acquisition and care of matériel and facilities.

All warfare is based on faking out the enemy.

Where you are strong, seem to be weak. Where you are capable, seem to be incapable. Come to places as though you were leaving them, and leave places as though you were coming to them.

Take as though you were about to give, disperse as though you were about to unite.

Finish as though you are about to begin, attack as though you were about to retreat.

Strike the enemy as though you were going to scratch his back. Grant a concession as though you were going to make a demand.

Rest as though you were about to work. Form an alliance as though you were about to break off discussions.

Hit where the enemy's not prepared, come out where the enemy is inattentive.

IF YOU INTEND TO WAGE A WAR,
YOU MUST FIRST COUNT THE COST.
—TS'AO TS'AO

If you resort to war, and victory is long in coming, your fighting men will lose their spirit.

A state that tries to support standing armies forever will waste its substance, and not even advisers and experts will be able to make things turn out well.

A state is impoverished especially by armies that it must maintain at great distances: maintain an army at great distances, and the nation's wealth will flow away.

If you train and supply a regular army at home, you will find that prices go up, and when prices go up, the people's money will lose its value.

As the people's money loses its value, they will be the more harassed by draft call heaped on call.

Then when your men have lost their spirit, and the people's money declines in value, or the homes on the Central Plains grow bare, the people will see their taxes rise toward thirty percent.

And the government will spend sixty percent of its revenues for broken chariots, worn-out horses, breastplates and helmets, bows and arrows, spears and shields, protective mantlets, draught oxen, and heavy wagons.

To fight a hundred times and win a hundred times is not the blessing of blessings. The blessing of blessings is to destroy the other man's army without getting into the fight yourself.

If you know the enemy and know yourself, you need not fear the result of a hundred battles. If you know yourself and don't know the enemy, you'll win one time and lose one time. If you know neither the enemy nor yourself, you must fear the result of every battle.

In the old days those who waged war well first made sure that they could not be defeated, and then they waited until the enemy could be defeated.

"Could not be defeated" lies in oneself. "Could be defeated" lies in one's enemy.

Therefore, those who wage war well can make sure that they cannot be defeated, but they cannot bring it about that the enemy can be defeated.

So one wins in war by not making mistakes. Not making mistakes is the way in which one assures victory. It is he who beats himself who will lose.

So he who wages war well sets up on ground where he

cannot be beaten and takes his opportunity to beat the enemy.

The winner in war looks for victories and then fights. The loser in war fights and then looks for victories.

How can the great mass of one's army never be defeated when it engages the enemy? By the proper use of orthodox moves and unorthodox moves, that's how.

How can troops be committed so that it's like throwing a grindstone against an egg? By knowing the hollow and the solid, that's how.

Normally, in battle use the orthodox move to engage the enemy, and use the unorthodox move to beat him. The orthodox move fixes or distracts the enemy. The unorthodox move strikes him when and where he does not expect it.

The tactic of the effectively sprung unorthodox move is as inexhaustible as heaven and earth, as unending as rivers and streams. The sun and moon that cease and begin again are like it; the four seasons that die and are born again are like it.

There are only five musical tones, but of the five tones we can never hear all possible changes; there are only five colors, but of the five colors we can never see all possible changes; there are only five flavors, but of the five flavors we can never taste all possible changes. In the craft of war, there are only the orthodox move and the unorthodox move, but of the orthodox move and the unorthodox move we can never exhaust all possible changes.

Thus orthodox becomes unorthodox, and unorthodox becomes orthodox. Their interaction is as endless as interlocked rings. Who can determine where one ends and the other begins?

Order is born of disorder, courage is born of fear, weakness is born of strength.[1] We organize disorder by numbering, we embolden fear by discipline, we strengthen weakness by controlling the shape.

He who is good at making the enemy move shapes him; makes the enemy follow his lead; offers something that the enemy is bound to seize. Offering some advantage, he moves him; holding power to annihilate, he waits for him.

[1] He seems to mean "strength is born of weakness," but the Chinese text definitely reads as here translated.

When the enemy would rest, make him work. When the enemy would eat, make him go hungry. When the enemy would halt, make him move around.

If you attack well, the enemy won't know where to defend against you. If you defend well, the enemy won't know where to attack you.

We shape the enemy's force and keep our own force unshaped. Then we can keep our forces concentrated and the enemy's divided. We concentrate our forces into one and divide the enemy's forces into ten: so that with ten in one, and one in ten, we will set many men against the enemy's few. And when we can attack a few of them with many of us, the enemy will be in trouble indeed.

We must not let it be known where we intend to fight. If it be not known, then the enemy will have to prepare in many places. And if the enemy prepare in many places, the numbers against which we must fight in one place will be few.

If the enemy prepares at the front, then his numbers at the rear will be few. If the enemy prepares at the rear, his numbers at the front will be few. If the enemy prepares on the left flank, then his numbers on the right flank will be few. If the enemy prepares on the right flank, then his numbers on the left flank will be few. If the enemy prepares everywhere, then there is nowhere his numbers will not be few.

Numerical weakness comes from having to prepare against the other man. Numerical strength comes from making the other man prepare against you.

Do not repeat a tactic which has gained you a victory, but shape your actions in an infinite variety. Water sets its flow according to the ground below it: set your victories according to the enemy against you. War has no constant aspect, as water has no constant shape. What is "genius"? To get the victory by changing according to your foe.

Shape your troops like water: water as it moves leaves the high places and seeks the low. Let your army leave the enemy's strong places and seek the weak.

William McNaughton

Ssu-ma Ch'ien
(d. *ca.* 85 B.C.)

HISTORICAL RECORDS

"The Fire-Bulls"

When T'ien Tan saw that his troops' spirit was moved to this pitch, he knew that he could join battle. Having mattocks distributed to his men, Tan took a mattock in his own hands, too, and worked beside the men. He sent his own wives and concubines to fill in the ranks, and he ordered that his personal stores of food be completely distributed to the soldiers.

After giving instructions to the regular troops to keep out of sight and not to move around, T'ien sent the women, children, and old men up on the city wall. Then he sent a delegation to the Yen troops to sue for peace. When the Yen troops received his offer of surrender, they raised great shouts of victory: "*Wan sui! wan sui!*" And T'ien Tan collected the populace's gold, which came to twenty thousand ounces all told, and he had the wealthy citizens of Chi-mo send it to the Yen general with the message: "We citizens of Chi-mo want to surrender to you. We beg that you not loot our family homes or mistreat our women, or let their peace and quiet be destroyed." When the Yen general received this, he was happy in the extreme, and he agreed to their plea.

Thus having been convinced that Chi-mo was surrendering, Ch'i Chieh the Yen general allowed discipline to relax, and the Yen army let down its guard. At this point T'ien Tan rounded up all the cattle in Chi-mo, more than a thousand head altogether. He dressed these animals in red silk robes, and he had multicolored dragon stripes painted all over them. He tied bayonets to their horns, and to their tails he tied torches of reeds soaked in oil. Now the defenders had cut a number of holes in the city walls, and T'ien Tan that night started the cattle out through these holes toward Ch'i Chieh's camp, and T'ien Tan's soldiers set fire to the reed bundles on the cattle's tails. He also sent five thousand crack troops out behind the cattle.

As the animals felt the heat of the burning torches, they went wild with rage and ran into Ch'i Chieh's camp. The Yen troops, in the dark, were terrified and confused. The light from the reed bundles as they burned flickered over the animals, and the Yen troops saw that the animals were covered with dragon stripes. Large numbers of the troops were killed or wounded by the bayonets tied to their horns. And then the five thousand troops, following behind the cattle with gags in their mouths, fell on the camp; and at the same time the people on the Chi-mo city wall started to beat drums, and the children and old men pounded on bronze vessels, and with all this tumult of sounds together, it may truly be said that "Heaven and Earth were hurled around."

The Yen army, receiving this attack totally unprepared, was thrown into panic and riot, and the troops fled in great disorder. The Ch'i troops pressed this advantage and killed the Yen general Chi'i Chieh. By this time the Yen army was completely disorganized and in a rout; they fled, they ran, and the Ch'i army moved out after them. As they moved through city after city, the populace revolted against Yen and came back under T'ien Tan's jurisdiction. The number of troops under his command thus grew greater and greater every day. Day after day the T'ien Tan army won; the Yen army lost day after day. T'ien Tan finally drove them back to the Yellow River and then did not press them farther. More than seventy cities that had fallen earlier to Yen were recaptured and returned to the former government.

William McNaughton

Chu Hsi
(1130–1200)

Chu Hsi was a statesman, historian, commentator on the Confucian classics, and China's most important post-classical philosopher (neo-Confucianism is sometimes called "Chu-Hsi-ism"). He also wrote poetry. Chu Hsi wrote *The Comprehensive Mirror Outlined and Explained,* basing it on *The Comprehensive Mirror for Aid in Government,* a history of China from 403 B.C. to A.D. 959, written by Ssu-ma Kuang in order to enable scholars to honor the Confucian precept, "Study history before you get into office." Later historians have added to Chu's work and kept it up to date.

THE COMPREHENSIVE MIRROR OUTLINED AND EXPLAINED

"Li Kuang Bluffs the Tartars"

In 144 B.C. General Li Kuang was in command of the fort at Yen-men. Li and his men were there to defend the Chinese border against the Tartars who lived in the country beyond Yen-men.

One time General Li took some men and rode into Tartar territory for reconnaissance. Before they had gotten a day's march into Tartar country, Li and his men saw several thousand Tartars coming toward them. Li had only a few men with him, and the men wanted to turn and get away.

"If they see us run now," General Li said, "they will attack us, and even if we can get away, they can harass us and do us a great deal of damage while we retreat."

Li acted as if he were unconcerned at the Tartars' approach, and he began to unfold a stratagem against them. When the Tartars were less than a mile away, Li ordered his men to get off their horses and to take off the saddles. While they were doing this, a Tartar officer rode within arrow range, followed by several of his own men. Li Kuang and ten or so of his soldiers remounted and, as if they were afraid of nothing, rode out toward the Tartar officer. The Tartar shot an arrow at Li and missed. Shooting back, Li knocked the Tartar officer off his horse. The other Tartars turned their horses and ran away.

Li Kuang did not bother to chase them. When Li and the ten soldiers who had just ridden out with him got back to their little camp, Li had the ten unsaddle their horses, too. The Tartars watched them from the distance.

When the Tartars saw how confident and secure the Chinese soldiers acted, they concluded that the whole Chinese army must be nearby. So though there were several thousand of them, the Tartars were afraid to attack Li and his little band in their camp.

During the night, when it was very dark, Li Kuang and his men sneaked out and went safely back to the fort at Yen-men.

William McNaughton

Lo Kuan-Chung
(fourteenth century)

We know very little about Lo Kuan-chung except that he is supposed to have written two of the "four miraculous works" of Chinese fiction: *A Tale of Three Kingdoms* and *A Saga of the Marshes.* Legend has it that he was a poet and a drifter; his nickname, which he may have given himself, was "Wanderer on Seas and Lakes." Lo's great novel, *A Tale of Three Kingdoms,* is based on public storytellers' material about the romantic "Three Kingdoms" period (A.D. 221–265); to this Lo added factual material from the histories. His main artistic contribution is considered to be the enlivening of characterizations.

A TALE OF THREE KINGDOMS

Chapter 46: Chuko K'ung-ming Borrows Some Arrows

Lu Su went off to find K'ung-ming. K'ung-ming said to him, "How do you think I can get a hundred thousand arrows made in three days? You must give me some help. Get me several boats."

So Lu quietly got ready about twenty light, swift boats. As had been ordered, the crew of each was given blue screens and bundles of grass. When the boats and crews were ready, Lu Su notified K'ung-ming. On the first day K'ung-ming took no action, nor yet on the second day. Before three A.M. on the third day, K'ung-ming, in a secret communication, summoned Lu Su to his boat.

When he arrived, Lu said, "I am ready for orders, sir."

"I want you to come with me," K'ung-ming said. "We're going to get the arrows."

"Where will we get them?" asked Lu Su.

"Be patient," said K'ung-ming. "You will find out in due time."

Men with long ropes tied together the twenty boats, and the boats moved to the north bank. There was a heavy fog that night, and the mist was especially dense along the river, so that one man could hardly see another. K'ung-ming kept the boats moving on despite the fog.

Before five A.M. the little fleet reached Ts'ao Ts'ao's camp. After ordering that the boats should line up with their prows to the west, K'ung-ming had the men beat drums and shout.

At this point Lu Su exclaimed, "Suppose they attack us!"

K'ung-ming smiled. "Is he going to bring his fleet out in this fog? Here, have some more wine. Let us enjoy ourselves. We shall go back when the fog lifts."

When the drums and voices were heard on the bank, the officers in charge of the two camps ran to the Command Post to tell the Commander. He said, "Coming up in a fog like this, they must have set up an ambush for us. Don't send any of our boats out to meet them, but collect our troops and issue orders to shoot at the enemy." He also ordered that six companies of archers and crossbowmen be detached from the infantry camps and sent to aid the marines.

They lined up the naval forces on the bank to prevent a landing. Soon the archers and crossbowmen arrived, and the legion and more of men began to shoot down into the river. Their arrows fell like rain. After a while, K'ung-ming issued orders for the boats to turn around so that the prows pointed east and to move in closer to shore so that many arrows might hit them.

K'ung-ming had the drums continue to beat until the sun was high and the fog began to break up. Then the boats got under way and sailed downstream. Each of the twenty boats bristled with arrows up and down both sides. Before they passed from earshot of Ts'ao Ts'ao's camp, the crews lifted up a great, derisive shout: "Thank you, Your Excellency, for the arrows!"

The forward patrols reported this to Ts'ao Ts'ao, and he hurried to the scene of the early morning's activity. But by the time he arrived, the light boats, catching the swift current, were far downstream, and he could no longer pursue them.

As they sailed on down and back to their own camp, K'ung-ming said to his companion, "Each of the boats must have five or six thousand arrows in it. We didn't do any work at all, and now we have over one hundred thousand arrows to use. Tomorrow we shall shoot them back at Ts'ao Ts'ao, but he may not be so happy about it."

"You are some kind of superhuman being," said Lu Su. "How did you know there would be a thick fog today?"

K'ung-ming replied, "If you want to be a general and don't understand the patterns of heaven, don't recognize the principles of earth, don't know the technique of unorthodox moves, don't follow the lightening and darkening of the day, don't anticipate the change of seasons, don't read the 'Array of Eight Ranks,' and don't appreciate the 'Aspects of an Army,' you will never succeed in war. I determined three days ago that there would be a fog today, so I set the limit at three days for getting the arrows."

Chapter 52: Chao Yun Captures Kuei Yang with a Trick

Chao Yun pretended to be very happy, and he poured out wine for the two men, Ch'en Ying and Pao Lung, until they had drunk too much. When the two of them were quite drunk, Chao had them bound with ropes. Then he called in the men under them and questioned these men about the whole affair. Eventually they admitted it had been a false surrender.

Chao Yun then had the whole force of five hundred men brought before him, and he gave them all food and wine. Then as commander he told them: "Those who intended to murder me were Ch'en Ying and Pao Lung. You men really had nothing to do with it. If you carry out the plan I propose, you will all receive significant rewards." These line soldiers all bowed and thanked General Chao. Chao then had Ch'en and Pao, the two generals who had "surrendered," beheaded.

General Chao ordered their five hundred men to proceed down the road to Kuei Yang, and he himself led a thousand troops behind them. During the night they arrived under the city wall at Kuei Yang and called at the gate. When the guards on the wall had been aroused, the men below said that the two generals of the army, Ch'en and Pao, had killed Chao Yun and had returned with their troops. They wished to report on the matter to the prefect.

The guards on the wall brought fires so that they could see more clearly, and they discovered that below the wall were indeed the soldiers and horses of their own side. Chao Fan then hurried to the gate and went out to meet them, and Chao Yun shouted to the men to Fan's right and left to seize him. Then Chao Yun and his force moved into the city and pacified the common people.

Chapter 70: "Old Huang Chung Captures a Hill"[1]

Ts'ao Hung then sent out Hsiahou Shang and Han Hao. The two men between them led five thousand troops and went in with them as reinforcements. . . . Huang Chung meanwhile had gotten from his spies a thorough knowledge of the local terrain. . . .

When Huang Chung heard that Hsiahou Shang and Han

[1] This anecdote may be the source of the Red Army's famous tactic "Lure the enemy to penetrate deeply." The tactic was used successfully time after time in the Chinese Civil War and probably was the key, on the military front, to Communist successes early in the 1946–49 phase of the war.

Hao had come with their armies, Huang rode out with his troops and faced them. Han Hao was in front of his division, and he cursed loudly at Huang Chung and called him "an immoral old bandit." Han spurred his horse and went after Huang with his spear. Hsiahou attacked at the same moment. Fighting with some strength against the two generals, Huang Chung fought with each of them ten or more times. Then, as if defeated, Huang Chung withdrew. Han and Hsiahou pursued him about seven miles and captured his camp.

Huang Chung then built another camp with brushwood. And the next day, Han and Hsiahou came after his army again. Huang again joined with them several times and then fled, in the end, as if defeated. And Han and Hsiahou chased him again some seven miles, and they captured another camp from him. They left Chang Ho to guard the first camp they had taken.

Chang rode forward from the rear camp to discuss the situation with Han and Hsiahou. Chang Ho said, "Huang Chung has retreated two days in a row, and I believe that he has some dangerous trick in his mind."

Spitting on the ground, Hsiahou replied, "You don't win a war by being timid. I think we've conferred enough. Watch the two of us: we're going out for a big win." So Chang Ho, shamed and humiliated, left Han and Hsiahou.

On the following day, Han and Hsiahou attacked again; and again Huang Chung retreated about seven miles, as if defeated. Han and Hsiahou kept after him hot as they could. The following day Han and Hsiahou took their troops out after Huang again, and Huang fled as though before the wind. Sometimes he seemed to try to throw up a defensive line, but he was always driven quickly off it. He fell back all the way to the pass; they camped right under it. Here Huang Chung set up defenses and stayed within them.

Meng Ta secretly sent a letter to inform Hsuan Te of all this in detail. The letter said, "Huang Chung has been beaten time after time in battle, until now he has had to pull all the way back to the pass." Hsuan Te was shaken and asked K'ung-ming about it. K'ung-ming said, "This is just the old general's trick: he's sucking their armies in." Chao Yun and the rest of them didn't believe it. Hsuan Te sent Liu Feng to the pass with reinforcements for Huang Chung.

When Huang saw Liu Feng, he said, "So you have come to help me direct this campaign. Why?" Feng answered, "My father heard that your troops have been beaten several times in a row, sir. So he sent me in." Smiling, Huang pointed to himself and said, "This old man has a plan. It's called 'suck the enemy in.' You watch: tonight in one drive we will get back every camp we have lost, and we will capture the enemy's food, provisions, and horses. I was just lending them the camps so they could lay in some supplies for us. Tonight I leave Ho Hsun to guard the pass, and General Meng will carry off the food and provisions and steal the horses for us. Young man, you have come just in time to see us smash the enemy."

That night an hour or so before midnight, Huang led five thousand troops out from the pass and straight down. In Hsiahou Shang's and Han Hao's camp the soldiers, seeing that Huang and his troops kept within the pass day after day, had finally let their guard down a little, and when Huang and his troops suddenly hit the camp full on, Hsiahou's men and Han's men couldn't even get their armor on or saddle their horses. Han and Hsiahou ran from their commands to escape, soldiers and horses rushed and trampled one another, and so many died that they could not be counted. And by the time the sky began to grow bright, Huang Chung had retaken the three camps in succession. In the camps the enemy had abandoned weapons, saddles, and horses beyond number, and Huang Chung ordered Meng Ta to move it all back beyond the pass.

Chapter 95: "The Empty City"

K'ung-ming took five companies and started toward Hsi-ch'eng. The patrols kept sending back reports that Ssuma Yi, with a large force, was moving toward Hsi-ch'eng. K'ung-ming had with him no ranking officers; he had only some civil officials and the five companies of troops. Half of the troops had started to move out the supplies, so he had in fact only two and a half companies.

As the intelligence came back that the enemy was close by, the lower officers with K'ung-ming grew nervous.

K'ung-ming himself walked up on the city wall to look things over. In the distance, he saw dust clouds rising against the sky. So the armies of Wei were coming to Hsi-ch'eng. He could tell that they were coming along two roads.

K'ung-ming issued the order that all banners be taken down and hidden away. He ordered that if any officer in command of soldiers in the city moved or made noise, that officer should be executed at once. Then he ordered that all the city gates should be opened. He ordered that twenty soldiers should be dressed in civilian clothes and should be set to cleaning the streets at each gate.

When the order on silence had been transmitted and all the other orders had been carried out, K'ung-ming put on the simple Taoist dress he sometimes liked to wear. Then he ordered a boy to carry his lute behind him, and another boy to come along with books, or to step and fetch things, and the three of them went up onto the wall. K'ung-ming sat down by one of the towers. He told one boy to light a stick of incense, and he took his lute from the other boy and began to play.

Ssuma's advance patrols approached the city gates. They saw K'ung-ming, and the two boys, and the stick of incense. They did not come into the city but went back and told what they had seen. Ssuma Yi smiled as if he didn't believe it. Ordering the army to halt, he himself rode on ahead. He was astonished: it was as the patrols had reported it. There sat K'ung-ming, smiling. A boy stood beside him holding a sword. Another boy stood to his other side and held up a yak's tail, the ordinary symbol of authority. And twenty or so people were working inside the gates, sweeping, as if nothing unusual was going on or was expected.

Ssuma Yi could not believe it! He thought of K'ung-ming's reputation and of his mastery of the art of deception. Ssuma rode back to his armies and ordered them to turn around, and he marched them off to the hills in the north.

As the march began, Ssuma's second son began to argue with him. "K'ung-ming does not have any force of troops in there. I am certain of it! Why are we withdrawing, Father?"

"K'ung-ming is a careful man," Ssuma replied. "He

does not take chances. The open gates can mean only one thing: ambush. If we send men through them, we will fall into his trap. What do you know about anything, anyway? No, we must withdraw."

So the two armies of Ssuma Yi turned away from Hsi-ch'eng. As he saw them move out, K'ung-ming laughed and clapped his hands. The civilian officials were astonished. They asked K'ung-ming how it could be, that a great army should march away at the sight of a single man. K'ung-ming replied:

"Ssuma Yi knows my reputation. He knows that I am a careful man and do not take chances. He saw what was going on, and he thought: 'This is a deception!' He probably expected an ambush. So he has marched away.

"He is right," K'ung-ming continued, "that I do not take chances. But in this case, what could I do? Now he will meet Kuan and Chang. I sent them into the hills to wait for him."

The officials were still very scared, but they praised K'ung-ming's clear vision, and his subtle schemes, and his clever techniques.

And then one of them said, "Might it not have been better if we had just run away?"

"With two and a half companies? How far would we have gotten?" asked K'ung-ming.

William McNaughton

A SAGA OF THE MARSHES

A Saga of the Marshes is a semi-historical novel about the Bridge-Mountain Gang, a colorful band of rebels and bandits who may remind the Western reader of Robin Hood and his Merry Men (there are Chinese counterparts of the Sheriff of Nottingham, too). The work is based on the legends and story-cycles that grew up around the exploits of the twelfth- or thirteenth-century bandit, Sung Chang and his group.

Chapters 65–66: "The Lantern Festival"

They held a meeting to discuss the Lantern Festival. Governor Liang said, "Twice the Bridge-Mountain Gang has come into our city. Shouldn't we cancel the Lantern Festival this year?"

Wen Ta replied, "There are proclamations stuck up all over the streets but without any signatures. The gang has done this because they are driven to it and have no other way. I am sure they have no plans. We should hold the festival." And so it was proclaimed in the city.

The city was the largest in Hopei, and the merchants of the world settled there as thick as fog or clouds. A tent was set up, and men set out five-color screens. Lanterns and rockets were prepared, and everywhere streamers went up on which were written the words of famous men. Old curiosities and toys were hung around.

They built a fairy fish mountain at the governor's mansion beside the Chou Bridge. Two dragon lanterns, one red, one yellow, twisted around the mountain, and every scale of each dragon was itself a tiny lantern. Pure water flowed from the dragons' mouths and into the stream beneath the bridge.

They built another fairy mountain at the Temple of the Brass Buddha, and another fairy mountain at the House of the Jade Cloud. The House of the Jade Cloud was the best wine shop in Hopei. Its roofs were three-eaved, the beams were subtly carved, and so were the pillars. You could hear music and laughter in it all day and all night, and the sounds of lutes and of other musical instruments filled the ears without ceasing.

Now the spies from the Bridge-Mountain Gang heard the news, and they reported back to the mountain with it, and when Wu Yung heard it, he was very happy. And he and the Iron-faced P'ei Hsuan counted off eight companies of men. The eight companies—four cavalry companies and four infantry companies—were to go each its own way.

Wu Yung said: "At nine P.M. on the fifteenth, when the watch announces the hour, be all ready at the city of Ta Ming Fu." And so they divided up.

Shih Ch'ien went over the city wall and into the city. He could find no inn that would take him, for he had no companions or luggage, so he had to sleep at the Temple of the

God of the Eastern Mountain, beneath the god's pedestal. By day he walked the streets.

One day Shih was watching workmen putting up pavilions and hanging lanterns, and he saw the gang's Hsieh Chen and Hsieh Pao carrying their wild game and walking through the streets, wide-eyed. And later he saw the gang's Tu Ch'ien and Sung Wan as they came out of a whorehouse.

He walked over to the House of the Jade Cloud. There was the gang's M. Kung, hair loose and flying, wearing an old torn sheepskin, holding a staff in his left hand and in his right hand a beggar's bowl. He was covered with filth and grime, and he begged of people as they passed. Soon Shih saw another beggar coming. He and K'ung looked at the beggar and saw that it was the gang's L. Kung.

M. Kung said, "Tsou Yuan and Tsou Jun were selling lanterns on the street yesterday." And then they went off, and as they walked by a temple, a Taoist came out, and they saw that it was the gang's Kung-sun Sheng. The gang's Ling Chen stood beside him as attendant. They all bowed in understanding to each other, and then each went his way.

The gang's Wang the Dwarf Tiger, and the Ten Foot Green Snake, and Sun Hsin, and Mrs. Ku, and Chang Ch'ing and Mrs. Sun, disguised as three country couples, walked around in the crowds, and talked and laughed as farmers do.

When the fifteenth came and in the drum tower the second watch announced nine P.M., Sung Ch'ien took a basketful of fireballs and torches to set fire here and there. He had stuck some toys on the basket, and he went around behind the House of the Jade Cloud. He went in and went upstairs and pretended he was selling toys. He found the gang's Hsieh Chen and Hsieh Pao carrying their hunting forks, rabbits hanging on them. Someone cried, "The robbers have come outside the West Gate!"

And then a great flame burst from the House of the Jade Cloud and reached toward the sky. The moon paled in the light from the blaze. Governor Liang ordered his horse and leaped on it to investigate. Just as he came out on the street before his mansion, he saw two tall men pushing carts, and they stopped in the middle of the road. Then the two men seized lanterns and threw them into the carts, setting another great fire.

Governor Liang decided then he should make for the East Gate. As he drew near, he saw two more tall men with swords attack the gate guards. They were joined by two more members of the gang, and they wounded maybe ten of the guards before the guards fled. So the four men had the East Gate. Governor Liang saw that he was in trouble, and he and his men turned and headed for the South Gate. Before he got there, people he met said that the gate guard there had been attacked by a great fat priest with an iron staff in his hands, and another priest with a face like a tiger's who fought with two swords. And bandits were pouring into the city through that gate.

And the governor turned his horse again and started back toward the governor's mansion. But seeing that Hsieh Pao and Hsieh Chen, wielding their three-forked iron spears, had cut off his way, he turned for refuge into the house of the magistrate Wang. Just as he got into the yard, he saw Liu T'ang and Yang Hsiung strike the magistrate with their clubs, and the magistrate staggered into the street and fell dead.

The governor turned his horse again and galloped toward the West Gate. But even as he passed the Temple of the City God, he heard fireballs bursting. The sky thundered, and the earth shook. Chou Yuen and Chou Jun were there, bamboo poles in their hands, setting fire to the eaves of the houses.

The governor rode on. Wang the Dwarf Tiger and the Ten Foot Green Snake ran out of a whorehouse. Sun Hsin and Mrs. Ku took weapons from where they had hidden them and joined the fight there.

At the Temple of the Brass Buddha, Chang Ch'ing and Mrs. Sun ran out and climbed up on the fairy mountain and set fire to it. By now the people in the city were running around like rats or wolves. From every house came the sound of weeping like gods, of mourning like devils. The flames leaped from a hundred places on every side.

Governor Liang finally reached the West Gate, and there was his guard with its leader Li Ch'eng. They rushed in disorder to the city wall at the south. They saw that the city was full of horsemen and fighting men, and that on their banners was written "The Great Sword Kuan Sheng."

In the flames, Kuan Sheng fought through this way and that. To his left was Huang Hsin. Like the wings of the wild goose, the armies came on, and now they were beneath the South Gate.

Governor Liang retreated and hid beneath the North Gate. He watched the fire from there. He saw The Leopard-headed Lin Ch'ung gallop by, his weapon held horizontally before him. He saw Ma Lin to his left, to his right saw Teng Fei, saw Hua Yung behind him.

The governor turned to the East Gate again. There he saw, amid many flaming torches, He Whom No Obstacle Can Stay, Mu Heng. To the left of him was Tu Hsing, to the right was Cheng T'ien Shou, and three tall men were in front, swords in hand, and they led more than a thousand men to charge the city. In terror the governor galloped to the South Gate, and there, reckless of his life, he forced his way through.

Meanwhile, Ch'ai Chin the robber and the jailer Ts'ai Fu went to the jailer's house. They carried out everything he owned, and they took with them his family and servants, for he had cooperated with them and had agreed to go with them to Bridge Mountain. And Ts'ai said at this time, "Great Lord, I beg you to save the city's common people. Do not let them suffer."

So Ch'ai Chin took this word to the counselor Wu Yung. When Ch'ai Chin found him and told him, Wu Yung issued an order to protect the city's common people. But already much damage had been done.

And soon the counselor Wu Yung issued other orders within the city. Proclamations were made to set the people's minds at ease, and the fires were put out. Wu Yung opened the city treasury and had the silver and gold and precious things piled upon carts. He opened the granaries and distributed rice to the common folk, and what was left he set on carts to take back to Bridge Mountain for the gang to use when they needed it.

William McNaughton

Chapter 3

CHINESE POEMS

Chinese poetry has sometimes been described, by foreign students, as a "mandarin exercise." Nothing, in fact, could be further from the truth. Chinese poetry begins in folk poetry: the earliest extant Chinese poem is a farmers' work song,[1] and half of the first anthology of Chinese poetry, *The Book of Songs,* is folk poetry. In 125 B.C. the Chinese government established a government bureau—the *yueh-fu* or music bureau—to collect "narrow-alley and street-corner songs" and to study them as a clue to public feeling, much as a modern administration might study Gallup polls. And the Chinese system of civil service examinations, at least when it was working well, kept bringing new blood into the mandarinate, so that the mandarin or scholarly class did not grow too far away from the people to remember the springs of their life or the style and drift of their ballads.

An idea of those springs can be found in a list of the things Chinese poets most often wrote about: homesickness; hatred of war; separation from family, friends, or loved ones; history and myth; the delights of a small farm and garden; mountains and rivers (the spectacular beauty of the Chinese landscape); physical love; the lot—usually unhappy—of the beauties in the imperial harem or other neglected wives or women; Taoist immortals (sennin); "embracing the ancient," i.e., visits to some historically famous spot and thoughts about the past; seeing a friend off on a journey; and "the moment," some small but vivid thing seen, felt or heard.[2]

[1] See McNaughton, *Chinese Literature: An Anthology,* p. 14.

[2] The list was worked out by Lenore Mayhew, to whom I am indebted for it.

Without trying to "paint every leaf on the tree," we can sketch the main outline of the history of Chinese poetry. After the earliest folk songs comes *The Book of Songs,* an anthology so fine that tradition describes it as having been put together by Confucius himself. This anthology contains folk songs, historical ballads, formal poetry by or about the aristocracy, and hymns or "odes of the temple and altar." Many of the poets represented here were fond of rhyme, and the commonest rhyme scheme of later Chinese poetry— a b c b—is frequently used, although many other schemes, as well as some unrhymed poems, can be found.

Next come the important forms *ku-shih,* or "old-style poems"—as they were named by later generations—and *fu,* or prose-songs. The *ku-shih* are ordinarily quite short, eight lines being the favorite length, and they rhyme on the even-numbered lines. The *fu* are rather longer, some running to a few hundred lines; the versification is freer, resembling free verse, or even rhythmic prose. An important part of the rhetoric consists in the piling-up of details.

In the fifth or early sixth centuries (A.D.), the Chinese became self-conscious about their language and began to write poems in something called the palace style, which had a very rigorous and formal prosody. By the T'ang dynasty (618–907) the palace style had developed into the formal showpiece of Chinese poetry, the *lü-shih,* or regulated verse. Eight lines long, the *lü-shih* rhyme on even-numbered lines, and every syllable is virtually locked into a musical relation with every other by rules governing the use of the tones of the Chinese language. Between one and four of the poem's two-line groups must have parallelism; that is, each syllable in the first line must relate in a definite way to the corresponding syllable in the next line. Both must mention a weather phenomenon, or a landscape feature, or an article of clothing, or an artifact; or both must be verbs of motion, or both verbs of quality, or both adverbs of manner. Another rigorous form, the *chüeh-chü,* was also very popular during this period. A *chüeh-chü* can be defined roughly as "the second half of a *lü-shih.*"[1] But a great

[1] For a fuller description of the forms see McNaughton, *Chinese Literature: An Anthology,* pp. 342–43. I argue my difference with the prevailing opinion that a *chüeh-chü is* "the first half of a *lü-shih*" in Lenore Mayhew and William McNaughton, "Where Love Is: Seventy-eight T'ang Dynasty Poems" (unpublished).

many poets preferred to write in less rigorous forms, and the T'ang dynasty left us a legacy of great poetry only a fraction of which is in *lü-shih* or *chüeh-chü.*

After the T'ang, Chinese versification was revitalized when poets, visiting the bars or wine houses, heard singers—possibly girls from Central Asia and the Middle East—who used musical forms new to China, or at least to the literati. These poets began to write poems to fit the tunes they heard, and a new poetic form, the *tz'u,* was born. Even today the Chinese do not use the words "compose" or "write" when they describe the composition of a *tz'u;* they say "fill in a *tz'u.*" *Tz'u* were influenced by the *lü-shih* poetic style—tone and parallelism were used—but the *tz'u* writer had about twelve hundred variations to choose from. Unlike *lü-shih,* a *tz'u* may have lines of different lengths. Thereafter, the *ch'ü*—a slightly freer form, also intimately related to music—came into use.

Until modern times, Chinese poets continued to write old-style poems, prose-songs, regulated verse, *chüeh-chü, tz'u* and *ch'ü.* Mao Tse-tung, for example, liked to "fill in" *t'zu.*

But the poetry of modern China is as diverse, experimental and free as that of most other modern nations. The main break with tradition is that since 1918 the Chinese have written poetry in their spoken language and not in classical Chinese, which is the Latin, so to speak, of China. Similar tendencies, of course, can be found in modern Western poetries, and propaganda on their behalf can be found in the early Imagist criticism. In fact, this may be where Hu Shih (1891–1965), who founded China's movement for poetry in the colloquial language, got his idea. He was studying at Columbia University and starting to write poetry in the heyday of the Imagists.

Anonymous

THE BOOK OF SONGS
(collected *ca.* 500 B.C.)

Rats

RATS,
stone-head rats lay off our grain,
three years pain,
enough, enough, plus enough again.
More than enough from you, deaf you,
we're about through and ready to go
where something will grow
untaxed.
Good earth, good sown,
and come into our own.

RATS,
big rats, lay off our wheat,
three years deceit,
and now we're about ready to go
to Lo Kuo, happy, happy land, Lo Kuo, good earth
where we can earn our worth.

RATS,
stone-head rats, spare our new shoots,
three years, no pay.
We're about ready to move away
to some decent border town.
Good earth, good sown,
and make an end to this endless moan.

Ezra Pound

Lily Bud

Lily bud floating, yellow as sorrow,
grief today, what of tomorrow?

Gone the bud, green the leaf,
better unborn that know my grief.

Scrawny eyes with swollen heads,
the fish traps catch but stars.

What man has food now
after these many wars?

Ezra Pound

Anonymous
(attributed to Mei Sheng, before 200–140 B.C.*)*

The Beautiful Toilet

Blue, blue is the grass about the river
And the willows have overfilled the close garden.
And within, the mistress, in the midmost of her youth,
White, white of face, hesitates, passing the door.
Slender, she puts forth a slender hand;

And she was a courtesan in the old days,
And she has married a sot,
Who now goes drunkenly out
And leaves her too much alone.

Ezra Pound

T'ao Ch'ien
(365–427)

Moving House

My old desire to live in the Southern Village
Was not because I had taken a fancy to the house.
But I heard it was a place of simple-minded men
With whom it were a joy to spend the mornings
   and evenings.
Many years I had longed to settle here;
Now at last I have managed to move house.
I do not mind if my cottage is rather small
So long as there's room enough for bed and mat.
Often and often the neighbors come to see me
And with brave words discuss the things of old.
Rare writings we read together and praise;
Doubtful meanings we examine together and settle.

Arthur Waley

The Tzu Yeh Songs (fourth century)

These were probably written by a professional female entertainer. The clever eroticism of the imagery seems to have eluded many readers.[1]

Cool autumn
      and the windows opened wide;
Low moon
      and the slanted lights inside.
Midnight:
   nothing heard,
      nothing seen—
A double laugh
      behind the screen.

Autumn moon's
      at the open shutter,

[1] See Lenore Mayhew and William McNaughton, *A Gold Orchid* (Rutland, Vt., and Tokyo: Charles E. Tuttle Co., 1972), p. 17.

The lights put out,
sheer robes gone wide.
Within silk curtains
someone smiles—
The lifted orchid's come untied.

Lenore Mayhew and
William McNaughton

Wang Wei
(701–761)

Beside Lake Yi

Where the lake ends, she sits now playing her flute.
At dusk she bade farewell to her husband.
Wistfully she stares across the water,
Watching a white cloud rolling up the blue
mountain side.

Chang Yin-nan and Lewis Walmsley

A Poetic Dialogue: Wang Wei and P'ei Ti—The Creek by the Luan House

Wang Wei:
Autumn rain and sudden winds.
The water plunges, bouncing off the rocks.
Waves leap aimlessly over each other.
The white heron is alarmed and lands.

P'ei Ti:
A man could hear the water-sound far off.
I walk down looking for the ford.
Ducks and egrets swim away, and then
veer back, longing to be near people.

Robert Bly

A Portrait of Ts'ui Hsing-tsung

I painted your portrait when your years were young;
Now I have painted you when you are old
Yet in this picture I discover a new man!
I understood you better in the old days . . .

Chang Yin-nan and Lewis Walmsley

Li Po
(701–762)

For a thousand years or more Li Po was the best-known Chinese poet in the Orient. In his youth he spent several years when he never set foot in a town, studying on Mount Omei with the Master of the Eastern Cliff. Professor Holmes Welch[1] calls Li Po a "Church Taoist," an alchemist and hygienist. In his youth Li Po is said to have been a swordsman. He served in the prestigious imperial Hanlin Academy and was exiled from the capital for drunkenness and misconduct. He has been called the people's poet, as Tu Fu is called the poet's poet. The magic of Li Po's best work is unquestioned. His brilliant cinematographic imagination can be seen in "The Girls of Yueh."

Old Poem

I climb to see the four seas
And earth and heaven
Filling up the void.
Autumn forests
obscure the thousand things,

[1] Holmes Welch, *Taoism: The Parting of the Way* (Boston: Beacon, 1957), p. 185.

Winter winds whirl in the waste;
Fiery flowers follow rivers to the East,
And the ten thousand happenings
are broken waves.

The once-bright sun is covered,
The white clouds ride the rootless air;
The plane tree nests the swallow and the wren,
The wild thorn feeds the drake.
Leave, come, go, arrive—
I carry a sword,
I make my songs.
The roads are hard.

Lenore Mayhew

The Girls of Yueh

I

At Chang-kan the young girl from the south
Has eyes beautiful as the moon,
Has eyes beautiful as the stars.
She wears no crowshead stockings.
Her sandaled feet are like frost.

II

In the south the young girls
are white and shining
And love the five boat games.
They pick flowers,
they speak with their eyes:
They ask the traveler to stay.

III

On the Yueh River
girls gather lotus.
One sees me,
sings her oar song
and comes back;

Smiles, but slides her boat
behind the lily flowers.
She pretends to blush
and will not come out.

IV

The girl from Tung Yang has white feet.
The boatman from Kuei Chi has white skin.
They are looking at each other.
The moon is not yet down.
The white world
wounds each heart.

V

At Mirror Lake the water is like the moon.
The Yueh River girl is like the snow.
She rows across the waves
wearing white powder.
In the broken water
her bright shadow trembles.

Lenore Mayhew

The River-Merchant's Wife: A Letter

While my hair was still cut straight across my
forehead
I played about the front gate, pulling flowers.
You came by on bamboo stilts, playing horse,
You walked about my seat, playing with blue plums.
And we went on living in the village of Chokan:
Two small people, without dislike or suspicion.

At fourteen I married My Lord you.
I never laughed, being bashful.
Lowering my head, I looked at the wall.
Called to, a thousand times, I never looked back.

At fifteen I stopped scowling,
I desired my dust to be mingled with yours

Forever and forever and forever.
Why should I climb the lookout?

At sixteen you departed,
You went into Ku-to-yen, by the river of swirling eddies,
And you have been gone five months.
The monkeys make sorrowful noise overhead.

You dragged your feet when you went out.
By the gate now, the moss is grown, the different mosses,
Too deep to clear them away!
The leaves fall early this autumn, in wind.
The paired butterflies are already yellow with August
Over the grass in the West garden;
They hurt me. I grow older.
If you are coming down through the narrows of the river Kiang.
Please let me know beforehand,
And I will come out to meet you
As far as Cho-fu-Sa.

Ezra Pound

Another Poem on the River-Merchant's Wife

I lived a young girl
Unaware of the things of the world;
Now I am married to you
in Chang-Kan,
And I walk the riverbank
to watch the wind's color.
In May
the south wind blows,
And I think of you
sailing down to Pa Ling;
And in August
in the west wind
I know you are leaving Yangtzu.
You come, but you go,
and I am mostly unhappy.

When will you be in Hsiang Tan?
My dreams follow the waves,
follow the winds—
Last night a big storm
Tore out trees
down by the river,
Turned the whole world black.
Where were you then?
If I could ride the clouds,
I would come and find you
east of Orchid Beach.
In the reeds the Mandarin ducks are happy;
The purple kingfishers embroidered on the gold
screen—there are two of them.

I am fifteen.
My face is pink
like the flowering peach,
And I am a river wife
Afraid of waves,
afraid of wind.

Lenore Mayhew

Tu Fu
(712–770)

Tu Fu is an incomparable poetic technician, considered by many to be China's greatest poet. He was a Confucian and served the government in minor posts, but his life was marred by illness and poverty.

Two for the Flowers Near the River

The riverside flowers are driving me crazy
because there's no way to describe their effect

I went to see Hu-ssu Jung
my neighbor and fellow drinker

he's on a ten-day bender
all I found was an empty bed

2

Mrs. Huang's garden
flowers engulfing the path

thousands
weighing the branches

butterflies move pause move pause
it's a dance

and the orioles
know the appropriate music

David Young

Po Chü-i
(772–846)

The Girl

Flowers and the absence of flowers . . .
Mists
            and the memory of mists . . .
At midnight here,
In sunlight gone—
Like a dream of spring,
Like the unfindable clouds of morning.

Lenore Mayhew

Han Shan
(dates unknown)

Han Shan is often pictured, in Chinese and Japanese paintings, as a grotesque little man laughing in the woods. He is said to have been a poor and eccentric scholar who lived at Cold Cliff and scrounged his food from a friend, a cook at a nearby temple. "Han Shan" is not a name but means "Cold Mountain."

Poem

In my first thirty years of life
I roamed hundreds and thousands of miles.
Walked by rivers through deep green grass
Entered cities of boiling red dust.
Tried drugs, but couldn't make Immortal;
Read books and wrote poems on history.
Today I'm back at Cold Mountain:
I'll sleep by the creek and purify my ears.

Gary Snyder

Niu Hsi-chi
(? ninth to the tenth century)

Written to the Tune of *Sheng Ch'a Tzu*[1]

Spring mountains
Fog
about to disperse
Sky clear
stars few

[1] The next six poems are *tz'u* (see the introduction to this chapter).

A fading moon
shines on your cheek
We cry at parting
as the day comes up

So many words!
but the feeling
strong as ever
Turning your head
to look back
you call
over and over
"Remember the Green-Skirt Girl
"and everywhere on earth
"be tender with the grass"

C. H. Kwock and
Vincent McHugh

Li Yü
(937–978)

The last emperor of the Southern T'ang dynasty, Yü lived three years as a prisoner after the dynasty fell, and wrote much beautiful poetry, some of it erotic and some of it about his plight. After the new emperor complained that he disliked "listening to somebody snore beside my bed," Li Yü was mysteriously poisoned.

I Grieve for the Beautiful People[1]

In the little yard the wind returns;
the garden weeds, the willow eyes
grow green.

[1] "The beautiful people," or "beautiful ones": probably his wives. When Li was deposed and moved into exile, he lost the perquisites of emperor, one of which was the imperial harem.

I lean against the railing,
                    the creak of old bamboo
                    and the new moon
                                    are the same as last year,
as if barbarian flutes
            had never scattered crystal cups.

On the surface of the pond
                the ice is melting,
the candle flares up, the incense turns black,
the painted hall lies under long shadows.
My hair is flecked with white,
and there is no comfort in thinking.

Lenore Mayhew

Ch'in Kuan
(1049–1100)

To the Tune "All the Garden's Fragrance" (Excerpt)

Red water pepper flowers growing lushly
yellow rushes everywhichway

Late night, the dew settling
the broad sky clearing
just a few thin clouds over this
shining southern river
where I row alone
in a raspberry-wood boat
passing misty banks and sandspits
losing track of distance

I have a thin gold fishhook
and I roll my line in slowly
hauling up one deep star

David Young

Anonymous Woman Poet
(Ming dynasty: 1368–1644)

Questions About a Bite

On your shoulder
plain as day
the marks of teeth
You tell me
Who bit you?
I won't scold you
You can save me the trouble
of asking you questions
day after day
What's bitten
is your flesh
What hurts
is my heart
What kind
of monster
would bite you
with such cruelty?

C. H. Kwock and
Vincent McHugh

Nalan Hsingte
(1655–1685)

I Remember the Beautiful Person

High peaks of sheer stone
rise level with the riders' heads;
Where the rivers meet
the water is frozen.
The horses neigh,

The friends speak,
one goes west,
one east
To the deep canyon where the road breaks off
And a rope bridge swings across.
Wild geese flying over the north pass
look like illegible calligraphy.
This year's flowers open in an anxious time.
Tears again.
The sun falls,
And over the Ming tombs
the disordered clouds
turn yellow.

Lenore Mayhew and William McNaughton

A Length of Rope ("The Great Wall"[1])

The moorland fires are gathered up
into the green clouds.
The West wind howls in the night.
Over the dark fields the wings of wild geese
pattern the autumn sky
Like mountaintops sketched on a screen.

Through how many panels of mountains and seas
Do the high parapets of the long wall
wind and wind?
Our eyes follow, slope after slope
and we understand
How it ate up the dragon hearts of our grandfathers.
And in the end they built it for whom,
for the benefit of what clan?

Lenore Mayhew and William McNaughton

[1] Since it was the convention to title *tz'u* with the name of the song or tune being "filled in," there was sometimes no apparent connection between the title of a poem and its subject. If a *tz'u*-writer thought it necessary, he could, as here, add a subtitle.

Liu Ta-pai
(1880–1932)

Tears

93

Thin clouds . . .
Who drew this brush across the distant sky?

94

People are in the flowers,
People are in the wind.
The wind opens cracks in people's hearts.

William McNaughton

Kuo Mo-jo
(b. 1892)

Short-story writer, playwright, historian, translator of Japanese, German, and English, and a Marxist since 1925, Mo-jo has held high posts in the government of the People's Republic of China. His discovery in 1919 of Walt Whitman was especially important to his poetry. Wen I-to called him the only truly modern Chinese poet.

Death's Inducements

I have a little knife.
It leans by the window and smiles at me,
It smiles and says to me:
"Mo-jo, don't trouble your heart!
"Come, come quickly to my mouth,
"I'll get rid of many troubles for you."

The blue, blue sea water outside my window
With incessant sound calls out to me,
It calls to me and says:
"Mo-jo, don't trouble your heart!
"Come, come quickly to my breast,
"I'll get rid of many troubles for you."

Kuo Mo-jo's note. "'Death's Inducements' is the first poem I ever wrote. I did it in early summer, 1918, I think it was."

William McNaughton

Night

Night! Night of blackness and gloom! You should be
Democracy!
You hug all us humankind.
You make no distinction "poor, rich,
"High, low," you make no
Distinction "beautiful, ugly, wise, stupid."
You are the great melting pot
of poor, rich, high, low,
Beautiful, ugly, wise, stupid,
All disorder's root and unhappiness' stem.
You are the master craftsman of liberation,
freedom,
Equality, rest,
all order's embryo and happiness' bud.
Night of blackness and gloom! Night! I really
Love you,
I will not leave you again.
I hate the light coming in
From outside; into this world
Without distinctions
The hard light will bring distinctions.

William McNaughton

Mao Tse-tung
(1893–1976)

Mao Tse-tung was the son of a moderately successful Hunanese peasant. Mao's contributions to modern Chinese history lie in his understanding that revolution in China would come from the peasants (not from the urban proletariat); that the Chinese Communist Party had to have an army; in his study of and writings on military strategy; and in his analysis of the land reform problem and his role in its solution. Mao became the leading power in the Chinese Communist Party in 1935. From 1949 to 1958 he served as official Chief-of-State in the People's Republic. He liked to write poetry but was modest about his work, calling it "old-fashioned"—which formally it is—and "no model for the young."

Snow
(to the melody "Shen Yuan Chun")

This is the scene in that northern land:
A hundred leagues are sealed with ice,
A thousand leagues of whirling snow.
On either side of the Great Wall
One vastness is all you see.
From end to end of the great river
The rushing torrent is frozen and lost.
The mountains dance like silver snakes,
The highlands roll like waxen elephants,
As if they sought to vie with heaven in their height;
    And on a sunny day
You will see a red dress thrown over the white,
    Enchantingly lovely!

Such great beauty like this in all our landscape
Has caused unnumbered heroes to bow in homage.
But alas these heroes!—Chin Shih Huang and Han
  Wu Ti
Were rather lacking in culture;
Rather lacking in literary talent

Were the emperors Tang Tai Tsung and Sung Tai
Tsu;
And Genghis Khan,
Beloved Son of Heaven for a day,
Only knew how to bend his bow at the golden eagle.
Now they all are past and gone:
To find men truly great and noble-hearted
We must look here in the present.

Andrew Boyd

Loushan Pass (February, 1935)

Note. The Red Army made a crucial move through Loushan Pass on the Long March. The local governor had put two divisions of government troops to block the move, and the Red Army got through after bitter fighting.

Cold is the west wind;
Far in the frosty air the wild geese call in the
morning moonlight.
In the morning moonlight
The clatter of horses' hooves rings sharp,
And the bugle's note is muted.

Do not say that the strong pass is guarded with iron.
This very day in one step we shall pass its summit,
We shall pass its summit!
There the hills are blue like the sea,
And the dying sun like blood.

Andrew Boyd

Three Poems of Sixteen Characters (1934–1935)

Note. This poem is read as a personal statement: "Mao determines to succeed where others have failed."

Mountains!
I whip my horse not leaving the saddle.
I turn my head. Surprise—
I'm three feet three inches from the sky!

Mountains!
Like seas in storm, like tides turned back
 the mountains roll off in great waves . . .
Thrown into a desperate charge
Ten thousand horses run as if drunk into battle.

Mountains!
They stick into the blue sky and their tops are not
 blunt.
With them you could prop up stellar space.

William McNaughton

Chu Hsiang
(1904–1933)

Bury Me

Bury me in a pond of lotuses.
By my ear there will be water worms' sounds,
And on the lamp of green lotus leaves,
The fireflies will blink on, blink off—

Bury me under tassel flowers
And I will always dream fragrant dreams—
Bury me on top of Mount T'ai

Where the wind's sound hums through a solitary
pine—
No, let my body be burned
And thrown into a spring river in flood,
With the fallen flowers let it swirl away
Someplace nobody knows.

William McNaughton

Hu P'in-ch'ing
(b. 1920)

Sun and Shadow

On a hot summer day
on the creek bank,
a shaft of sun
straight, dark-green, gold,
and the long shadow
of it that lies in the clear thin stream
seem like
a poem, amazing and bright,
and the meaning that gives it form,
that lies in some dim corner of the soul,
is still obscure.

William McNaughton

Cheng Ch'ou-yu
(b. 1933)

Pei-a-nan, An Aboriginal Village

My wife is a tree, so am I;
And my wife is an excellent spinning wheel
Whose shuttles of squirrels spin the drifting clouds.
Up on high: what she loves to spin is those clouds.

And how I wish my job to be
Ringing my bosom's
        grade-school bell,
Because I have reached this age—
When woodpeckers stand on my shoulders.

Wai-lim Yip

There are virtually no biographical data available on the next two poets, both of whom now work in the People's Republic. Perhaps this lack is due to a belief that personal publicity encourages "bourgeois individualism."

Yen Yi

Snow[1]

Up there
Who's cutting down the Tree of Jade?[2]
Up there who's drilling

[1] From Yen's book *The Poplar's Song* (Peking, 1963).
[2] In Chinese lore there is supposed to be a tree in the moon, sometimes called the "Tree of Jade."

in the silver hills?
Are the gods
imitating us and building their own wall?
These silver filings—
Where do they come from
Flying and turning in the air
And to earth
Mixed with the sweat of the builders of the sky
Changing the earth into a silver world?

William McNaughton

Li Ying

Evening[1]

The sun is a red lantern
Half-covered with Gobi sands.
The surveying team's fires blink
In front of the tents. I love the sound
of water boiling in camp kettles.
I love the reflections
cast by the red flames.
A hundred thousand years—
The first horsemen go by here.
Our tents are comfortable,
our hearths, our apartments.
Little Wang puts up a poster
Above, high above the door:
"Desert Highway No. 1
"—Tomorrow longer than the Great Wall."
Watching him
Little Li says: "Look out there: cities!
"Listen: somebody's honking
on the highway, the headlights

[1] From Li's book *The Red Willows* (Peking, 1963).

"Are reflected
in the water!"
Both men laugh.
Over their heads
The stars shine.
A red lantern
Half-covered
in Gobi sands
is the moon.

William McNaughton

Chapter 4

CHINESE RELIGIOUS AND PHILOSOPHICAL WRITINGS

Since I have summarized in the Introduction the ideas that make up Chinese religion and philosophy, I will deal here with the men who invented, developed or transmitted them, and with the works in which we can see that invention, development and transmission.

More than any other religion, Confucianism honors literature, both secular and religious, quite apart from its dogmatic content. This is, I suppose, part of the reason some people deny that it *is* a religion. Right at the center of the Confucian canon are a collection of folk songs, only a small percentage of which is "religious," and a compilation of historical documents, a sort of "original materials for study of the history of the Chou dynasty." The first of these canonic works is *The Book of Songs;* the second, *The Book of Documents,* and tradition has it that both were compiled by Confucius himself. (Because of their status simply as literature, I have put my selections from *The Book of Songs* in Chapter 3.)

Of primary importance to understanding Confucianism are two other works: the record of Confucius's conversations (called the *Analects*), and the *I Ching,* or *Book of Changes.* In many modern scholars' view the *I Ching* is too "irrational" to be associated with Confucius, "the first humanist." Nevertheless, its fundamental vision seems to me to be consistent with Confucius's views, as I infer them from the *Analects.* The *I Ching,* together with commentaries acquired through the ages, provides a set of images of the Chinese mind quite as useful in studying that mind as are the images in the *Divine Comedy* for studying Thomist philosophy and the medieval Catholic mind.

Confucius was born in 551 B.C. and died in 479. His home was in the little state of Lu, an early center of Chinese culture. Confucius is supposed to have played a guitar, or similar instrument, and to have enjoyed singing, conversation, and ginger. He taught for a living, and some of the early masterpieces of Chinese literature—*The Book of Songs,* for example—may have been texts he put together for his students. He liked to travel and may have heard some of the folk songs in *The Book of Songs* on his travels.

We do not know much about the lives of Lao-tzu and Chuang-tzu, the founders of Taoism. Lao-tzu is supposed to have kept the royal archives for the Eastern Chou dynasty and to have left when he saw the arts of government decay there. There is a legend that Confucius visited him to ask about rites. Chuang-tzu may have worked in the government of his own state (Sung) for a while, as a minor clerk.

We have already discussed philosophical Taoism (pp. 35–36.)The other kind of Taoism—cultistic Taoism—is a mixture of popular beliefs, superstition, debased yogic practices (from India), health-food fads, messianic sex cults, primitive alchemy and, perhaps, experimentation with drugs and herbs. All these interests and beliefs were held together, in earlier times, by a common goal: to make the physical body live forever, or at least for a very long time. Cultistic Taoists of later times can be sometimes identified by their deification, or canonization, of Lao-tzu, and by their jargon, which is full of "the Tao" and other terms from Lao-tzu's *Tao Te Ching.*

In reading about Taoism it is important to understand the word "sennin" or "hsien-jen." (Sennin is the Sino-Japanese form, which I prefer since it fits better into English and since, in the Anglo-American literary tradition, it is the anterior form, having been introduced in some of Ezra Pound's early translations.) A sennin is a Taoist immortal or, if you reject the folk lore, a Taoist hermit. The word is written, in the Chinese writing system, with a man beside a mountain, and sennin were men who left the normal human pursuits of wealth, career, and glory and retreated into one or another of China's magnificent wild mountains, there to "cultivate the Tao" and to practice Taoist magic arts. The sennin were believed to possess all sorts of magical powers and to live forever, or at least for a few centuries. In the stories below (from *Lives of the Taoists*), the main characters are touched with these popular beliefs, but at least some of them—so it seems to me—really represent philosophical Taoism rather than cultistic Taoism. In any event, the stories are an excellent source of material on early Chinese folklore. None of them, so far as I know, has ever appeared in English before.

Of the material in this chapter, the most difficult is, perhaps, that on Zen Buddhism. This material consists of *mondo* (to rely on the more familiar Sino-Japanese form again), or anecdotes about the Zen masters; and *koan*, or the anecdotal material used as an aid to meditation and, potentially, as a catalyst of enlightenment. Nothing I can say will make the material any easier—it is a tenet of Zen that "words just get us farther away from it"—but I think that the reader who just relaxes and reads will comprehend more easily than the one who concentrates and worries the stories for their meaning. The Zen material includes a number of important anecdotes of the Zen master Rinzai (Chinese "Lin-chi" d. A.D. ? 867), which have not previously been translated into English.

CONFUCIANISM

THE I CHING, OR BOOK OF CHANGES

The *I Ching* is considered in China to be one of the five great classics of Confucianism. It is supposed to be the work of four great Chinese culture heroes: the legendary Emperor Fu Hsi (2852–2738 B.C.), who worked out the hexagrams; Wen Wang, "the Elegant King" (thirteenth to twelfth century B.C.), who added The Words; the Duke of Chou (twelfth century B.C.), who wrote commentaries on The Lines; and Confucius, who added "The Boar's Head" (or "Decisions") section. Confucius's school is supposed to have written the section called The Image, and commentaries have been added through the ages. The book is used as an oracle, its images used to start one's mind off in thinking about some particular problem of the moment.[1]

Hexagram 1: Ch'ien, The Creative

The Hexagram. Ch'ien, the Creative, is above; Ch'ien, the Creative, is below.

The Words. Seed. Growth. Fruit. Sacrifice.

The Boar's Head. The Creative is truly great. In it are the seeds of everything in the physical universe. It works in beginnings and so leads Heaven.

Clouds pass, the rain flows. The things of the physical universe, in their degrees, shift from form to form. In this is the great understanding of ends and beginnings.

Cloudiness, sunshine, flexibility, rigidity, *humanitas,* equity: each of the six stages comes to the full at its own time. One can ride on them like six dragons toward Heaven.

The Creative: its *tao* is CHANGE. . . .

The Image. The heavens are regular and constant in their courses. . . .

Hexagram 47: A Tree in a Box—Oppression

The Hexagram. K'an, the Abysmal, Water, is below; Tui, the Joyous, Lake, is above.

The Words. Growth. Sacrifice.

The Boar's Head. Oppression is when you've got something hard and dead on top, and things underneath it trying to grow through.

To be in danger and keep one's pleasure in things, to be oppressed and yet keep on growing—only the superior man can do this. . . .

The Image. There is no water in the lake: oppression.

The superior man follows his will in terms of whatever mandate has come.

[1] For more details, see William McNaughton, *The Confucian Vision* (Ann Arbor: University of Michigan Press, 1974), pp. 149–150.

Hexagram 48: The Well-Curb and Well

The Hexagram. Sun, the Gentle, Wind, Wood, is below; *K'an,* the Abysmal, Water, is above.

The Words. You can change the capital, but you don't change the Well. The Well doesn't lose, it doesn't gain. They go and come, and the Well is the Well.

. . . The Well: a symbol of social structure, as men developed it to meet the most basic needs of the race—social structure independent of political structure. . . . If social and political forms have not drawn on—have not gone down to—these eternal basic needs, the polity and the society will be ineffectual and will be reduced to nonforms: chaos and anarchy.

The Boar's Head: Going down into the water and bringing water up—this is the Well. The Well nourishes and does not wear out. . . .

The Image. Wood, and above it water—this is the Well. The superior man does everything he can to take care of the common man, whose lot it is to labor and sweat.

William McNaughton

THE BOOK OF DOCUMENTS

Modern scholars describe *The Book of Documents,* traditionally said to have been compiled by Confucius, as a mixture of authentic materials and of forgeries in later centuries. It is one of the Five Classics.

What does Heaven hear? What our common people hear. What does Heaven see? What our common people see. What does Heaven hate? What our common people hate. (II, iii, 4.)[1]

Don't bring chaos into our political traditions by being "clever." Look at facts in detail, listen to facts in detail—

[1] The numbers after each extract indicate book, chapter, and section in which the material appears.

and don't make the words lean to one side so as to change the scope or significance of any fact. (V, xvii, 7.)

What happened to the common people in Miao? There the ruler did not govern with force of personality and moral example, he governed with punitive laws. Actually it was nothing but power and oppression, sheer as tigers' claws, but he called it "the Law."

The Great Emperor wiped out Miao's ruler and brought order . . . Then judges started to make decisions in the law-courts—well, the question was not, "What will intimidate the people?" The question was, "What will make the people prosperous?" Decisions were made with restraint and reverence.

And then officials didn't have to pick and choose words to describe what they were doing. . . . (V, xxvii.)

William McNaughton

THE RECORD OF RITUALS

The Record of Rituals is the fifth of the Five Classics. It was compiled in the second century B.C.

For the official who splits words so as to break the law; who names things wrong so as to change governmental functions; or who tries to sneak around established and traditional practices so as to subvert the governmental authority, the punishment shall be death.

William McNaughton

Confucius

THE ANALECTS

The *Analects* is a record of Confucius's conversations, perhaps kept by his students.

The superior man figures totalities, not angles. The little man figures angles, not totalities. (II, 14.)

The superior man understands equity. The little man understands profits. (IV, 16.)

Confucius said, "I can't fault the Emperor Yü. He ate poor food but served the spirits with complete filial piety. He wore bad clothes, but his religious cap and gown were beautiful. His house was falling apart, but he spent his time building canals. I can't fault the Emperor Yü." (VIII, 21.)

Tzu-lu asked about serving ghosts and spirits. Confucius said, "If one cannot yet serve men, how can he serve the spirits?"

Tzu-lu said, "May I venture to ask about death?"

Confucius replied, "If you do not understand life, how can you understand death?" (XI, 11.)

Tzu-lu said, "The Prince of Wei wants you to help him form a government. What will you do first?"

Confucius said, " 'Will' do? *Must* do: name things right."

Tzu-lu said, "I guess that's a joke. It's irrelevant. Why name things right?"

Confucius said, "Yu, you are a yokel. If a superior man hears about something he doesn't understand, he shows some reserve.

"If you don't name things right, you cannot communicate accurately about them with language. If you cannot communicate accurately about them, what has to be done cannot be done properly. If what has to be done doesn't get done properly, ritual and music will not spring up. If ritual and music do not spring up, the law will not punish the guilty or protect the innocent. If the law doesn't punish the guilty or protect the innocent, the common people will not know how to move hand or foot.

"Therefore, when the superior man names a thing, you can talk about it; and when he talks about a thing, you can act on it. You don't have to look through a superior man's words for his meaning like something lost in the grass, and the meaning won't change on you from one time to the next." (XIII, 3.)

Tzu-lu spent the night at Stone Gate. The gatekeeper said, "Where are you from?"

Tzu-lu said, "I'm studying with Confucius."

"Oh," said the gatekeeper. "He's the one that knows you can't do anything but keeps working on it, isn't he?" (XIV, 41.)

Tzu-kung asked if there were a single principle that one could follow throughout one's life. Confucius said, "Reciprocity is it. What you yourself don't want, do not do to the other man." (XV, 23.)

William McNaughton

Mencius

THE MENCIUS

Later Confucians put this book, by the philosopher Mencius (372–289 B.C.), into a group called "The Four Books," which were considered to explain essential Confucianism. The other three were the *Analects, The Doctrine of the Mean,* and *The Great Learning.*

Mencius said, "The common people are the important thing. Next come the spirits of the grain and of the land, and last comes the ruler.

"That's why, get the peasantry, and you can get the empire." (VII, ii, xiv.)[1]

William McNaughton

TAOISM

Lao-tzu

(?570 B.C.–?)

TAO TE CHING (THE TAO AND ITS POWER)

The tao you can tao is not the Tao. The name you can name is not the Name.

The thirty spokes join on the one hub, and their usefulness for the carriage is just where they aren't. You take a clay lump to make the dish, and the clay's usefulness is just where it isn't. You cut material into doors and windows to make a room, and its usefulness as a room is just where it isn't.

The tree you can barely reach around grows from the thinnest shoot. The tower that's ten stories tall rises from a layer of dirt. The longest journey begins with a single step.

The ten thousand things interact, and so I watch for the rebound.[2]

William McNaughton

[1] Most of this material is from McNaughton, *The Confucian Vision.*

[2] From McNaughton, *The Taoist Vision* (Ann Arbor: University of Michigan Press, 1971).

Chuang-tzu
(365–290 B.C.)

THE BUTTERFLY DREAM

One time, Chuang-tzu dreamed he was a butterfly, flitting around, enjoying what butterflies enjoy. The butterfly did not know that it was Chuang-tzu. Then Chuang-tzu started, and woke up, and he was Chuang-tzu again. And he began to wonder whether he was Chuang-tzu who had dreamed he was a butterfly or was a butterfly dreaming that he was Chuang-tzu. [1]

William McNaughton

Man Is Born in Tao

Fishes are born in water
Man is born in Tao.
If fishes, born in water,
Seek the deep shadow
Of pond and pool,
All their needs are satisfied.
If man, born in Tao,
Sinks into the deep shadow
Of non-action
To forget aggression and concern,
He lacks nothing;
His life is secure.

Moral: "All the fish needs
Is to get lost in water.
All man needs is to get lost
In Tao."

Thomas Merton [2]

[1] McNaughton, *op. cit.*
[2] Thomas Merton, *The Way of Chuang Tzu* (New York: New Directions, 1965).

HORSES' HOOFS

Horses' hoofs are made for treading frost and snow, their coats for keeping out wind and cold. To munch grass, drink from the stream, lift up their feet and gallop—this is the true nature of horses. Though they might possess great terraces and fine halls, they would have no use for them.

Then along comes Po Lo.[1] "I'm good at handling horses!" he announces, and proceeds to singe them, shave them, pare them, brand them, bind them with martingale and crupper, tie them up in stable and stall. By this time two or three out of ten horses have died. He goes on to starve them, make them go thirsty, race them, prance them, pull them into line, force them to run side by side, in front of them the worry of bit and rein, behind them the terror of whip and crop. By this time over half the horses have died.

The potter says, "I'm good at handling clay! To round it, I apply the compass; to square it, I apply the T square." The carpenter says, "I'm good at handling wood! To arc it, I apply the curve; to make it straight, I apply the plumb line." But as far as inborn nature is concerned, the clay and the wood surely have no wish to be subjected to compass and square, curve and plumb line. Yet generation after generation sings out in praise, saying, "Po Lo is good at handling horses! The potter and the carpenter are good at handling clay and wood!" And the same fault is committed by the men who handle the affairs of the world!

In my opinion, someone who was really good at handling the affairs of the world would not go about it like this. The people have their constant inborn nature. To weave for their clothing, to till for their food—this is the Virtue they share. They are one in it and not partisan, and it is called the Emancipation of Heaven.

Burton Watson[2]

[1] Frequently mentioned in early texts as an expert judge of horses.

[2] Burton Watson, *The Complete Works of Chuang Tzu* (New York: Columbia University Press, 1968).

Liu An
(d. 122 B.C.)

Ching Ti was the first emperor to recognize the *Tao Te Ching* as a classic. Liu An was his nephew and Prince of Huai-nan.

HUAI-NAN TZU[1]

Now this Tao covers Heaven and carries Earth. It spreads to the four regions and strikes the eight uttermost points. . . . Be indifferent: "antiact and never lack effect." Go easy: antigovern and nothing will remain ungoverned. Now this *wu-wei* [antiaction] we're talking about, it means not to get ahead of things when you act. This "never lack effect," it's based on what things do of themselves. This "antigovern," it means don't change nature or natural process. This "nothing will remain ungoverned" is based on the fact that things adjust each other.

William McNaughton

Ko Hung
(early fourth century)

Ko Hung was the author of a monumental encyclopedia on the art of achieving immortality: *Pao-p'u-tzu—Embrace the Simple, the Unrefined.* One day a student, T'eng Sheng, asked him, "Do these sennin [Taoist immortals] really exist?" Hung wrote the *Shen-hsien chuan* (Lives of the Spiritual Sennin, or Lives of the Taoists) to answer his question.

[1] The title just means "The Man from Huai-nan." The book is named after the title of Liu An, its author (or, as some say, its patron).

LIVES OF THE TAOISTS

Li Ah

Li Ah was a native of Szechwan. Over several generations people noticed that Li Ah never got any older. He often begged in the Central Market at Chengtu, and what he took in by begging, he gave away afterward to the poor and the destitute. He went away at night and came back in the morning. Nobody in the market knew where he stayed.

Sometimes people looked Li Ah up and asked him to foretell the future for them. At such times Ah never said a word, but people just looked at his face, and they could tell what was going to happen. If Li Ah's face had a happy expression, then everything was going to turn out all right. But if it had a sad expression, things were going to go badly. If Li Ah laughed, there would be some really good luck; but if he sighed a little, then there would be some deep misfortune. Having learned the future from Li Ah like this, people waited for the event, and Li Ah was never wrong.

Now one time there was a strong young man who thought maybe Ah was different from other men, and so the strong young man often came around and did things for Ah. Once, out of curiosity, he followed Ah far enough to see where Ah stayed at night. He discovered that Ah lived at Green City Mountain.

Later the strong young man decided he would follow Ah and take Ah for his *guru,* and so he went off with him. But the strong man didn't have the Tao yet, and he was afraid they might meet tigers and wolves. So he hid his father's big sword in his things and brought it along. Ah saw it, and he was displeased with the young man.

"If you're going to come along with me and follow my way," Ah said, "why are you afraid of tigers?"

Ah took the sword and hit a big rock with it. The sword broke into pieces.

The strong young man was very unhappy. Next morning, as he and Ah went out together, Ah said to the young man, "You're unhappy that the sword is broken, aren't you?"

"What I'm afraid of," said the strong young man, "is that my father's going to be mad at me. It was his sword."

Well, then Ah took the pieces of the sword in his left hand and hit the ground with them. Suddenly the sword was exactly as it had been before.

As they were going back toward Chengtu, on the road before they got to town, they met a man driving his cart at a reckless speed. Li Ah stuck his leg under the cart, and wheel rut and leg both were broken. Ah (the record says) thereupon died. The strong young man looked on in horror. But in a moment Li Ah got up and rubbed his leg. Soon the leg was as good as it had ever been.

At this time the strong young man was eighteen years old, and Ah looked to be in his early fifties. When the strong young man was in his eighties, Li Ah still looked exactly the same. Later, they say, this Li Ah was called off to the K'unlun Mountains. He went away, and nobody ever saw him again.

Mr. Whiterock

Mr. Whiterock, so-called, was the younger brother of Chung-huang Chang-jen. During the "P'eng Tsu Period"—if I may so call it—Whiterock was over two thousand years old. He was not interested in the art [Tao] of flying around in the sky; he was only interested in the secret of immortality.

Mr. Whiterock never lost his delight in the pleasures of ordinary human experience. His discipline had as its main point getting together with a few friends and having a good time; it had as its zenith a medicine of gold smelt.[1]

At first Mr. Whiterock lived in poverty, and so he couldn't afford any medicine. He raised sheep, cattle, and pigs, and in ten years or so, going easy on expenditures for clothes and folderols, he had put together goods and capital to a total worth of around ten thousand gold pieces. Then he could buy all the medicine he wanted, and take it.

He often boiled up white rocks and made a meal, because he lived on Whiterock Mountain. So people at that time started calling him "Mr. Whiterock." He also ate dried meat and drank wine, and ate rice and other grains. He could walk a hundred to a hundred and thirty-five miles a

[1] That is, he was an alchemist who tried to concoct an elixir of immortality out of melted gold.

day. To look at his face, you'd think he was a man in his early forties. He liked to get up in the morning and pay his respects to the spirits. He liked to read the hermetic classics and books on the origin of matter.

Once P'eng-tsu said to him, "Why don't you take the medicine that lets you fly around in the sky?"

"Fly around in the sky?" Whiterock replied. "The only thing I'm interested in is living a long time. In the sky do they have better times than we have down here? All those Most Venerables to worship and serve. Service and worship—it's worse in the sky than it is on earth." So people of that time called Mr. Whiterock "The Retired Sennin," because he didn't bother trying to get up in the sky or getting appointed a celestial mandarin. And also, I suppose, because he didn't really care if he'd heard it all or not.

William McNaughton

CH'AN (ZEN) BUDDHISM

Bodhidharma

(d. A.D. 528)

According to tradition, Bodhidharma introduced Ch'an Buddhism to China. Modern authorities, somewhat skeptically, call him "a semi-legendary figure."

Bodhidharma sat looking at the wall. Shen-kuang came up and said, "My mind is not pacified. Sir, will you pacify my mind?"

"Bring your mind here," replied Bodhidharma, "and I will pacify it."

Shen-kuang said, "I have searched for my mind for a long time, and I cannot find it."

"There!" said Bodhidharma. "I have pacified your mind already."

Tao-hsin
(579–651)

Fa-yung lived at an isolated temple up on the wilds of Mount Niu-t'ou. Tao-hsin went to see him. As they were standing around talking, a wild animal roared in the woods just a few feet from the two men. Tao-hsin jumped.

"Ah ha," Fa-yung said, "I see it is still with you."

Later Tao-hsin noticed that Fa-yung liked to sit on a particular rock and meditate. When Fa-yung was busy elsewhere, Tao-hsin went out and painted Buddha's holy name on the rock.

The next time Fa-yung was going out to sit on his rock and meditate, Tao-hsin contrived to walk with him. They got to the rock, and Fa-yung started to sit down. Then he saw Buddha's name on the rock. For a moment he hesitated.

"Ah ha," said Tao-hsin, "I see it is still with you, too."

Hui-neng
(638–713)

Hui-neng said to Ming the monk: "What did your original face look like, before your mother and father were born?"

P'an-shan
(eighth century)

In the market P'an-shan heard someone say to the butcher, "Give me the best piece of meat you've got."

"No piece in my shop," replied the butcher, "is not the best piece."

At this P'an-shan was enlightened.

Pai-chang
(724–814)

Pai-chang went one day to see his teacher, Ma-tsu. As they were talking, a flock of wild geese flew over. Ma-tsu asked Pai-chang, "What are those things?"

"They're wild geese, sir," replied Pai-chang.

"Where are they going?" asked Ma-tsu.

"They have flown away, sir," replied Pai-chang.

Ma-tsu grabbed Pai-chang's nose and twisted it. Pai-chang cried in pain.

"You say they have flown away," said Ma-tsu, "but all the same they have been here from the beginning."

At this instant Pai-chang was enlightened.

Pai-chang decided to send out one of his monks to set up a new monastery. He called them all together and told them that whoever could give the best answer to his question would be chosen to set up the new monastery. Then Pai-chang put a vase of water on the ground and said, "Without calling its name, tell me, what is this?"

"Well," said the head monk, "nobody could say it's a tree stump."

Kuei-shan, the cook monk, tipped over the vase with his foot and walked away.

Pai-chang said, "The head monk loses."

Nan-ch'üan
(748–834)

Nan-ch'üan was living in a little hut in the mountains. One morning he was getting ready to go out and do some work in the fields, and a strange monk stopped by to visit him.

"Make yourself at home," said Nan-ch'üan to the visitor. "There's food in the hut. You can cook yourself lunch. Then why don't you bring the leftovers up the road there, where I'll be working?"

Nan-ch'üan worked in the field until noon, past noon, finally until evening, and the visitor never came. Nan-ch'üan went home at dusk very hungry. When he got home he discovered that the visitor had cooked and eaten a meal, then had thrown away all the food and had broken all the utensils. The visitor was sleeping in the hut.

The exhausted Nan-ch'üan lay down beside his visitor to sleep. The visitor got up and left.

Years later Nan-ch'üan told his students about this visitor. "He was such a good monk," said Nan-ch'üan. "I miss him even today."

Yueh-shan
(751–834)

One morning Yueh-shan lectured to the monks. After the lecture one monk stopped Yueh-shan and said, "Sir, I, uh, I have a problem. I was wondering if you could help me solve it?"

Yueh-shan replied, "I'll solve it at tonight's lecture."

That evening when the monks had filed into the lecture hall and sat down, Yueh-shan said to the group, "The monk who told me this morning he had a problem—will he please come to the front of the room now?"

The monk walked up and stood beside Yueh-shan in front of the group. Yueh-shan grabbed him roughly and said, "You monks, look! This fellow has a problem!"

Then Yueh-shan pushed the monk aside and went off to his own room.

Kuei-shan
(770–853)

With his disciple, Yang-shan, Kuei-shan founded the Kuei-yang branch of Zen.

Zen master Kuei-shan sent for the monastery's treasurer. The treasurer came in, and Kuei-shan said, "I sent for the treasurer, not you."

The treasurer did not know what to do.

Kuei-shan sent for the head monk. When the head monk came in, Kuei-shan said, "I sent for the head monk, not you."

The head monk did not know what to do, either.

Chao-chou
(778–897)

One day a monk came up to the Zen master Chao-chou. The monk said, "The dog there, does it have a Buddha nature?"

Chao-chou replied, "Moo!"[1]

A monk asked an old lady where a certain temple was. The temple, a popular place for pilgrims to visit, was supposed to bring wisdom to anyone who worshiped there.

"It's straight ahead," said the woman. The monk walked on, and the old woman said, "A common churchgoer, like any other."

Somebody told Chao-chou about this incident, and Chao-chou said, "Let's investigate this."

Next day Chao-chou went and asked the old woman where the temple was, and the same thing happened. Chao-chou came back and said, "I have investigated that old woman."

A new monk came to Chao-chou and said, "I have just entered the monastery, sir. Will you be my teacher?"

Chao-chou said, "Have you eaten?"

"Yes," replied the monk. "I have eaten."

"Then you'd better wash your bowl," Chao-chou said.

At this the monk was enlightened.

[1] "Moo": "No," or "It does not have." In Chao-chou's time the word would probably have been pronounced "miu," which doesn't change the point. Verbally the orthodox or expected answer would have been "Yes."

A monk said to Chao-chou, "What is the significance of Bodhidharma's trip to the East?"[1]

"The cypress tree in the front yard," replied Chao-chou.

T'ung-shan
(d. 869)

A monk asked T'ung-shan, "What is Buddha?"

"Three pounds of flax," replied T'ung-shan.

Te-shan
(779–865)

Te-shan was a great scholar and authority on the *Diamond Sutra.* When Te-shan heard of the Ch'an (Zen) school with its unorthodox doctrines, he decided he should go south and challenge it. So he packed up his translation and notes on the *Diamond Sutra,* slung them on his back, and set out.

On his way Te-shan stopped at an inn. He asked the old lady who kept the inn for some tea and cakes.

"Your reverence," asked the old lady, "what are all those writings you're carrying?"

Te-shan replied, "It's the manuscript of my translation, notes, and commentary on the *Diamond Sutra.*"

"The *Diamond Sutra,*" said the old lady. "That's the one that says the past mind is gone, the present mind is ungraspable, and the future mind is unreachable."

"Yes," said Te-shan.

"Well," said the old lady, "which mind will you have your tea and cakes with?"

Te-shan could not answer the old lady's question. After a while he asked her if there were any Zen masters around. She told him where to find Lung-t'an.

[1] The monk's question is a common way of asking, "What does Buddhism mean, really?"

That evening Te-shan went to see Lung-t'an. Te-shan asked him a lot of questions, and they sat up talking until very late. Lung-t'an finally said, "It's pretty late. Maybe you should go to bed."

Te-shan bowed and opened the screen to leave. Outside it was pitch-dark. Lung-t'an gave Te-shan a light to help him find his way. As Te-shan took the light in his hand, Lung-t'an leaned down and blew it out. Te-shan thereupon was enlightened.

"What has happened?" asked Lung-t'an.

"From now on," replied Te-shan, "I will not doubt the teacher's words."

Next day Te-shan burned his notes and commentaries.

Huang-po
(early ninth century)

Huang-po was Lin-chi's teacher.

Huang-po was talking to the monks. "You bunch of drunks!" he said. "Go on pilgrimages, go on pilgrimages—if I'd gone on as many pilgrimages as you have looking for Zen, where would I be today? Don't you know that in the whole country, there's not a single teacher of Zen?"

A monk walked up to Huang-po and said, "But look, there are men who reform the students and govern them, aren't there? What about such men?"

Huang-po answered, "I didn't say there was no Zen. I said there are no teachers of Zen."

Lin-chi
(d. 867)

Lin-chi was founder of the Lin-chi (Japanese Rinzai) Zen sect.

A monk asked Ts'ui-wei, "Why did Bodhidharma come east?"

Ts'ui said, "Please hand me that meditation armrest."

Later on the same monk asked Lin-chi why Bodhidharma had come east. Lin-chi replied, "Give me that meditation mat."

Lin-chi said, "Monks, there have been men who were willing to sacrifice their bodies and lose their lives for the Law. Twenty years ago, when I was studying with Huang-po, I asked him three times, 'Exactly what is *the* great idea of Buddhism?' And three times he let me have it with the stick, *whop*! It was as if he had caressed me with a branch of sweet artemisia.[1]

"I would really enjoy a good thumping right now. Who would be willing to give it to me?"

A monk came out of the group of listening monks and walked to the front of the room. He said, "*I* will."

Lin-chi picked up the stick and held it out to the monk. The monk hesitated a moment. Lin-chi beat him.

Lin-chi said, "Followers of the Way! Don't be stupid and let them destroy your original face. Don't let one of these old Zenmasters get his stamp on you. They sit around saying, 'I understand Zen. I understand the Tao.' They start talking about it, and the words pour out like a waterfall.

"All of that just makes hell-karma. The man who studies the Way simply and correctly doesn't grab at the world's little excesses. The only thing he worries about and the only thing he wants is, to see and understand simply and correctly.

"See and understand simply and correctly, and then in a globe of light the end has begun."

[1] There is supposed to have been a Taoist ritual in which a child was caressed with such a branch to ensure him a happy life.

Lin-chi said to the monks, "I hear you saying all over the temple, 'We must work on the discipline! We must confirm the results!'

"You are fooling yourselves. If anything can be gotten from the discipline, it is only the karma of birth and death.

"You say that you are all working hard at the ten thousand operations of the six perfections.[1] It seems to me that you are just making more karma. If you seek Buddha and seek the Law, you are laying up karma in hell. If you seek the Bodhisattva, you are making more karma, too. If you read the sutras and read the lessons, you are making more karma.

"Buddhas, Masters and Patriarchs are people who do not have things they have to do. And so for *them* what is corrupt and what is composed, as well as what is uncorrupt and uncomposed, are pure phenomena."[2]

Lin-chi said, "What I'm saying is this. There isn't any Buddha. There isn't any Law. There isn't any discipline to work on, and there aren't any goals to achieve.

"What are you always looking to somebody else for? Blind men! You put a head on top of your head!

"What is it that troubles you? Adepts, there you are. You are the same as a Buddha or Patriarch, but you're always worrying about something. You're always looking around for something.

"Make no mistake about this: there isn't any Law out there. In here there isn't any Law you can get either.

"Do you know what would be better for you than hanging onto my words the way you do? It would be better if you would just relax and stop rushing around. Don't try to keep going what has gotten going. And what hasn't gotten going, don't try to get it going. If you would do that, it would be better for you than ten years of visiting holy places."

[1] The six perfections: in your conduct to be charitable, moral, patient, zealous, and wise; and to meditate.

[2] Composed: that is, aggregate and so subject to decomposition and destruction.

Yen-t'ou
(828–878)

Three monks were standing in the temple yard. One of them saw a bucket of water and pointed to it. The second monk said, "The water is clear, the moon is reflected."

"No," said the first monk. "It is not water and not moon."

The third monk, Yen-t'ou, tipped the bucket over.

Tao-wu
(fl. *ca.* 850)

One time when Yun-yen was sick, Tao-wu went to see him.

"Suppose you die," said Tao-wu, "and leave only your body with us. Then where can I see you?"

Yun-yen replied, "Well, it will not be where nothing is born and nothing dies."

Tao-wu said, "What you should say is, there is no place where nothing is born and nothing dies, and we don't need to see each other again anyway."

Hsuan-sha
(d. 908)

Hsuan-sha wrote a letter to his old teacher, Hsueh-feng, and asked a monk to take it to him. Receiving the letter, Hsueh-feng called his monks together and, as they watched, he opened Hsuan-sha's letter. In the envelope were three blank sheets of paper.

Hsueh-feng showed the sheets to the monks and said, "Do you get it?" None of the monks said anything.

Then Hsueh-feng looked at one of the sheets and began to say, as if reading,

"When spring comes, the flowers bloom;
"When autumn comes, the fruit ripens."

The monk from Hsuan-sha went home and told him what had happened.

"The old man is getting stupid," said Hsuan-sha.

Fa-yen
(early tenth century)

Fa-yen was founder of the Fa-yen branch of Zen.

A young monk went to Fa-yen and said, "My name is Echo, sir. Could I venture to ask your Holiness what is meant by the name Buddha?"

"Oh, so you are Echo, are you?" replied Fa-yen.

Mu-chou
(tenth century)

Mu-chou was walking down the road. He passed a strange monk walking in the opposite direction. A few steps farther on, Mu-chou turned and called back, "Venerable sir!"

The monk turned around.

"Idiot," Mu-chou muttered, and walked on.

Yun-men
(d. 996)

Yun-men founded the Yun-men branch of Zen.

A monk said to Yun-men, "What is Buddha?"
Yun-men replied, "An ass-wipe stick."

Wu-tsu Fa-yen
(d. 1104)

Somebody asked Wu-tsu Fa-yen what Zen was like. Fa-yen replied: "It is like the art of burglary. One time a burglar's son noticed that his father was getting old. The son decided that he should learn to burgle and rob, so that if the old man got sick or died, he would be able to support the family.

"The father thought that this was a good idea, and so he took the son with him the next time he went out on a job. The two of them broke through a fence, sneaked into a rich family's house, and found a large chest full of expensive clothes.

" 'Get in there and bring out the clothes,' said the father.

"As soon as the son was inside, the father locked up the chest and began to shout and make a lot of noise. Then he left the room, went back through the hole in the fence, and returned home.

"Inside the chest the son was frightened out of his wits. He was also furious with his father. Hearing people stirring in the room, the son got an idea. He made a noise like a rat. The family ordered a servant girl to take a light and look inside the chest.

"When the girl opened the chest, the young burglar blew out the light, knocked the girl aside, and ran from the room. The family raised a hue and cry, and the young man found himself running down the street with many citizens running after him. Turning a corner, he saw a well with a large rock lying beside it. The young man waited until the footsteps of his pursuers were very close, then he dropped the rock into the well and hid nearby. The pursuers all gathered around the well to see if they could see the burglar who had drowned himself in the well. Then they went away.

"When the young man got home, he said to his father, 'What did you do that for?' He also said some harsher things. The father said, 'Just tell me what happened.' And so the son told him.

" 'Well,' said the father, 'you said you wanted to learn the art of burglary.' "

One time Wu-tsu Fa-yen said, "The water buffalo's head, horns, and four hooves have all passed through the window lattice. Why can't the tail pass through?"

William McNaughton

PART TWO: JAPAN

Chapter 5
JAPANESE STORIES

Japanese tales date back to the tenth century. Among them are "The Tales of Ise," which give a brief dramatic or narrative setting, either real or imaginary, to a number of poems, and a journal, "The Tosa Diary," a travel diary, which suggests, if it does not fully tell, a good artistic tale. In the centuries that followed, a vast number of tales and journals were written in which the authors' emotions and visions were expressed in the form of prose poems.

Modern Japanese fiction has broken with this approach: One of its main developments has been to create a prose *as* prose, pure and simple. The two tales below represent significant points in this shift. In addition, their authors exemplify stages in the growth of a modern Japanese sensibility. Both are very good stories and each has been the source of an important contemporary motion picture of international renown. One is the main source of *Rashomon*; the other, of *Ugetsu*, which one scholar of the cinema calls perhaps the most perfect film ever made.

Ueda Akinari
(1734–1809)

The earlier works of Ueda Akinari fall into the "Osaka period," of which he is the last major author.

In his later works—most notably the *Ugetsu Monogatari*, or *Tales of Moonlight and Rain*, from which "Homecoming" is taken—he initiated the "Edo (Tokyo) style." Son of an unknown father and of an entertaining girl in the pleasure district of Osaka, Ueda Akinari was adopted by an oil-and-paper merchant named Ueda, who gave him his name. When he was four years old, he fell victim to smallpox, which left him with several paralyzed fingers, and he learned to write only with great difficulty. His adoptive father told him that he owed his survival to the intercession of the fox-god Inari, and for the rest of his life Akinari was devoted to this god—and to no other religious vision, some say. He sold oil and paper, practiced medicine and tried unsuccessfully to earn a living at literature. His friends called him "Mr. Gruff," but he himself chose "The Crab" as his pen name, "because," as he said, "everybody goes straight ahead, but I go sideways."

TALES OF MOONLIGHT AND RAIN

Homecoming

1

In Shimōsa Province, in a village called Mama in the district of Katsushika, there lived a man called Katsushiro. His family, established there since his grandfather's time, owned considerable farmland and had led quite a prosperous life. But Katsushiro, by nature a freedom-loving, carefree man who hated the drudgery of tilling the soil, had neglected the farm, and the family fortune dwindled.

A poor man now, Katsushiro felt the stinging pain of the arrows of scorn shot at him by his many relatives—indeed, so much so that he began devising various ways and means of recouping the family fortune.

At about this time there was a traveling merchant named Sasabe no Soji, who made annual trips from Kyoto to Shimōsa to purchase supplies of silk cloth made and dyed in the village of Ashikaga, for sale in the capital. Since Sasabe had relatives in Mama, he often visited the village. Katsushiro thus knew him well, and in the course of a casual conversation he revealed to Sasabe his desire to become a tradesman and travel to Kyoto. Sasabe, to Katsushiro's great delight, readily agreed to help him in such a venture and inquired how soon he would be prepared to leave.

Katsushiro sold what little farmland he still owned and, with the money, purchased a considerable amount of Ashikaga silk for sale in Kyoto and made other preparations for his journey.

Katsushiro's wife, Miyagi, was a beautiful woman who attracted the attention and admiration of everyone. She was by nature wise, affectionate, and loyal. She had her misgivings about her husband's plan to go to Kyoto with trading goods and tried earnestly to talk him out of it. But since Katsushiro was more determined than ever, she could not stop him. While worrying about her own future livelihood, alone at home during his absence, she nevertheless bravely helped him in all sorts of ways to prepare for his long journey.

On the last night before he left, they said tender farewells to each other. . . .

The cock crowed as they said their last farewells, and Katsushiro started out from his eastern province in the early dawn, hurrying westward toward Kyoto.

2

In the summer of that year (1455), civil war broke out in Kamakura at the court of Ashikaga regent, Shigeuji, who ruled over the eastern half of the shogun's domain, and who was reputedly intriguing to seize control over the whole country. Forces under the high councillor, Lord Uesugi, loyal to the Ashikaga shogun Yoshimasa, in Kyoto, rebelled, reducing the regent's palace to ashes. Shigeuji, defeated in the first clash of arms, fled to Shimōsa, where he put up a strong defense, seeking allies.

The whole Kantō area thus became enveloped in the flaming ravages of war. Warriors shifted their allegiance as the fortunes of war seesawed. Old men fled into mountain fortresses. Young men were forced into the service of battling warlords. Weeping women and children wandered about in confusion and terror, stunned by the blazing destruction of a village one day, a fresh assault by ruthless plunderers the next. . . .

As war cries and screams of terror resounded throughout the area, men became rougher and more ruthless, inspiring fear and dread everywhere. Some of them, attracted to Miyagi's beauty, tried to seduce her by deceptive tricks. But she repulsed them all, firmly and with invincible resolve, thus preserving her virtue and integrity from the lust of evil men. She locked herself in her home, refusing to see anyone. Even her housemaid left her. . . .

3

Katsushiro meanwhile had arrived in Kyoto with Sasabe, where he sold all of his stock of silk cloth. Since at that time fancy, colorful clothing was in great demand in the capital city, he made a big profit on the sale.

Then he began to make preparations to return to the village of Mama, where Miyagi awaited him. But just then rumors spread to Kyoto about the successful attack of Uesugi's army upon the regent and about the war of pursuit and destruction that was going on. He also heard rumors here and there about how his native Shimōsa province had been turned into a fiery battlefield filled with plundering warriors and weapons, mayhem and massacre. . . .

Nevertheless, he started homeward from Kyoto in the beginning of August of the same year, as he had promised his wife. But as he entered the Kiso highway which passed between towering mountains, he was set upon at a place called Misaki by marauding highwaymen, who robbed and stripped him of everything he possessed—money, goods, clothing—sparing only his life.

At the same time he heard from others in the neighborhood that new wartime barriers had been established here and there along the highway to the east, and that travelers were strictly forbidden to pass. . . .

Katsushiro therefore retraced his steps toward Kyoto and went to Ōmi province. There he fell ill with a high fever. At a place called Musa, in Ōmi, there lived a wealthy man called Kodama Kihei, who happened to be Sasabe's father-in-law. To him, therefore, Katsushiro appealed for shelter in his illness. Kodama was kindness itself. Not only did he welcome Katsushiro into his house; he also summoned a physician to provide him with medical treatment. . . .

When his fever subsided and he began to feel better, Katsushiro thanked his host profusely for his compassion and generosity. But it was still difficult for him to walk steadily. And so, contrary to his original intention, he remained at Kodama's house for the rest of the year. . . . He remained there for seven years. . . .

4

Early in 1461, hostilities broke out in Kawachi among the rival, related heirs of the Hatakeyama clan leadership, causing frightful disturbances in the neighborhood of Kyoto. This was followed in the spring by the spread of a virulent epidemic. The streets were filled with the bodies of the dead. Fear rose in the hearts of the living that the world might be coming to an end. Cries of lamentation rent the air.

All this set Katsushiro to thinking seriously about his own situation. Why should he, bereft of all worldly possessions, and without any future prospects, continue to tarry in a distant province, dependent on the blessings and goodwill of people entirely unrelated to him? . . . And so, during a sunny spell in late spring, he bade them farewell, and in about ten days he reached his home.

5

The sun was sinking in the west. It was quite dark, for rain clouds hovered in the sky and seemed about to burst into a downpour. But Katsushiro remembered the village of Mama well, having lived there so long. As he plodded over the early summer grassland, he saw that the spliced bridge he knew so well had fallen into the stream. The old familiar sound of horses' hooves could no longer be heard. The farms, destroyed and abandoned, were utterly desolate. The old roads were gone. Most of the farmhouses that had once stood here and there could no longer be seen. Those that still stood seemed to be inhabited, but they were no longer the same.

Confused, wondering which of the houses was his, he stood searching for it with bewildered eyes. Then, some twenty paces away, he saw clearly through the starlight seeping down from rifts in the clouds a towering pine tree, its trunk split by lightning.

That split pine marked the spot where his house stood. Glad to be home at last, he walked cheerfully on and found his house seemingly intact, the same, it seemed to him, as it had always been.

Someone seemed to be living in it. From a crack in the old front door, a beam of light could be seen. For a moment he wondered whether some strangers were now occupying his house. But then he suddenly thought, could it possibly be that his wife was still alive? How strange indeed that she had endured, alone, unchanged, in this desolate place! The thought stirred him tremendously. Approaching the door, he coughed slightly.

It seemed that someone inside the house, sensing that there was a caller, had come to the door.

Suddenly a voice demanded, "Who's there?"

The voice sounded very old, but Katsushiro realized with a palpitating heart that it was definitely the voice of Miyagi.

"This is Katsushiro," he replied. "I have just returned. It is marvelous that you have endured unchanged in this desolate place."

Apparently Miyagi, too, remembered her husband's voice, for the door opened, revealing to him the dark, grimy figure of a woman with deep-sunken eyes, her tousled hair tumbling down her back. She was almost unrecognizable to Katsushiro as his wife Miyagi.

On seeing him, Miyagi uttered not a word but began to weep bitterly.

Katsushiro, dazed and groping for words, said after a while, "Had I known that you were living here in this condition, would I have spent the long months and years away? Long ago, in Kyoto, I heard about the rebellion in Kamakura, about how the regent's forces fled here to Shimōsa to defend themselves, and how they were viciously attacked by the rebellious lord of the province. . . .

"Shimōsa province, I was told, had long since been despoiled and was being overrun ceaselessly by horses' hooves. Perhaps, I thought, you had burned along with the house, or you had drowned yourself in the sea. So I gave up the thought of returning home and went back to Kyoto. Thus for seven years I lived on the kindness of others. Lately, I've felt an intense longing for you, so I came back to see for myself what had happened to you. I did not even dream that you were still alive. But perhaps I'm only dreaming now."

Miyagi wiped the tears from her eyes and said, "Soon after we parted, before that autumn you promised to return, this became a fearful place. The people of the village fled from their farms to the sea, to the mountain fortresses. Most of the few who remained became bestial in their greed. Taking advantage of my being alone, they tried to attack me, using clever tricks. I resisted firmly, determined not to surrender my virtue just to prolong my life. Many, many were the times I endured insufferable tortures.

"The *Tanabata* festival of stars,[1] heralding the approach of autumn, came and went, but you did not return. I waited through the winter, and then spring came. But still there was no word from you. I thought of going to Kyoto myself to search for you. But the barriers were so strictly closed to travelers that not even the bravest of men could hope to slip through. How much less could a lone woman hope to succeed in getting past. The pine tree standing like a sentinel in front of this house, and the woman sitting and waiting inside—both have fallen into decay, with only foxes and owls as companions to this day. But now that you have returned, all the long, lonely, fearful years of bitterness are over, and I rejoice to see you again.

"I myself have found happiness by persevering until I could be reunited with you, but sad indeed is the lot of a woman who has died in anger and sorrow, waiting in vain for her husband's return."

She began to weep again, and Katsushiro comforted her by putting his arms tenderly around her shoulders. "The summer night is short," he said, "and soon it will be dawn."

Thus they lay down to sleep together.

6

The wind, rustling in the pine grove, wafted in through the torn paper of the window and the night was cool. Katsushiro, weary from the long journey home, soon fell into a deep sleep.

[1] The festival, originally held on the seventh day of the seventh lunar month, is now celebrated on July 7. In Chinese myth, two lovers, the Herd Boy and the Weaving Girl—represented by stars—were separated by the Heavenly River (the Milky Way) every night of the year except this one. Now the festival is a "prayer ceremony" for children's artistic development.

Then, as dawn began to light the sky, he opened his eyes with a lingering feeling of drowsiness. He felt somewhat chilly, so he reached for the blanket, to draw it up to his chin. His hand touched instead something strange and rustling, and he was suddenly wide awake. He felt cold drops on his face. Looking up at the ceiling, expecting raindrops, he saw that the roof of the house had been blown off, apparently by winds. Through the opening the last remaining silvery beams of the setting moon were filtering in.

As he got up to look around, he saw that the door of the house, for all practical purposes, might just as well have been missing. The bamboo fence outside lay crumbled, tall bushes growing wildly amidst the fragments. Everything seemed wet with dew, so much so that he could have squeezed drops from his sleeve. The walls of the house were covered with spreading arrowroot and ivy vines. What had once been a garden was now overgrown with weeds. The house itself was in a state of ruin, like a wild field in the fall.

Suddenly, thinking of his wife, Miyagi, with whom he had slept the night before, he wondered where she could have gone. She was nowhere to be seen.

Then for a moment the thought occurred to Katsushiro that this morning's disenchantment must be devilry perpetrated by the fabled fox. Yet there was no mistake about it. This was the house he had lived in long ago. The large back room extending from the porch to the paddy crib which he himself had put up remained precisely as he had built it. Aghast, he almost forgot to watch his step as he walked on.

Thinking the matter over closely, he came to the conclusion that Miyagi must already be dead, and that bewitching foxes and badgers had taken over the house, making it so desolate. Something mysterious, perhaps assuming the likeness of Miyagi, must have revealed itself to him last night. Was it possible that the spirit of his wife, who loved him, had returned to the earth to spend the night with him? Perhaps after all he had not erred in thinking that she was no longer of this earth. He felt as though he were dreaming, for the tears would not come to his eyes.

As he walked around the house, smitten with loneliness, bereft of the wife whom he had always loved, he came upon the section that had once been their bedroom. The floorboards were ripped open and there was a mound of piled earth, so contrived as to be protected from the rain and dew. Perhaps last night's spirit had risen from here. The thought was at once dreadful and reassuring.

Among the holy things placed on the grave mound was a piece of planed wood covered with Nasuno paper on which were written several words, some of which were faded and scarcely legible but which Katsushiro recognized as the handwriting of his wife. There was no posthumous holy name, nor the date of death, only thirty-one syllables of poetry expressing her grief just before she died:

To think that my life
Has lasted to this day.
Deceived by my love,
I have waited, waited vainly,
For my husband's return.

For the first time Katsushiro was sure that his wife was dead. Crying out loudly and bitterly, he collapsed in grief.

7

After a while Katsushiro began to feel wretched that he did not know the day, month, and year of Miyagi's death. Someone in the village no doubt remembered and could tell him, he thought. Wiping his tears, he walked out of the house. The sun had risen high in the eastern sky. Going to the first house in the neighborhood, he saw the master, but he was a man whom Katsushiro had not known in the past. The stranger confronted him with a brusque demand: "Who are you, and where did you come from?"

Katsushiro made a polite salutation and explained. . . .

"I am very sorry for you indeed," the man replied. "But I have lived here for only about a year. . . . But there is an old man who is said to have been in this village since very long ago. He sometimes goes to that house of yours to pray. I am sure he can provide the information you seek."

"And where does he live, may I ask?" Katsushiro said.

"About five hundred paces from here, near the beach, there is a well planted hemp farm. He lives in a small house there."

Katsushiro walked briskly to the place indicated and

found an old man of about seventy years of age, his back considerably bent, sitting on a straw mat in front of a stove in the yard and sipping tea. As soon as the old man saw Katsushiro, he shouted, "Well, Katsushiro, why did it take you so long to return?"

Katsushiro recognized him immediately as Uruma, a man who had lived in the village since olden times. He first congratulated him on his longevity, then told him about how he had been unexpectedly detained at Kyoto, and about his strange experience the night before. He thanked the old man for burying his wife and for offering prayers for the peace of her soul, and his eyes filled with tears.

Old Uruma said, "War broke out the summer after you left on that distant journey. The villagers fled in terror. . . .

"As for myself, I could hardly walk even a short distance because my legs were weak, so I, too, resolutely stayed indoors.

"This place became desolate, like the dwelling place of fearful demonlike spirits of trees. For a young and beautiful woman like Miyagi to have had to endure it was the most wretched thing that this old man has known in his life.

"Autumn came and went, and winter and spring, too. She passed away on the tenth of August.

"I felt very sorry for her. I made a coffin for her, dug a grave with my own hands, and buried her. I placed a poem she had written before she died on the mound as a grave marker, along with the usual religious offerings. I never learned how to write, so I could not record the date of her death. And there were no temples within reach, so I could not ask a priest to come and perform the burial rites, or to bestow upon her a posthumous holy name.

"Five years have passed since then. Judging from what you have told me about last night, I guess Miyagi's spirit must have returned to earth to tell you of the long year of suffering she endured. I think you should go back there and pray for the peace of her soul with all your heart."

So saying, old Uruma rose to his feet, picked up his staff, and led Katsushiro to Miyagi's grave.

Kneeling before the grave together, they wept and prayed.

Kenji Hamada

Akutagawa Ryunosuke
(1892–1927)

At school Akutagawa Ryunosuke excelled in "Sino-Japanese" and read the best poets of China in their own language. In college he studied English and came to know Western literature extremely well. His favorite Western authors were Ibsen, Baudelaire, Strindberg, and Anatole France, and he translated France and William Butler Yeats into Japanese. For four years, Ryunosuke taught English in a technical college and then resigned to devote his time to literature, and to work as a newspaper correspondent. Ryunosuke took the modern, de-poeticized Japanese prose, developed by the Japanese naturalists, and, following Mori Ogai, Natsume Soseki—and Occidental models—pushed to a limit the modern objective kind of fiction, a fiction remote from the diary-journal-autobiographical, quasi-autobiographical, or pseudo-autobiographical fiction of the tradition. Nevertheless he is often called a "poet-in-prose," and the intensity and concentration of his stories are truly remarkable. This may be what makes them film so well. In his later years, Ryunosuke was troubled by poor health, obsessions, and hallucinations. At dawn on July 24, 1927, he committed suicide by taking cyanide. The explanation he left: "a vague uneasiness."

IN A GROVE

Testimony of a Woodcutter Questioned by the Police Lieutenant

"I swear, Lieutenant, what I'm telling you is true. It was me that discovered the body. That morning, as usual, I went to the other side of the mountain to chop down cedars. The body was in a grove in the shadow of the mountain. The exact spot? About five hundred yards, I think, from the stop at Yamashina. It's a wild place where there are scattered clumps of bamboos and stunted cedars.

"The body was lying on its back, and had on a pale-blue hunting-cloak. He wore that steel-gray headgear they wear in the capital. You could only see one gash on the body, but it was a deep wound across his chest. The dead bamboo-leaves strewn around the body looked like they'd been dyed a dark red. No, the blood wasn't running from the wound anymore. It was already dry around the edges. There was a large horsefly sticking on the wound as if he didn't hear me coming.

"Didn't I find a sword or something? No. Nothing at all. Only, at the foot of the next tree there was a straw rope. . . . Oh, yeah, besides the rope there was also a comb. That's all I found around the body. But the grass and dead bamboo-leaves had all been trampled down. He must have really fought hard before they killed him. What'd you say? Didn't I see a horse? No. It wasn't a place a horse could get into. There was a thick underbrush between the spot and the road."

Testimony of a Wandering Monk Questioned by the Same Police Lieutenant

"I can assure you, Lieutenant, that the man I saw yesterday was the one found dead today. Yes, it was around noon, I think, halfway between Sekiyama and Yamashina. He was walking toward Sekiyama. There was a woman with him riding a horse. The woman wore a veil, so I wasn't able to see her face. I only remember her dress, which was sort of lilac-colored. The horse was a chestnut, and the mane was cut short. At least I think it was. How big was the horse? Hmmm, about five feet, but I'm not really sure. Being a monk, I'm not an expert on the material world. The man? He was armed with a sword and carried a bow and arrows. And I especially remember the black-lacquered quiver in which he had put about twenty arrows. Yes, I distinctly remember it.

"How could I have foreseen the fate that would befall him? Is not human life like a flash of lightning or the early morning dew? . . . I grieve for this man, but I cannot find words to express my grief."

Testimony of an Old Woman Questioned by the Same Police Lieutenant

"The man I arrested? There's no question—he's a famous bandit called Tajomaru. But when I found him he was lying there moaning on the stone bridge of the Awataguchi Road. It looked like he had fallen from his horse. What time was it? Oh, around ten o'clock last night. Last time I saw him—he got away from me that time—he was wearing the same dark-blue hunting-jacket, with the same sword in the same tight sheath. This time, as you've already discovered, he also carried a bow and arrows. Oh, yes? The victim had the same weapons? In that case there's no doubt. The murderer is Tajomaru. The bow, wrapped with leather, the black-lacquered quiver, and the seventeen falcon-arrows all belonged to the dead man. And the horse, like you said, was a chestnut with a shaved mane. To be thrown from that animal, that was Tajomaru's destiny. The horse, dragging a long rein on the ground, was grazing on the grass by the side of the road, just a little beyond the stone bridge.

"This Tajomaru, of all the bandits that work around the capital—everybody knows he's a woman-hunter. Last fall in the mountain behind Toribe Temple, people found a woman and a young girl dead. The woman had come to pray. The rumor was that Tajomaru had killed them. If it was really Tajomaru that killed the man, we should try to find out what happened to the woman on the horse. Excuse me, I may be stepping out of line. But this point should be cleared up."

Testimony of an Old Woman Questioned by the Police Lieutenant

"Yes, it's my son-in-law's body. He was not from the capital. He was an officer in the Wakasa Provincial Government. His name was Kanazawa no Takehiro. He was twenty-six years old. No. He was such a sweet person, no one would have wanted to do him harm.

"My daughter? Her name is Masago. She is nineteen years old. Oh, she's a brave girl, as brave as any man. Besides Takehiro, she's never known any other man. Her skin is golden-brown, and she has a beauty mark below her left eye. Her face is small and oval.

"Takehiro and my daughter left yesterday for Wakasa. But what fate led them into such a disaster? And what's happened to my daughter? I know I have to accept my son-in-law's death . . . but I'm worried about my daughter. . . . Please, I am an old woman . . . please find my daughter, if you have to dig up the grass and trees. . . . That bandit, what is his name? Tajomaru! How I hate him! He not only killed my son-in-law, he also . . ." (Sobs cut off her words.)

Tajomaru's Confession

"Yeah, I killed him. But not the woman. You want to know where she is? How should I know? I don't know anything about her. Hey, what are you going to do? Wait a minute! It won't do you any good to torture me, I can't tell you something I don't know. You know I killed him, why should I hide anything about the girl? I'll tell you what I know.

"Early yesterday afternoon, I passed by the couple. A light breeze lifted her silk veil and uncovered her face. Only for a moment . . . then I couldn't see her anymore. I guess partly because I only saw her so briefly, but she looked like a Bosatsu. Suddenly I decided to take the woman, even if I had to kill the man.

"What? To kill a man's not as big a thing as you think. If you rape the woman, you've got to kill the man. Me, I swing the sword I have in my belt, you don't have to use one. You, you kill by power, by money, even by a kind word. Obviously, there's no blood. Your victim goes on living. But all the same you've killed him. I wonder which one of us, you or me, is guiltier." (A sneer crosses his face.)

"But what's even better is to rape the woman without killing the man. The way I felt then, I decided to take the woman and not hurt the man, if I could. Since I couldn't attack her right there on Yamashina Road—you know what the road is like—I decided to lead them into the mountain.

"It was easy. Pretending to be another traveler, I told

them this. 'There, down in the mountain, there's an old tomb. While I was digging around, I found a lot of mirrors and swords. To keep away thieves, I buried the treasure in a grove in the shadow of that mountain. I'm looking for a buyer, and I'll sell him anything he wants, dirt-cheap.' The man seemed very interested in my little story. So . . . what do you think happened? Look out for greed! In a few minutes, the couple on horseback was following me to the mountain.

"When we got to the grove, I told them that was where I'd buried the treasures and told them if they wanted to see them to follow me. The man, blinded by greed, had no reason to hesitate, but the woman wanted to wait where she was, without getting off her horse. I can see why she didn't want to come with us, what with all that thick underbrush. And that's just what I was hoping for. So, leaving her alone, I went into the grove, the man following me.

"At first, the grove was nothing but bamboos. About sixty yards from there was a small clearing of cedars . . . no spot could have been better for my plan. While clearing out the underbrush, I told him, looking quite sincere, that the treasures were under the cedars. Soon there were fewer bamboos, and we reached the clearing. . . . As soon as we got there, I threw him on the ground. Armed with a sword, the man looked very strong. But I really caught him off guard with such an unexpected attack. Like *that,* I had him tied to the foot of a tree. The rope? I'm a thief, I always have a rope tied to my belt, in case I need, say, to escape over a fence. To keep him from shouting, I just stuffed his mouth full of dead bamboo leaves.

"After I'd made sure he was tied tightly, I went back to the woman and told her to come with me because her husband had gotten sick. I don't need to tell you, my plan worked. As soon as she'd taken off her veil, she started toward the grove. I was holding her hand. When she saw her husband tied to the tree, she unsheathed her dagger—she'd taken it from underneath her clothes, I don't know when. I've never met such a bold woman. If I'd looked away for a moment, I would've been dead. She would have stabbed me in the stomach. I moved fast, but it was hard to keep from getting hit, the way she was fighting. But no one fools around with me, I am Tajomaru. I made her drop her dagger without even taking my sword from its scabbard.

Troublesome as she was, once I had her weapon there was nothing she could do. So I got what I wanted without killing.

"Without killing. I didn't have any reason to kill the man, then. I was about to leave the grove, the woman crying, when she caught hold of my arms like a madwoman. I heard her say in a broken voice that she wanted either me or her husband to die. She could not stand being shamed before two men—it was more painful than death. But that's not all. Breathing hard, she said she wanted to stay with whoever lived. At that moment, I was struck with a wild desire to kill her husband." (A dark emotion makes him shudder.)

"Listening to my story, you probably think I'm a much meaner man than you. That's because you've never seen this woman's face—and especially because you didn't see the way her eyes shone when she was begging me. When our eyes met, I burned with the desire to marry her even if I had to fall dead right then. Marry her . . . I couldn't push the idea out of my mind. Everything changed then. It wasn't just lust, like you probably think. If I'd only wanted to rape her, I would have left them after giving her a good kick. And I wouldn't have stained my sword with his blood. But when I stared at her in the dim light of the grove, I knew I couldn't leave that spot until I had killed her husband.

"I didn't want to kill him while he was tied up, like I was a coward. So I untied him and challenged him to a fight. (You found the rope under the tree. I forgot to take it with me.) His face grim, he took out his long sword and without saying a word threw himself at me. I don't need to tell you about it. On the twenty-third thrust, my sword went into his chest. The twenty-third thrust! Even now, I'm impressed with this. No one else ever lasted more than twenty with me." (He smiles a satisfied smile.)

"As the man fell to the ground, I turned toward the woman, the bloody sword in my hand. But then—what? . . . She was gone! Where had she gone? I looked around through the cedars for her, but the dead bamboo-leaves on the ground showed no sign of her. I couldn't hear anything but the moans of the man dying.

"Maybe, from the first blows of our swords, she ran from the grove looking for help. This time, as you know, it was my life that was in danger, so I grabbed up the sword, bow, and arrows and quickly headed for the mountain road we'd come from. The woman's horse was still grazing quietly. What did I do next? I don't need to tell you. The only other thing I want to say is, before I got to the capital, I sold the sword. That's my confession. Sooner or later I'll be hanged. So, condemn me." (His attitude is arrogant.)

Penitent Statement by a Woman at the Kiyomizu Temple

"After he violated me, the man in the dark-blue hunting-jacket laughed at my husband, who was tied to a tree. How my husband must have wanted to get at him! But the more he struggled to get loose, the more the rope cut into his skin. Without thinking, I ran . . . no, I *wanted* to run with all my strength to my husband. Before I had a chance, the bandit kicked me and I fell to the ground. At that moment, I saw a strange look in my husband's eyes. Really strange. . . . That look, even now, every time I remember it, makes me tremble. Unable to say a word to me, my husband showed all his feelings with that brief look. What flashed in his eyes? It wasn't anger, it wasn't sorrow. Could it have been anything else but a cold glimmer of contempt? As though in a trance I cried out, and then I fainted.

"I don't know how much time had gone by when I finally came to. The man in the dark-blue hunting-jacket had disappeared. My husband was still tied to the foot of the cedar. Painfully, I lifted myself from the dead leaves onto my elbow, and I stared at my husband. His look had not changed—now mixed with the cold contempt, there was hatred. Ashamed, sad, furious—how could I tell what I was feeling then? I stood up shakily, and I moved close to my husband. I said to him: 'You! Now that you have seen me fall into this shame, I can no longer stay with you! I must kill myself. Now. But . . . I want you to die, you as well as me. You have seen my shame. I can't let you go on living after me.'

"I said that with all my strength. But without flinching, my husband kept on staring at me with hatred. Heart pounding, I looked for my husband's sword. The bandit must have taken it, I couldn't find it in the underbrush. I couldn't find the bow and arrows, either. But I did find a knife. I picked it up and said again to my husband, 'I want your life. I will die right after you.'

"When I said this, he finally moved his lips. I could not hear what he said because his mouth was full of dead bamboo-leaves. But from the slight movement of his lips, I knew what he wanted. Still filled with contempt, he said, 'Kill me!'

"As though in a dream, I plunged the knife into his chest through his light-blue hunting-jacket.

"I must have fainted again. When I finally woke up, I looked around me. My husband, still tied, had been dead a long time. Through the branches of the bamboos and cedars, a ray of light from the setting sun strayed across his gray face. Holding back my tears, I untied the rope around his body. Then . . . what happened to me? I have no more strength to talk of it. I tried so many ways, but I couldn't kill myself. I put the knife to my throat, I threw myself into a pond at the foot of the mountain. I tried everything. But since I'm still alive, why should I brag about it?" (She smiles a sad smile.) "Even the Bosatsu, endlessly merciful, will he turn away from me, cowardly woman that I am? I who killed my husband, I who have been violated by a bandit, what can I do . . . now? But, I . . . I . . ." (She breaks into violent sobs.)

The Dead Man's Story Through the Mouth of a Shamaness

"The bandit, having gotten what he wanted, sat down where he was and tried many ways to console my wife. I, of course, couldn't say what effect this had. My body was tied to the foot of a cedar. I winked at my wife several times. 'Don't listen to him. Everything he says—it's lies!' I wanted her to understand that. But sitting weakly on the dead bamboo-leaves, she stared steadily at her knees. It looked like she was listening to the bandit. At least, it looked that way to me. I was shaking violently, burning with jealousy. The bandit chose his words cleverly. He said, 'Your husband won't want you anymore, now that your body's soiled. Wouldn't you like to leave him and marry me? It was the love that you aroused in me that made me so bold . . .' The bandit dared to use arguments like this.

"Hearing his words, my wife, as though enraptured, lifted her head. I have never seen my wife look so beautiful. But what do you think my wife, 'so beautiful,' said to this bandit in front of her husband tied up there? Drifting through these voids, each time I remember, I become filled with rage. She said, 'Take me where you want!' " (There is a long silence.)

"But my wife's crime is even worse. Without that, I wouldn't be suffering so much in this darkness. As she was about to leave the grove, holding the bandit's hand, she suddenly turned white, and she pointed her finger at me tied to the tree. She said, 'Kill that man! If he's alive, I can't live with you!' My wife said these words over and over again as if she were mad. 'Kill him!' These words, like a storm, even now blow me over and over into a remote darkness. Has a word so horrible ever come from a human mouth? Has a word so damned ever struck a human ear? A word . . ." (He breaks into a derisive laugh.) "Hearing these words, the bandit himself turned pale. Saying it again—'Kill him!'—my wife caught hold of the bandit's arm. Staring at my wife, he said nothing—not yes, not no. The next moment, with one kick, he knocked her down on the dead bamboo-leaves." (He breaks again into a derisive laugh.) "The bandit, slowly crossing his arms, turned to me and said, 'What do you want me to do? Do you want me to kill her or let her live? Show me with your head, do you want me to kill her? . . .'

"For this single sentence, I could have forgiven the bandit." (There is another long silence.)

"When I hesitated, my wife cried out and ran deeper into the grove. Not losing a second, the bandit ran after her, but he couldn't even catch her sleeve. I watched, as if I were in a dream.

"After my wife had fled, the bandit picked up my sword, my bow, and my arrows and cut the rope that he had tied me with. 'This time, it's my turn'—I remember this phrase that he murmured as he left the grove. After he was gone, everything was quiet again. Then suddenly I said, 'Is someone crying?' Taking off the rope, I listened, but it was I that was crying." (For the third time, a long silence.)

"From the foot of the cedar, I painfully lifted my exhausted body. In front of me was the knife my wife had dropped. Picking it up, with one blow I drove it into my chest. A warm and sour lump rose into my throat. But I didn't feel any pain. As my body got cold, the silence around me grew deeper. What silence! In the sky above this grove in the shadow of the mountain, not a single bird came to sing. Only the last rays of the setting sun drifted through the bamboos and the cedars. This ray, too, faded. I couldn't see the bamboos or the cedars anymore. Lying on the ground, I was surrounded by a deep silence. At that moment, someone quietly came up to me. I tried to turn my head toward him. But darkness had already spread around me. Someone, this same someone, his hand unseen, gently pulled the knife from out of my chest. My mouth filled again with blood. I sank into this eternal darkness. . . .

Joan M. Rabinowitz

Chapter 6
JAPANESE NOVELS

An epic has been defined both as a tale of the tribe and as a poem including history. Whatever the definition, the fact remains that many literatures contain works that seem to pull the whole culture together, at least for a given moment in its history; that seem to present the society, its values, and its members so well that they summarize the past development of the society and imply its future growth. It is this sort of summary and implication that people have in mind when they describe Lady Murasaki's *The Tale of Genji* as the beginning of Japanese literature. The poet Matsuo Basho, who visited Murasaki's retreat at Ishiyama-dera, punned on her name (Murasaki means purple) when he wrote the haiku:

> Beyond the giant pines
> At Ishiyama-dera:
> The purple dawn.

Lady Murasaki's novel is in fact one of the dawns of Japanese literature, and it is as well one of the real masterworks of world literature. Few societies have ever been described so clearly, in such luminous detail, as is Japanese court society in *The Tale of Genji,* whose main character, Genji, is a prince in the court at Kyoto. The novel as a whole is dominated by the conflict between natural human attachment to things and the ideal Buddhist attitude of *detachment,* and it is permeated with the Japanese aesthetic ideal: appreciation of the beauty of things in an impermanent world. Except for the Yugao episode, the material below presents some of the lighter moments of the novel. The Yugao episode is particularly interesting because of the light it shed on contemporary psychological beliefs and theory.

The next excerpt, from a modern rewriting of the famous historical "epic" *The Tale of the Heike*, presents the Samurai society, the Japanese military society that succeeded the court society. The basic story is about the struggle between two powerful clans, the Heike and the Genji, a struggle that led to a century of civil war. It is imbued with the Zen spirit.

Like many *Chinese* novels,[1] *The Tale of the Heike* was first put together (probably early in the thirteenth century) from legends, tales and ballads that were part of the popular culture. One of the most famous episodes is the Kesa-Gozen story, which appears virtually *in toto* in the excerpts reprinted here. The reader may already know the film treatment of the story in the splendid Japanese film, *Gate of Hell*.

The other excerpt marks an important point in the progression to the modern Japanese novel. Yasunari Kawabata, known perhaps to the reader as the 1968 Nobel Prize-winner, writes from a full command of the resources of traditional Japanese literature.

Murasaki Shikibu[2]
(978–?)

Murasaki Shikibu learned Chinese by listening in on her brother's lessons. She married between 994 and 998 and had two daughters. After her husband died, she was placed in the service of the Empress Akiko, from which position she must have seen much of the life recorded in *The Tale of Genji*. Her translator, Arthur Waley, thinks the novel was probably written between 1001 and 1020—that it took, in other words, almost two decades to complete. Mura-

[1] See William McNaughton, *Chinese Literature: An Anthology* pp. 569–70, 607, 653–54.

[2] "Shikibu" is not a name; it is the title that appears in English translation as "Lady."

saki's name is missing from a court list dated 1031; she may have been dead by then.

THE TALE OF GENJI

Part I, Chapter 2: The Broom Tree

The servants dusted and aired the eastern side-chamber of the Central Hall and here made temporary quarters for the Prince. They were at pains to improve the view from his windows, for example by altering the course of certain rivulets. They set up a rustic wattled hedge and filled the borders with the choicest plants. The low humming of insects floated on the cool breeze; numberless fireflies wove inextricable mazes in the air. The whole party settled down near where the moat flowed under the covered bridge and began to drink wine.

Ki no Kami went off in a great bustle, saying that he must find them something to eat. Genji, quietly surveying the scene, decided this was one of those middle-class families which in last night's conversation had been so highly commended. He remembered that he had heard the lady who was staying in the house well spoken of and was curious to see her. He listened and thought that there seemed to be people in the western wing. There was a soft rustling of skirts, and from time to time the sound of young and by no means disagreeable voices. They did not seem to be much in earnest in their efforts to make their whispering and laughter unheard, for soon one of them opened the sliding window. But Ki no Kami, crying "What are you thinking of?", crossly closed it again. The light of a candle in the room filtered through a crack in the paper-window. Genji edged slightly closer to the window in the hope of being able to see through the crack, but found that he could see nothing. He listened for a while, and came to the conclusion that they were sitting in the main women's apartments, out of which the little front room opened. They were speaking very low, but he could catch enough of it to make out that they were talking about him.

"What a shame that a fine young prince should be taken so young and settled down forever with a lady that was none of his choosing!"

"I understand that marriage does not weigh very heavily upon him," said another. This probably meant nothing in particular, but Genji, who imagined they were talking about what was uppermost in his own mind, was appalled at the idea that his relations with Lady Fujitsubo were about to be discussed. How could they have found out? But the subsequent conversation of the ladies soon showed that they knew nothing of the matter at all, and Genji stopped listening. Presently he heard them trying to repeat the poem which he had sent with a nosegay of morning glory to Princess Asagao, daughter of Prince Momozono.[1] But they got the lines mixed up, and Genji began to wonder whether the lady's appearance would turn out to be on a level with her knowledge of prosody.

At this moment Ki no Kami came in with a lamp, which he hung on the wall. Having carefully trimmed it, he offered Genji a tray of fruit. This was all rather dull, and Genji, by a quotation from an old folk song, hinted that he would like to meet Ki no Kami's other guests. The hint was not taken. Genji began to doze, and his attendants sat silent and motionless. . . .

Genji's followers, who had drunk heavily, were now all lying fast asleep on the verandah. He was alone in his room, but could not get to sleep. Having at last dozed for a moment, he woke suddenly and noticed that someone was moving behind the paper-window of the back wall. This, he thought, must be where she is hiding, and, faintly curious, he sauntered in that direction and stood listening. "Where are you? I say, where are you?" whispered someone in a quaint, hoarse voice, which seemed to be that of the boy whom Genji had noticed earlier in the evening. "I am lying over here," another voice answered. "Has the stranger gone to sleep yet? His room must be quite close to this; but all the same, how far off he seems!" Her sleepy voice was so like the boy's that Genji concluded this must be his sister.

"He is sleeping in the wing, I saw him tonight. All that we have heard of him is true enough. He is as handsome as can be," whispered the boy. "I wish it were tomorrow; I

[1] We learn later that Genji courted this lady in vain from his seventeenth year onward. Though she has never been mentioned before, Murasaki speaks of her as though the reader already knew all about her. This device is also employed by Marcel Proust.

want to see him properly," she answered drowsily, her voice seeming to come from under bedclothes. Genji was rather disappointed that she did not ask more questions about him. Presently he heard the boy saying, "I am going to sleep over in the corner room. How bad the light is," and he seemed to be trimming the lamp. His sister's bed appeared to be in the corner opposite the paper-window. "Where is Chujo?" she called. "I am frightened; I like to have someone close to me." "Madam," answered several voices from the servants' room, "she is taking her bath in the lower house. She will be back presently." When all was quiet again, Genji slipped back the bolt and tried the door. It was not fastened on the other side. He found himself in an anteroom with a screen at the end, beyond which a light glimmered. In the half-darkness he could see clothes boxes and trunks strewn about in great disorder. Quietly threading his way among them, he entered the inner room from which the voices had proceeded. One very minute figure was couched there who, to Genji's slight embarrassment, on hearing his approach pushed aside the cloak which covered her, thinking that he was the maid for whom she had sent. "Madam, hearing you call for Chujo[1] I thought that I might now put at your service the esteem in which I have long secretly held you." The lady could make nothing of all this, and, terrified out of her wits, she tried hard to scream. But no sound came, for she had buried her face in the bedclothes.

"Please listen," said Genji. "This sudden intrusion must of course seem to you very impertinent. You do not know how much I like and admire you, and if tonight I could not resist the temptation of paying this secret visit, pray take the strangeness of my behavior as proof of my impatience to pay a homage that has long been due." He spoke so courteously and gently and looked so kind that not the devil himself would have taken umbrage at his presence. But feeling that the situation was not at all a proper one for a married lady, she said (without much conviction), "I think you have made a mistake." She spoke very low. Her bewildered air made her all the more attractive, and Genji, enchanted by her appearance, hastened to answer: "Indeed I have made no mistake; rather, with no guide but a long-

[1] Chujo means "Captain," which was Genji's rank at the time.

felt deference and esteem, I have found my way unerringly to your side. But I see that the suddenness of my visit has made you distrust my purpose. Let me tell you then that I have no evil intentions and seek only for someone to talk with me for a while about a matter which perplexes me." So saying, he took her up in his arms (for she was very small) and was carrying her through the anteroom when suddenly Chujo, the servant for whom she had sent before, entered the bedroom. Genji gave an astonished cry and the maid, wondering who could have entered the anteroom, began groping her way toward them. But, coming closer, she recognized the rich perfume of his dress and knew that this could be none other than the Prince. And though she was sorely puzzled to know what was afoot, she dared not say a word. Had he been an ordinary person, she would soon have had him by the ears. Nay, she thought, even if he were not a prince I should do best to keep my hands off him; for the more stir one makes, the more tongues wag. But if I should touch this fine gentleman . . . and all in a flutter she found herself obediently following Genji to his room. Here he calmly closed the door upon her, saying as he did so, "You will come back to fetch your mistress in the morning."

Chapter 4: Yugao

—HERE IN THE NIGHT
IN A GARDEN OF THE OLD CAPITAL
I FEEL THE TREMBLING GHOST OF YUGAO
—GARY SNYDER

It was at the time when he was secretly visiting the lady of the Sixth Ward.[1] One day on his way back from the Palace he thought that he would call upon his foster-mother, who, having for a long while been very ill, had become a nun. She lived in the Fifth Ward. After many inquiries he managed to find the house; but the front gate was locked and he could not drive in. He sent one of his servants for Koremitsu, his foster-nurse's son, and while he was waiting he began to examine the rather wretched-

[1] Lady Rokujo. Her identity becomes apparent in the course of the story.

looking by-street. The house next door was fenced with a new paling, above which at one place were four or five panels of open trelliswork, screened by blinds which were very white and bare. Through chinks in these blinds a number of foreheads could be seen. They seemed to belong to a group of ladies who must be peeping with interest into the street below.

At first he thought they had merely peeped out as they passed; but he soon realized that if they were standing on the floor they must be giants. No, evidently they had taken the trouble to climb onto some table or bed; which was surely rather odd!

He had come in a plain coach with no outriders. No one could possibly guess who he was, and, feeling quite at his ease, he leant forward and deliberately examined the house. The gate, also made of a kind of trelliswork, stood ajar, and he could see enough of the interior to realize that it was a very humble and poorly furnished dwelling. For a moment he pitied those who lived in such a place, but then he remembered the song "Seek not in the wide world to find a home; but where you chance to rest, call that your house"; and again, "Monarchs may keep their palaces of jade, for in a leafy cottage two can sleep."

There was a wattled fence over which some ivylike creeper spread its cool green leaves, and among the leaves were white flowers with petals half unfolded like the lips of people smiling at their own thoughts. "They are called *Yugao,* 'Evening Faces,' " one of his servants told him. "How strange to find so lovely a crowd clustering on this deserted wall!" And indeed it was a most strange and delightful thing to see how, on the narrow tenement in a poor quarter of the town, they had clambered over rickety eaves and gables and spread wherever there was room for them to grow. He sent one of his servants to pick some. The man entered at the half-opened door, and had begun to pluck the flowers when a little girl in a long yellow tunic came through a quite genteel sliding door. Holding out toward Genji's servant a white fan heavily perfumed with incense, she said to him, "Would you like something to put them on? I am afraid you have chosen a wretched-looking bunch," and she handed him the fan. Just as he was opening the gate on his way back, the old nurse's son Koremitsu came out of the other house, full of apologies for having kept Genji waiting so long. "I could not find the key to the gate," he said. "Fortunately the people of this humble quarter were not likely to recognize you and press or stare; but I am afraid you must have been very much bored waiting in this hugger-mugger back street." And he conducted Genji into the house. Koremitsu's brother, the deacon, his brother-in-law Mikawa no Kami, and his sister all assembled to greet the Prince, delighted by a visit with which they had not thought he was ever likely to honor them again. . . .

Having arranged for continual masses to be said on the sick woman's behalf, he took his leave, ordering Koremitsu to light him with a candle. As they left the house he looked at the fan upon which the white flowers had been laid. He now saw that there was writing on it, a poem carelessly but elegantly scribbled: "The flower that puzzled you was but the *Yugao,* strange beyond knowing in its dress of shining dew." It was written with a deliberate negligence which seemed to aid in concealing the writer's status and identity. But for all that, the hand showed a breeding and distinction which agreeably surprised him. "Who lives in the house on the left?" he asked. Koremitsu, who did not at all want to act as a go-between, replied that he had only been at his mother's for five or six days and had been so much occupied by her illness that he had not asked any questions about the neighbors. "I want to know for a quite harmless reason," said Genji. "There is something about this fan which raises a rather important point. I positively must settle it. You would oblige me by making inquiries of someone who knows the neighborhood." . . .

Koremitsu, anxious to carry out his master's every wish, and intent also on his own intrigue, contrived at last by a series of ingenious stratagems to effect a secret meeting between Genji and the mysterious lady. The details of the plan by which he brought this about would make a tedious story, and, as is my rule in such cases, I have thought it better to omit them.

Genji never asked her by what name he was to call her, nor did he reveal his own identity. He came very poorly dressed and—most unusual for him—on foot. But Koremitsu regarded this as too great a tribute to so unimportant a lady, and insisted upon Genji riding his horse while he walked by his side. In doing so he sacrificed his own feelings;

for he too had reasons for wishing to create a good impression in the house, and he knew that by arriving in this rather undignified way he would sink in the estimation of the inhabitants. Fortunately his discomfiture was almost unwitnessed, for Genji took with him only the one attendant who had on the first occasion plucked the flowers—a boy whom no one was likely to recognize. Lest suspicions should be aroused, he did not even take advantage of his presence in the neighborhood to call at his foster-nurse's house.

The lady was very much mystified by all these precautions and made great efforts to discover something more about him. She even sent someone after him to see where he went to when he left her at daybreak, but he succeeded in throwing his pursuer off the scent and she was no wiser than before. He was now growing far too fond of her. He was miserable if anything interfered with his visits, and though he utterly disapproved of his own conduct and worried a great deal about it, he soon found that he was spending most of his time at her house.

He knew that at some time or another in their lives even the soberest people lose their heads in this way; but hitherto he had never really lost his, or done anything which could possibly have been considered very wrong. Now to his astonishment and dismay he discovered that even the few morning hours during which he was separated from her were becoming unendurable. "What is it in her that makes me behave like a madman?" he kept on asking himself. She was astonishingly gentle and unassuming, to the point even of seeming rather apathetic and deficient, perhaps, in depth of character and emotion. Though she had a certain air of girlish inexperience, it was clear that he was not by any means her first lover; and certainly she was rather plebeian. What was it exactly that so fascinated him? He asked himself the question again and again, but found no answer.

She for her part was very uneasy to see him come to her thus in shabby old hunting clothes, trying always to hide his face, leaving while it was still dark and everyone was asleep. He seemed like some demon-lover in an old ghost tale, and she was half afraid. But his smallest gesture showed that he was someone out of the ordinary, and she began to suspect that he was a person of high rank, who had used Koremitsu as his go-between. But Koremitsu obstinately pretended to know nothing at all about his companion, and continued to amuse himself by frequenting the house on his own account. . . .

It was the fifteenth night of the eighth month. The light of an unclouded full moon shone between the ill-fitting planks of the roof and flooded the room. What a queer place to be lying in! thought Genji, as he gazed round the garret, so different from any room he had ever known before. It must be almost day. In the neighboring houses people were beginning to stir, and there was an uncouth sound of peasant voices: "Eh! how cold it is! I can't believe we shall do much with the crops this year." "I don't know what's going to happen about my carrying-trade," said another. "Things look very bad." Then (banging on the wall of another house), "Wake up, neighbor. Time to start. Did he hear, d'you think?" and they rose and went off each to the wretched task by which he earned his bread. . . .

Now, louder than thunder, came the noise of the threshing-mills, seeming so near that they could hardly believe it did not come from out of the pillow itself. Genji thought that his ears would burst. What many of the noises were he could not at all make out; but they were very peculiar and startling. The whole air seemed to be full of crashings and bangings. Now from one side, now from another, came, too, the faint thud of the bleacher's mallet, and the scream of wild geese passing overhead. It was all too distracting.

Their room was in the front of the house. Genji got up and opened the long, sliding shutters. They stood together looking out. In the courtyard near them was a clump of fine Chinese bamboos; dew lay thick on the borders, glittering here no less brightly than in the great gardens to which Genji was better accustomed. There was a confused buzzing of insects. Crickets were chirping in the wall. . . . "I am going to take you somewhere not at all far away where we shall be able to pass the rest of the night in peace. We cannot go on like this, parting always at break of day." "Why have you suddenly come to that conclusion?" she asked, but she spoke submissively. He vowed to her that she should be his love in this and in all future lives, and she answered so passionately that she seemed utterly transformed from the listless creature he had known.

It was hard to believe that such vows were no novelty to her.

Discarding all prudence, he sent for the maid Ukon and bade her order his servants to fetch a coach. The affair was soon known to all the household, and the ladies were at first somewhat uneasy at seeing their mistress carried off in this fashion; but on the whole they did not think he looked the sort of person who would do her any harm. It was now almost daylight. The cocks had stopped crowing. The voice of an old man (a pilgrim preparing for the ascent of the Holy Mountain) sounded somewhere not far away; and, as at each prayer he bent forward to touch the ground with his head, they could hear with what pain and difficulty he moved. What could he be asking for in his prayers, this old man whose life seemed fragile as the morning dew? *Namu torai no doshi,* "Glory be to the Savior that shall come": now they could hear the words. "Listen," said Genji tenderly. "Is not that an omen that our love shall last through many lives to come?" And he recited the poem: "Do not prove false this omen of the pilgrim's chant: that even in lives to come our love shall last unchanged."

Then, unlike the lovers in the "Everlasting Wrong" who prayed that they might be as the "twin birds that share a wing" (for they remembered that this story had ended very sadly), they prayed, "May our love last till Maitreya comes as a Buddha into the World." But she, still distrustful, answered his poem with verse: "Such sorrow have I known in this world that I have small hope of worlds to come." Her versification was still a little tentative.[1] . . .

They drove to an untenanted mansion that was not far off. While he waited for the steward to come out Genji noticed that the gates were crumbling away; dense shinobu-grass grew around them. So somber an entrance he had never seen. There was a thick mist and the dew was so heavy that when he raised the carriage-blind his sleeve was drenched. "Never yet has such an adventure as this befallen me," said Genji, "so I am, as you imagine, rather excited," and he made a poem in which he said that though love's folly had existed since the beginning of the world, never could man have set out more rashly at the break of day into a land unknown. "But to you this is no great nov-

[1] We gather later that she was only nineteen.

elty?" She blushed and in her turn made a poem: "I am as the moon that walks the sky not knowing what menace the cruel hills may hold in store; high though she sweeps, her light may suddenly be blotted out."

She seemed very depressed and nervous. But this he attributed to the fact that she had probably always lived in small houses where everything was huddled together, and he was amused at the idea that this large mansion should overawe her. They drove in, and while a room was being got ready, they remained in the carriage which had been drawn up alongside of the balustrade. . . .

The mist was gradually clearing away. They left the coach and went into the room that had been prepared for them. Though so quickly improvised, their quarters were admirably clean and well-provided, for the steward's son had previously been a trusted house-servant of Genji's and had also worked at the Great Hall. Coming now to their room, he offered to send for some of Genji's gentlemen, "For," he said, "I cannot bear to see you going unattended." "Do nothing of the kind," said Genji. "I have come here because I do not wish to be disturbed. No one but yourself is to know that I have used this house," and he exacted a promise of absolute secrecy. No regular meal had been prepared, but the steward brought them a little rice porridge. Then they lay down again to sleep together for the first time in the unfamiliar and so strangely different place.

The sun was high when they woke. Genji went and opened the shutters himself. How deserted the garden looked! Certainly here there was no one to spy upon them. He looked out into the distance: dense woods fast turning to jungle. And nearer the house not a flower or bush, but only unkempt autumn grasslands, and a pond choked with weeds. It was a wild and desolate place. It seemed that the steward and his men must live in some outbuilding or lodge at a distance from the house; for here there was no sign nor sound of life. "It is, I must own, a strange and forsaken place to which we have come. But no ghost or evil fairy will dare molest you while I am here."

It pained her very much that he still was masked;[1] and,

[1] That is, covered part of his face with a scarf or the like, a practice usual with illicit lovers in medieval Japan.

indeed, such a precaution was quite out of keeping with the stage at which they had now arrived. So at last, reciting a poem in which he reminded her that all their love down to this moment when "the flower opened its petals to the evening dew" had come from a chance vision seen casually from the street, half turning his face away, for a moment he let her see him unmasked. "What of the 'shining dew'?" he asked, using the words that she had written on the fan. "How little knew I of its beauty who had but in the twilight doubted and guessed. . . ." So she answered his poem in a low and halting voice. She need not have feared, for to him, poor as the verses were, they seemed delightful. And, indeed, the beauty of his uncovered face, suddenly revealed to her in this black wilderness of dereliction and decay, surpassed all loveliness that she had ever dreamed of or imagined. "I cannot wonder that while I still set this barrier between us, you did not choose to tell me all that I longed to know. But now it would be very unkind of you not to tell me your name."

"I am like the fisherman's daughter in the song,"[1] she said. 'I have no name or home.'" But for all that she would not tell him who she was, she seemed much comforted that he had let her see him. "Do as you please about it," said Genji at last; but for a while he was out of temper. Soon they had made it up again; and so the day passed. . . .

It was an evening of marvelous stillness. Genji sat watching the sky. The lady found the inner room where she was sitting depressingly dark and gloomy. He raised the blinds of the front room and came to sit with her. They watched the light of the sunset glowing in each other's eyes, and in her wonder at his adorable beauty and tenderness, she forgot all her fears. At last she was shy with him no longer, and he thought that the newfound boldness and merriment became her very well. She lay by his side till night. He saw that she was again wearing the plaintive expression of a frightened child; so, quickly closing the partition door, he brought in the great lamp, saying: "Outwardly you are no longer shy with me; but I can see that deep down in your heart there is still some sediment of rancor and distrust. It is not kind to use me so," and again he was cross with her.

What were the people at the Palace thinking? Would he

[1] *Shinkokinshu,* 1701.

have been sent for? How far would the messengers pursue their search? He became quite agitated. Then there was the great lady in the Sixth Ward.[1] What a frenzy she must be in! This time, however, she really had good cause to be jealous. These and other unpleasant considerations were crowding into his head, when, looking at the girl who lay beside him so trustfully, unconscious of all that was going on in his mind, he was suddenly filled with an overwhelming tenderness toward her. How tiresome the other was, with her eternal susceptibilities, jealousies, and suspicions! For a while at any rate he would stop seeing her. As the night wore on, they began sometimes to doze. Suddenly Genji saw standing over him the figure of a woman, tall and majestic: "You who think yourself so fine, how comes it that you have brought to toy with you here this worthless common creature, picked up at random in the streets? I am astonished and displeased," and with this she made as though to drag the lady from his side. Thinking that this was some nightmare or hallucination, he roused himself and sat up. The lamp had gone out. Somewhat agitated, he drew his sword and laid it beside him, calling as he did so for Ukon. She came at once, looking a good deal scared herself. "Please wake the watchman in the cross-wing," he said, "and tell him to bring a candle." "All in the dark like this? How can I?" she answered. "Don't be childish," said Genji, laughing, and clapped his hands.[2] The sound echoed desolately through the empty house. He could not make anyone hear; and meanwhile he noticed that his mistress was trembling from head to foot. What should he do? He was still undecided, when suddenly she burst out into a cold sweat. She seemed to be losing consciousness. "Do not fear, sir," said Ukon. "All her life she has been subject to these nightmare fits." He remembered now how tired she had seemed in the morning and how she had lain with her eyes turned upward as though in pain. "I will go myself and wake someone," he said. "I am tired of clapping with only echoes to answer me. Do not leave her!" and drawing Ukon toward the bed, he went in the direction of the main western door. But when he opened it, he found that the lamp in the cross-wing had also gone out. A wind had

[1] Lady Rokujo.
[2] To summon a servant.

risen. The few attendants he had brought with him were already in bed. There was indeed only the steward's son (the young man who had once been Genji's body servant), and the one young courtier who had attended him on all his visits. They answered when he called and sprang to their feet. "Come with a candle," he said to the steward's son, "and tell my man to get his bow and keep on twanging the string as loud as he can." . . .

Genji's man had been an Imperial Bowman, and making a tremendous din with his bow he strode toward the steward's lodge crying "Fire! Fire!" at the top of his voice. The twanging of the bow reminded Genji of the Palace. The roll call of night courtiers must be over; the Bowman's roll call must be actually going on. It was not so very late.

He groped his way back into the room. She was lying just as he had left her, with Ukon face downward beside her. "What are you doing there?" he cried. "Have you gone mad with fright? You have heard, no doubt, that in such lonely places as this, fox spirits sometimes try to cast a spell upon men. But, dear people, you need not fear. I have come back, and will not let such creatures harm you." And so saying he dragged Ukon from the bed. "Oh, sir," she said, "I felt so queer and frightened that I fell flat down upon my face; and what my poor lady must be going through I dare not think." "Then try not to add to her fright," and Genji, and pushing her aside, he bent over the prostrate form. The girl was scarcely breathing. He touched her; she was quite limp. She did not know him.

Perhaps some accursed thing, some demon had tried to snatch her spirit away; she was so timid, so childishly helpless. The man came with the candle. Ukon was still too frightened to move. Genji placed a screen so as to hide the bed and called the man to him. It was, of course, contrary to etiquette that he should serve Genji himself and he hesitated in embarrassment, not venturing even to ascend the dais. "Come here," said Genji impatiently. "Use your common sense." Reluctantly the man gave him the light, and as he held it toward the bed, he saw for a moment the figure that had stood there in his dream still hovering beside the pillow; suddenly it vanished. He had read in old tales of such apparitions and of their power, and he was in great alarm. But for the moment he was so full of concern for the lady who now lay motionless on the bed that he gave no thought to that menacing vision, and lying down beside her, began gently to move her limbs. Already they were growing cold. Her breathing had quite stopped. What could he do? To whom could he turn for help? He ought to send for a priest. He tried to control himself, but he was very young, and seeing her lying there all still and pale, he could contain himself no longer. Crying, "Come back to me, my own darling, come back to life. Do not look at me so strangely!" he flung his arms about her. But now she was quite cold. Her face was set in a dull, senseless stare. . . .

He sent for the steward's son and said to him: "Someone here has had a fright and is in a very bad way. I want you to go to Koremitsu's house and tell him to come as quickly as he can. If his brother the priest is there, too, take him aside and tell him quietly that I should like to see him at once. But do not speak loud enough for the nun their mother to hear, for I would not have her know of this excursion." . . .

It was past midnight. A violent storm began to rise, sighing dismally as it swept the pine trees that clustered round the house. And all the while some strange bird (an owl, he supposed) kept screeching hoarsely. Utter desolation on all sides. No human voice; no friendly sound. Why, why had he chosen this hideous place? . . .

The candle was burning badly. He lit it again. Over by the screen in the corner of the main room, something was moving. There it was again, but in another corner now. There was a sound of footsteps treading cautiously. It still went on. Now they were coming up behind him. . . .

Why had fate seen fit to treat him thus? He felt that it must be as a punishment for all the strange and forbidden amours into which he had been drawn, despite himself, in these last years that now this unheard-of horror had befallen him. And such things, though one may keep them secret for a time, always come out in the end. He minded most that the Emperor would be certain to discover sooner or later about this and all his other affairs. Then there was the general scandal. Everyone would know. The very gutter boys would make merry over him. Never, never must he do such things again, or his reputation would utterly collapse. . . .

At last Koremitsu arrived. . . .

Ukon, hearing Koremitsu's voice, suddenly came to herself, and remembering what had happened, burst into tears. And now Genji, who while he alone was there had supported and encouraged the weeping maidservant, relieved at last by Koremitsu, could contain himself no longer. Suddenly realizing again the terrible thing that had befallen him, he burst into uncontrollable weeping. "Something horrible has happened here," he managed to say at last, "too dreadful to explain. I have heard that when such things as this suddenly befall, certain scriptures should be read. I would have this done, and prayers said. That is why I asked you to bring your brother. . . ."

"He went up to the mountain yesterday," said Koremitsu. "But I see that there has been terrible work afoot here. Was it in some sudden fit of madness that you did this thing?" Genji shook his head. So moved was Koremitsu at the sight of his master weeping that he too began to sob. Had he been an older man, versed in the ways of the world, he might have been of some use in such a crisis, but both of them were young and both were equally perplexed. At last Koremitsu said: "One thing at least is clear. The steward's son must not know. For though he himself can be depended upon, he is the sort of person who is sure to tell all his relatives, and they might meddle disastrously in the affair. We had best be clear of this house as quietly as we can." "Perhaps," said Genji, "but it would be hard to find a less frequented place than this." "At any rate," Koremitsu continued, "we cannot take her to her own house; for there her gentlewomen, who loved her dearly, would raise such a weeping and wailing as would soon bring a pack of neighbors swarming around, and all would quickly be known. If only I knew of some mountain temple, for there such things are customary[1] and pass almost unnoticed." He paused and reflected. "There is a lady I once knew who has become a nun and now lives on the Higashi Yama. She was my father's wet-nurse and is now very old and bent. She does not of course live alone; but no outside people come there." A faint light was already showing in the sky when Koremitsu brought the carriage in. Thinking that Genji would not wish to move the body himself, he wrapped it in a rush mat and carried it toward the carriage. How small she was to hold! Her face was calm and beautiful. He felt

[1] The bringing of a corpse. Temples were used as mortuaries.

no repulsion. He could find no way to secure her hair, and when he began to carry her, it overflowed and hung toward the ground. Genji saw, and his eyes darkened. A hideous anguish possessed him.

He tried to follow the body, but Koremitsu dissuaded him, saying, "You must ride back to your palace as quickly as you can; you have just time to get there before the stir begins," and putting Ukon into the carriage, he gave Genji his horse. Then pulling up his silk trousers to the knee, he accompanied the carriage on foot. It was a very singular procession; but Koremitsu, seeing his master's terrible distress, forgot for the moment his own dignity and walked stolidly on. Genji, hardly conscious of what went on around him, arrived at last in ghostly pallor at his house. "Where do you come from, my lord?" "How ill you look." . . . Questions assailed him, but he hurried to his room and lay behind his curtain. He tried to calm himself, but hideous thoughts tormented him.

Part II, Chapter 1: The Sacred Tree

About this time Princess Oborozuki left the Court for a while and went to stay at her father's house. She had for some time been suffering from slight attacks of malaria and it was thought that she could be treated for this illness more conveniently at her home than amid the bustle of the Court. Priests were summoned and their incantations were at once effective. Among the many people who wrote to congratulate her upon her recovery, Genji was naturally one, and as both of them happened for the moment to have a good deal of time on their hands, a correspondence ensued which led in the end to his paying her a somewhat reluctant visit. This was followed by others, and he was soon seeing her every night. She was well made, tending even to plumpness, so that the slight pallor and thinness that had ensued from her recent indisposition only enhanced her charm. It happened that at the time Kokiden was also staying in the house. This made Genji's visits particularly imprudent, but it was just this added risk that attracted him and induced him to repeat them. It was not of course long before several inmates of the house became aware that something was going on, but they were too frightened of Kokiden to say anything to her about it, nor had the Minister of the Right any suspicion whatever.

One night when Genji was with her a violent storm suddenly came on. The rain fell in such torrential floods as to be quite alarming, and just after midnight tremendous crashes of thunder began. Soon the whole place was astir. The young princes and Kokiden's gentlemen-in-attendance seemed to be wandering all over the house, while the ladies-in-waiting, terrified by the thunderstorm, were clinging to one another hysterically in the passage just outside. There were people everywhere, and Genji began to wonder how he was ever going to escape.

It was now broad daylight. Oborozuki's maids had entered the room and seemed to be crowding around the great curtained bed. Genji was appalled by the situation. Among these ladies were two who knew the secret, but they quite lost their heads in this emergency and were unable to be of any use. The thunderstorm was over and the rain was now less violent. The Minister was now up and about. He first paid his elder daughter a visit, and then, just at a moment when the rain was falling rather heavily, stepped lightly and briskly into Oborozuki's room. The rain was making such a noise that they did not hear him, and it was not till a hand was thrust through the bed-curtains that they realized what had happened. "We have had a very bad thunderstorm," he said, pulling the curtain slightly aside as he spoke. "I thought of you in the night and had half a mind to come around and see how you were getting on, but somehow or other I didn't. Your brothers were on duty at the Palace last night. Just fancy . . ." So he went on, speaking in an excited inconsequential manner, which, even in his present quandary, Genji could not help contrasting with the gravity and good sense of that other Minister, Aoi's father, and he smiled to himself. Really, if he had so much to say he had better come right inside and have done with it. Oborozuki, determined to screen her lover if she could, now crept to the edge of the bed and issued cautiously from between the curtains. Her face was so flushed and she looked so ill at ease that her father was quite alarmed. "What have you been doing?" he said. "You are not looking at all well. I'm afraid we stopped the treatment too soon. These attacks are very troublesome to get rid of. . . ." As he spoke his eye suddenly fell upon a man's pale violet-colored belt that had got mixed up with her clothes, and at the same time he noticed a piece of paper with writing upon it lying near the bed. How did these things come to be in his daughter's room? "Whose is this?" he asked, pointing at the paper. "I think you had better give it to me; it may be something important. I shall probably know the writing." She looked where he was pointing. Yes, there was Genji's paper lying conspicuously upon the floor. Were there no means of heading her father away from it? She could think of none and did not attempt to answer his question. It was evident that she was acutely embarrassed, and even though she was his own child he ought to have remembered that she was now a lady of some consequence, whose feelings, however reprehensible might be her conduct, he was bound in some measure to respect. Unfortunately there was not in his nature a particle either of moderation or restraint. He stooped to pick up the paper, and as he did so, without the slightest hesitation or compunction, he opened the bed-curtains and peered right in. There, full length upon the bed and apparently quite at his ease, lolled a charming young man, who, when the curtain stirred, merely rolled quietly over and hid his face in the pillows. Enraged, astonished as the Minister was, even he had not quite the courage to press the discovery home. Blind with fury, he thrust the paper into his pocket and rushed out of the room.

Genji was indeed extremely concerned about the consequences of this incident, coming as it did in the wake of so many other indiscretions. But his first care was to comfort his companion, which he did as best he could.

Self-restraint had never been a characteristic of the lady's father, and now that he was getting old he found it more than ever impossible to keep anything to himself. It was therefore only to be expected that, without considering the consequences or turning the matter over in his mind for a single moment, he went and told the whole story to his daughter Kokiden.

Kokiden had always detested Genji, and she now burst out angrily. . . . She went on . . . for so long and with so much rancor that her father, who never remained angry for more than a short time, soon began to sympathize with Genji rather than with her and was sorry that he had mentioned the matter at all. "I think that for the present," he said, "you had better not speak of this to anyone, not even to His Majesty, your son. Prince Genji's conduct is certainly outrageous; but you are very fond of your sister and you cannot denounce him without getting her, too, into trouble. Leave the matter to me. I intend to speak to her very seriously, and if this has no effect, then we shall have done our best and she must take the consequences." But it was too late to mend matters; she was indeed only further exasperated by his attempt to conciliate her. That Genji should have been carrying on this intrigue in her own house, and that, too, at a time when he knew she was in residence, showed an impudent contempt for her authority which deeply wounded her, and all that she now thought of was how best she might use this discovery to his undoing.

Arthur Waley

Yoshikawa Eiji
(b. 1892)

THE HEIKE STORY

Like no other epoch that preceded it, this age gave itself up entirely to pleasure and gambling, poetry tournaments, the blending of perfumes and incense, pageants, miming, dice games, outings at the four seasons to view the beauties of nature, cockfighting, and archery matches. Earlier, court circles regarded seasonal excursions and poetry parties as the natural complement to living; yet never had men at large regarded all things as their playthings as during this new age which sought to transmute even its religion and politics into exquisite pastimes—all, with the exception of war. At the word "war," both high and low trembled, for the seeds of conflict were now sown far and wide: among the powerful armed clergy; to the east; to the west, where pirates of the Inland Sea periodically made their forays; and close at hand in the very capital itself, where the Court and the Palace were at odds with each other. Lately it was openly rumored that the Genji and Heike in distant provinces were mobilizing their soldiers, and that a storm was brewing.

People were uneasy. Something ominous permeated the air itself. Still, in the midst of that foreboding and effeteness, a feverish hunger for pleasure seemed to consume everyone, and the crowded Kamo racecourse was one sign of it. According to the old chronicles, horse racing became a royal sport about the year 701, indulged in by guards on the grounds of the Imperial Palace during the May Festival. In these troubled times, however, horse racing was no longer confined to the course at Kamo in May, but took place in shrine compounds, on the estates of the courtiers and noblemen who entertained the emperor or the ex-emperor and their ladies, on the broad stretch of Second Avenue, or was even improvised at imperial picnics. As races were held on straight courses, wide enough for ten horses to run abreast, it was even possible to have contests on any of the main avenues of Kyoto.

One sovereign, it was also written, was so carried away by his fever for horse racing that he set aside twenty of his manors in the provinces for the breeding of racehorses, and in the capital itself, ordered the building of lavish stables requiring an army of grooms and attendants to maintain them. The late monarch as well as his son, the present ex-emperor, were no less addicted to this sport, and the royal visit today to Kamo was to select a horse, in anticipation of the races in May, from all the thoroughbreds sent from numerous stud farms in the provinces.

"Is Tadamori here?" the ex-emperor inquired, ignoring the courtiers around him. "I see no exceptional ones today. What do you think?"

Tadamori, who stood modestly apart, merely raised his head to reply: "Your Majesty, there is just one."

"Just one—that black colt from the manor of Shimotsuke?"

"Yes, your Majesty."

"The one I have been watching for some time—the colt tethered to that post? Yet these gentlemen and horse-fanciers all warn me against him; they say those four white fetlocks bring bad luck."

"A common saying, your Majesty, but not worth considering—" Tadamori began, regretting his habit of plain-speaking. "Of all these horses, I see none equal to that colt; that fine head, that eye, and the sweep of the tail."

The monarch hesitated. He was anxious to have the black colt taken to his stables and trained for the May races, at which he hoped to win against the emperor's horses. But, like his courtiers, he was also superstitious.

"If your Majesty wishes, I will take the colt to my stable and keep him until the day of the races," Tadamori ventured, recalling his own impulsive words and the effect they had had on the assembled noblemen.

"That should do no harm. Take him and be sure of his training, until the races," Toba replied. . . .

On returning home, Tadamori stood by the black colt, stroking its nose. . . .

"I'm afraid you've been lonely since your mother left."

"Remember, Father, we promised not to talk of that. Now about that colt—"

"Hmmm—a fine horse. Better exercise him morning and evening."

"I have that in mind. To tell you the truth, Wataru of the Genji, who is with me in the Guards, tells me he wants to train the colt. He's been begging me to ask you to obtain His Majesty's consent, for he wants to ride that colt in the Kamo races." Tadamori thought for a moment and then said: "Wataru . . . but don't you want to ride him yourself? You, rather than Wataru?"

"Those four white fetlocks—if it were not for them . . ." Kiyomori hesitated, drawing his thick brows into a nervous frown that startled his father. Tadamori was surprised by the discovery that this careless son of his had ideas of his own.

"I'm sure Wataru can be trusted. I can't say how His Majesty will feel about this, but I shall ask—that is, if you still have no intention of riding the colt yourself," Tadamori said, a little disappointed. Calling some retainers, he gave them directions for the feeding and grooming of the four-year-old, and shortly after went to his rooms, now empty of his wife and her reproaches. Resting in the lamplight, he called his young sons to him and played with them, as had now become his habit.

Several days later Tadamori told Wataru himself of the ex-emperor's consent, and later instructed Kiyomori to take the colt to Wataru's home. Leading the horse by its reins,

Kiyomori started on his way to Iris Lane on Ninth Avenue. Passersby turned to remark: "A magnificent horse—for the Court or the Palace?" But Kiyomori spoke to no one, glad to be rid of an ill-omened horse.

Wataru was expecting Kiyomori and was cleaning out the stable when his friend arrived. He was beside himself with joy.

"It's almost dark. I'm sorry my wife hasn't returned yet, but you must stay and drink with me. This is an occasion to celebrate. We shall drink to it in imperial wine!"

Kiyomori stayed until the lamps were lit and the wine made him tingle to his fingertips. . . .

Aware of his flushed cheeks, he unsteadily resumed his way along the now dark Iris Lane. . . . Then an arm suddenly reached around and gripped him silently. A highwayman! People talked about being attacked at this crossroads at night! Kiyomori's hand slid to his sword.

"Don't be alarmed, Heita. Come with me to the house we visited the other night." There was a low laugh at Kiyomori's ear. It was Morito. Kiyomori could hardly believe his ears. What was Morito doing in this deserted quarter of Kyoto, his face muffled up like a brigand's?

"Surely, you'll come along to that house on Sixth Avenue?" Morito persisted. Kiyomori's thoughts leapt at the proposal, but a sudden distrust of this fellow made him hesitate.

"Come, I saw you this evening on your way to Wataru's, and I followed you," Morito added, as he began to lead the way. His suspicions allayed, Kiyomori followed him, drawn by something compelling in Morito, and soon felt that good luck had waylaid him.

In the house of call near the palace they drank recklessly, and caroused as they had done that other night. When he was alone at last with one of the women, Kiyomori, a little bolder than at his last visit, ventured to ask:

"Where is my friend? Where does he sleep?"

The woman tittered. "He never spends his nights here."

"Has he gone home then?"

The woman appeared sleepy and too tired to reply. "He's always like that. How should I know what he does?" she said, flinging her arms around Kiyomori's neck.

Kiyomori struggled free. "I'm leaving, too! That Morito is playing some trick on me!"

Kiyomori quickly left the house. . . .

The following day Morito did not report for duty at the Guards, nor did he appear for several days, and Kiyomori brooded over this. Now, whenever he arrived at the palace, it was Wataru who always greeted him eagerly whenever they met in the palace corridors, and with a look that bespoke his happiness. . . .

That year, in mid-August, Wataru of the Genji invited some ten of his closest friends in the Guards to come and share a large jar of wine with him and view the moonlight in his garden. His friends, however, knew that there was another reason for the invitation. In the autumn, the emperor and the ex-emperor were going on a pilgrimage to the Ninna-ji Temple. They were also attending the races that would be held in the temple compound. The official date of this event had already been announced—the 23rd of September—and the Guards knew that Wataru was waiting impatiently for a chance to prove himself and the black four-year-old with the white fetlocks.

"It's to drink to his success," Wataru's friends told each other. One of them jokingly added: "He's afraid to appear stingy, since it's customary for riders to give a large party for relatives and friends after the 'whip ritual' has been performed. Wataru has no love for these priests. He scoffs at those 'holy Buddhas,' as he calls them, saying he doesn't need their help. So instead of all the prayers and incantations, and a big banquet, he calls this a moon-viewing party!" The remark was greeted with much laughter.

Another Guard said: "Listen, you know how he feels about his young wife, Kesa-Gozen, who once served at Court. He is so infatuated with her that even on night duty all his thoughts are at home. We once asked to meet her, but all he would do was smile and say she was his 'secret love' and not to be seen, and so forth. I think he wants us to meet her tonight."

Thus talking and chaffing among themselves, the guests arrived at Wataru's house, where the gate stood wide open in welcome and the paving stones had been freshened with a sprinkling of water. Gathered in Wataru's guest room, the young men fell silent and remained subdued while trays of food were brought in. It was not until the wine arrived that they once more were at their ease and talked and joked among themselves.

Heita Kiyomori and Sato Yoshikiyo were also there. Kiyomori noticed that Morito was not present, and was about to ask about him, but thought better of it. He had recently sensed that Wataru and Morito were uneasy in each other's company. . . . Morito's behavior troubled Kiyomori. He feared for Morito, in whom, he knew, a keen mind battled with violent primitive lusts. Furthermore, he had observed the furtive look that came into Morito's eyes whenever he and Wataru were together. This look contrasted oddly with Morito's habitual swaggering. Nowadays, too, Morito went about with bloodshot eyes and haggard cheeks, and Kiyomori had concluded that he was nervously fatigued, from either excessive studying or else heavy drinking and dissipation. He concluded that Wataru disliked Morito and had not invited him.

The wine was passed around and the young warriors were now at their ease. "Come, host," they called, "isn't it time for her to appear? Stop tantalizing us!"

Wataru was pressing wine on Yoshikiyo, who sat with his cup untouched.

Lifting his cup at last, Yoshikiyo addressed Wataru: "I once attended a poetry contest at the palace when a lady named Kesa-Gozen was applauded for her poems, so she is not entirely unknown to me. Now that she is the mistress of a household, I doubt that she has opportunities for composing verse. A pity that such talent should be lost to us. You must have her attend the poetry parties, Wataru, for we crude warriors most lack an appreciation of literary accomplishments and, what is more, despise them. . . . Might I then say that this warrior and his poet wife are like a graceful painting—the pine and the chrysanthemum—a most felicitous wedding? These men envy you. Can you blame them for being so jealous?"

Yoshikiyo laughed heartily. The wine made him expansive and less somber than usual. The guests grew boisterous, clamoring: "Yoshikiyo, talking of poetry again? Whenever that fellow opens his mouth, our wine grows cold!"

"Come, come, good host, bring out the real thing!"

"Quickly let her appear before us—your friends!"

They boisterously entreated and demanded that Wataru

bring out his wife, until he finally asked, "Shall I call dancing girls to entertain us in my humble home?"

"No, no! Let us have a glimpse of the lady—Kesa-Gozen—she who is lovelier than all the famous dancing girls in this capital!"

Wataru, laughing, begged for mercy, protesting: "She is shy—she will not leave the kitchen, where she warms the wine for my guests and busies herself with pleasing them. I fear she will not come and let these lamps shine on her."

"Let us see the light in your kitchen, rather than the autumn moon," the guests shouted. One of them staggered to his feet and made for the kitchen, but Wataru sprang after him and dragged him back with promises to fetch his wife. The guests continued to badger Wataru, who was quite sober now. Assuring them that he would present her fittingly as a warrior's wife, he begged them to wait a little longer and left the room. When he reappeared, he seated himself on the veranda which faced the garden, saying:

"The black colt that you know was entrusted to me now shows every sign of being a winner. I now look forward to entering him in the Ninna-ji races when the emperor makes his pilgrimage, and hope to celebrate that occasion with you. Now tell me what you think of the colt."

Wataru's guests grew silent. They knew how Wataru had labored over the horse's training, even staking his reputation on it. No one complained that he had broken the promise made a while ago, and they called out together, "Let's see him!"

Following his example, they seated themselves on the verandah facing on a small inner garden. The August moon shed enough brilliance for them to see the horse. Wataru faced the garden and called to someone.

Clop, clop, clop rang out the hooves as the horse drew near. Crickets stopped chirping. The bushes near a bamboo fence stirred; dew rolled down among the leaves with a sound like the scattering of pearls. The garden gate swung open and a woman appeared, leading the colt by its reins. Noiselessly she stepped through the moonlight and then stopped in the middle of the garden.

The guests drew in their breath and made no sound—surprised, delighted, and amazed.

There stood the horse in the moonlight. His coat shone like jet, like the wet plumes of a raven. A noble beast with fine legs and magnificent muscles. There was no comparing him now with the colt of the spring. His long tail almost swept the earth, and the four white fetlocks gleamed as though he were treading snow.

The guests, however, were not watching the horse, but the figure that stood silently bowing to them. This, then, was Kesa-Gozen?

She did not appear shy. A smile hovered on her lips as she turned to face the rearing horse, quieting it until it stood motionless.

Was it a trick of moonlight that made her look like the Kannon in the Dream Hall?[1] Her fingers gleamed white to their very tips, and her long hair was as glossy as the horse's coat.

"Ah," Kiyomori sighed to himself, "I would have a wife, too, were there another such as she in this world!" He swallowed hard and then blushed furiously at the sound he made in his throat. . . .

On the 14th of September, shortly before midnight, there was a sound of feet hurrying toward Kiyomori's room. It was Heiroku, a steward, who called out that a messenger had arrived on horseback from the palace. The young master was to put on his armor and report immediately. . . .

Kiyomori arrived at the Guard Office. Leaving his horse with a retainer, he shouldered his way through the dense crowd of Guards and armed men who surrounded the building, hoping to catch in the babble of voices some explanation for the summons.

"You never can tell about people. It was only last month that we Guards met at Wataru's house in Iris Lane."

Faces—faces—faces. Nothing but excited faces and excited talk.

"Yes, I was there that night. We were quite drunk and badgered Wataru into letting us see the moon in his kitchen instead of the moon in his garden. . . ."

"It was just like Wataru to introduce his wife in the graceful way he did."

"Even the light of the moon seemed too harsh for her as she turned her unsmiling face toward us."

[1] Kannon: Japanese form of Kuan-Yin, Buddhist goddess of Mercy.

"She was all elegance, like a white peony, though she had just come from her kitchen. . . ."

"Like a spray of pear blossoms in spring!"

"Ah, how pitiful! How pitiful, indeed!"

With more show of feeling than was usual among the Guards, one of them lamented: "Though she was another man's wife, I do say she was lovely beyond words. And that Kesa-Gozen murdered . . ."

Kiyomori could not believe his ears. Kesa-Gozen dead? Murdered? Her image in his heart was so real that he refused to believe she was dead. The unspeakable worst had happened to her. He felt he had more words in praise of her beauty than any man there. But she was another man's wife and he had believed he did wrong in even thinking of her. Now that everyone spoke of her, he no longer was afraid of admitting to himself that he had adored her. Roughly he pushed his way through the crowd as though bent on business that concerned him alone.

"Is it true? Is there no mistake about it? The murderer—who is the murderer?" Kiyomori demanded.

Someone spoke to him. "The master calls you."

Kiyomori turned and hurried toward the inner gate, where his father waited. He did not recognize his father in the man who spoke.

"Post yourself at the foot of Kurama Road, near First Avenue," Tadamori commanded. "Watch out for every man that passes. Consider every man suspect. Leave no one unsearched. Don't let the murderer escape. He may be disguised, but there's no mistaking him."

Kiyomori could not wait further. "Who is this man I am to capture?" he interrupted breathlessly.

"A warrior, Endo Morito."

"What, Morito killed Kesa-Gozen?"

"Yes, he," Tadamori replied heavily. "He has disgraced the name of the Imperial Guards—and of all things, because of an infatuation for another man's wife."

At that moment Morito's uncle, Endo Mitsuto, came rapidly through the inner gate, his eyes averted and his face sickly. He slipped by quickly as if eager to escape, but every eye scrutinized him as though he were the murderer's accomplice.

Armed retainers, other than his own, now gathered around Tadamori. He had conferred with His Majesty's aide and was now prepared to give the men an account of the events of that night.

Kesa-Gozen had been murdered early that night of the 14th, about the Dog Hour (eight o'clock). The place: her own home in Iris Lane. Her husband was away at that time.

Morito, who had had a nodding acquaintance with Kesa-Gozen's mother, either before her daughter left the Court to be married or soon after her marriage to Wataru, it was never known exactly when, fell wildly in love with Kesa-Gozen.

People believed that Morito's exceptional gifts as a scholar, widely recognized, would win him an imperial grant and enable him to enter the university, where he would attain to the highest honors conferred there. Lately, however, his fellow students and friends in the Guards had begun to look askance at him and avoid him, for Morito had for some time been acting strangely.

Ardent and persevering by nature, Morito was not only a scholar, but an eloquent speaker, daring and confident to the point of condescending to all his acquaintances. In matters pertaining to amour, he was more than self-assured, and when carried away by his passions, he was a formidable man with his magnificent physique—a madman, deaf to all reason.

His one-sided love affair with Kesa-Gozen, the headlong infatuation of a man not to be turned from his purpose, was her doom. He passionately importuned her, until she grew afraid; intimidated her by insinuating that Wataru would pay the price for her resistance, until his threats finally determined the course she would take. She secretly made up her mind that she would meet his challenge with one of her own.

Morito, desperate and on the brink of losing his mind, demanded a final answer from her, and Kesa-Gozen was prepared to give it. She lucidly considered the consequences of the promise she would give him, and this is what she said:

"There is no choice for me now. Hide yourself, on the night of the 14th, in my husband's bedroom, at the Dog Hour. Earlier in the evening I shall see that he bathes and washes his hair, ply him with wine, and then see him to bed. While he lives, there is no way in which I can meet your wishes. I shall wait for you in another part of the house while you go through with it. My husband is deadly with a sword; therefore creep quietly to his pillow, feel for his wet hair, and then with one blow strike off his head. Be sure you strike clean."

Morito feverishly assented. Early on the night of the 14th he did exactly as he was told. He had no trouble whatever and felt no need to examine the head that he grasped by its damp locks. Nonetheless he stepped out on the verandah to look at the head by the light of the moon.

He screamed. Froze. The head of his beloved dangled from his hand.

In that one horrid cry torn from the depth of his being were mingled his shame, his grief, his despair, and the agony of the mortal wound he had dealt himself. He sank numb to the floor. At that instant the colt in the stable neighed shrilly, pawed wildly, and would not stop neighing.

Morito finally rose to his feet. Moaning incoherently in the direction of the dark room, he took the cold thing, clammy with its wet hair and fresh blood, and drew it close to him under his arm, then leaped to the garden, cleared the hedge and bushes in a bound, and vanished into darkness like a malevolent ghost. . . .

The story of Kesa-Gozen's death soon reached every ear in Kyoto. It was talked about everywhere. Strangers, as well as those who knew her, tenderly mourned for her, denouncing Morito as a ghoul—a raving madman. Him they could never forgive, they said, and loathed him the more because he had once shown such promise. But more than the curiosity, the horror, and the pity that Kesa-Gozen's death aroused was the realization of how lightly most men and women regarded a woman's fidelity. There were few who were not profoundly moved, and who did not shudder at the thought of what she had done to preserve her womanliness.

The common folk of the Shiokoji grieved for her. Even the harlots of Sixth Avenue, who nightly hawked their bodies for a living, wiped the tears from their tawdry painted faces in pity, and not a few of them mingled discreetly with the crowds at Kesa-Gozen's funeral to leave nosegays for the dead one.

The courtiers, and the highborn ladies, too, were moved by the tale of Kesa-Gozen, though many appraised it cynically, for in the sheltered decadence of their lives what was a woman's virtue but an elegant commodity, a graceful pawn, casually bestowed and lightly withdrawn, for the pleasure of men? What then, they said, was so noble in Kesa-Gozen, who had defended her honor with her life? Was it not the natural timidity of a woman that drove her to this extremity? There were some who said with a shrug that a woman's whim to die in her husband's stead at the hands of a crazed lover was scarcely a matter for the courtiers to fuss over, that if the affair was to be regarded seriously at all, it was a sign of corruption in the Guards. What had happened to the Guards these days, these warriors who were assigned to keep watch at the palace or sent as messengers between the palace and the Court? If there were profligates there, Morito certainly was not the only one! What else could one expect of those warriors? . . .

The stalled beast turned loose in the fields to fend for itself reverts in time to its wild state. Man's barbarous nature asserts itself even more swiftly, and this was true of Morito, whose transformation back to savagery seemed to come overnight.

"Should I go on living? Am I better off dead? What am I to do with this self? They still pursue me—give me no time to think. . . . I must rest, and yet they keep following. I stop to take breath, and they still—" "I—I—I," he repeated to himself, not realizing that that self with which he identified himself no longer existed.

On that night when he escaped from the house in Iris Lane and mysteriously eluded his pursuers, Morito could not remember which way his feet took him. He slept in the open, hid himself in hollow trees, and ate whatever he could find in his wild flight. His clothes were now in tatters, his bare feet caked with blood and mud, and his eyes gleamed like those of some wild beast.

This was the man of letters, the gifted Morito, for whom there had been such high hopes. Who could find in this shape the scholar, the proud Morito? Who could believe that this was he who looked down on his fellow men with scorn? Yet the shape still breathed, walked, and moved. That which lived merely existed.

His ears were now sharpened to every bird cry, and the sight of rabbits and deer no longer startled him. He felt himself one with the birds and beasts of this wild solitude. But the slightest sound of men approaching made his hair bristle. There they were—coming! Taking a fresh hold on the round object that he carried, Morito would stand frozen for an instant, his bloodshot eyes wild, searching this way and that.

A sleeve of his outer robe was torn off to make a wrapping for the thing he held tight to him. It was the head of Kesa-Gozen. He had not laid it down for even a moment since that night. The blood had seeped through and dried hard until, drenched with dew and stained with earth, it looked like lacquer. More than a fortnight had passed since Morito had fled, and the head now gave out the odor of putrefaction. But he clung to it day and night, and when he drowsed, he seemed to see Kesa-Gozen once more in the flesh.

Nothing about her had changed. He heard the silken rustle of her garments as she drew near and whispered to him. He breathed her fragrance; felt the warmth of her body as she leaned toward him. Though spiders spun webs around his pillow of dead leaves, and pale sunless fungi grew about his head, they seemed less real than the fantasies that visited him in his delirium.

Once more they were boy and girl, hovering like butterflies over the flowerbeds of the palace gardens. Then he saw himself as the pitiful youth, lovelorn to madness—to death. And in his dreams he moaned: "O Kesa-Gozen, why will you not look on me? There is no one to deliver me from this torment but you, O heartless one! Why did you marry Wataru? Pity me! Give me but one night by your side. Let me once steal this forbidden blossom, then let this offense, more grievous than all the Ten Sins, cast me down to the bottomless, fiery pits of hell, for what agony can exceed this which I now endure?"

And in his fevered dreams he saw her closed eyes and sought her lips with his own. Between the folds of her tumbled robes he glimpsed her pale limbs, the curve of her naked breasts; reaching out for her, he would find her no longer there, and the dream would dissolve, leaving him tortured with thirst for her. Awake once more he would break into an agony of weeping, until all nature at midnight seemed to lament with him.

It was still dark when Morito, worn by tears and a night

of haunted dreams, awoke. Rising, he staggered and stumbled on blindly, not knowing where he was, when all his nerves tingled suddenly in response to curious new sensations. An icy current seemed to thunder through his brain and a wild roaring filled his ears, echoing and reechoing in his head.

The Narutaki Rapids—on the road to Takao with its maples!

Dawn had come, and a pale moon hung in the sky. Morito looked about him, filling his eyes with the crimson of maples all over the hillside. Never had the morning light seemed so crystal-clear. He was sane once more. Then the events of that night—the 14th of September—came back to him vividly as though he once more stood at the scene. The thundering of the Narutaki Rapids and the baying of waters suddenly sounded like the terrible lamentations of a despairing mother—Wataru's hoarse cries of hate, the mocking laughter of his fellow Guards, and the angry cries of the people.

Facing the rapids, Morito cried out as though in reply: "Let me die! . . . I cannot face the world alive!"

Swaying, he clung to a boulder and looked down into the boiling current, and as he gazed he spied a group of stonecutters making their way from the opposite shore, leaping from rock to rock as they approached in his direction. Like a flash, Morito turned and took flight, swiftly clambering to the crest of a hill.

Arrived at the top, he placed the bundle he was carrying on the ground, then fell heavily to his knees, struggling for breath. Sweat poured down his body, and he rubbed his hairy chest, panting.

Die, he must, now that he had regained his senses, he thought.

"Forgive me, my beloved," he then cried, lifting his hands in prayer. One by one he whispered the names of those he knew, entreating their pardon, then took the wrapping from the head.

"Now look at Morito, who will atone with his own life," he whispered. "Look once more at the world, for I, too, will soon be dust."

Numbly he stared at what he saw. The hair, matted with blood into lacquerlike strands, clung stiffly to the cheeks and forehead.

"Ah, my beloved, can this be you?"

The head resembled nothing more than a large clump of clay. As the sky filled with light, he saw how the flesh had shrunk under the tangled lattice of hair; the bones jutted out, and the skin was mottled. The ears had shriveled and looked like dried mussels; the eyes seemed carved from blue wax stained white. Nowhere could he discover the features he had once adored.

And he prayed: *"Dai-nichi Nyorai, Dai-nichi Nyorai!"* ("Great Illuminator!")

From the death mask before him his eyes traveled heavenward. In front of him rose the sun like a ball of fire. The roofs of the capital, the Eastern Hills, and the spired pagodas lay shrouded in mist, and all he could see was the immense flaming wheel of light. Then he suddenly remembered. . . .

The hermitage—more exactly speaking, a modest villa, where the Abbot Kakuyu frequently stayed—stood in a pocket of the Togano-o Hills, on the road to Takao, just where the Narutaki Rapids flow to join the Kiyotaki Rapids. . . .

The abbot was hard at his painting one day when his servant announced a guest. Putting aside his brush and inkstone, Toba Sojo turned to receive the caller, a youthful Guard from the Cloister Palace, Sato Yoshikiyo.

"I envy you your life, your reverence. Whenever I come to visit you, I am convinced that man's life was meant to be lived close to nature."

"Why envy me?" Toba Sojo replied. "I can't see why you don't choose the life that you most desire."

"More easily said than done, your reverence."

"Is that so? He who lives in the mountains yearns for the city, and the city-dweller would rather live in the mountains," the abbot chuckled, "and nothing is ever to one's liking. . . ."

"Oh, your reverence, there go your pictures—the wind!"

"Those scraps of paper? Never mind them. And now, have you come up here to see the maples and to compose a poem or two?"

"No, your reverence, I am on my way to Ninna-ji Temple on matters that have to do with the imperial pilgrimage."

"Yes? It's amazing how His Majesty doesn't tire of all this horse racing. I shouldn't be surprised if the human race turns into a horde of evils running neck and neck, and the Guards become a herd of wild horses, runaway colts, and vicious stallions. A frightening thought indeed!"

Toba Sojo turned abruptly to call in the direction of a room at the rear of the villa: "Boy, are the persimmons I asked for ready? Bring some fruit to our guest."

There was no reply, but a faint murmur of voices could be heard at the back of the house. Then a youth who appeared from around the corner of the house approached the verandah. Some stonecutters who lived in the vicinity, he said, had come in terror to report that since morning they had seen a strange, wild-looking man wandering barefooted in the nearby hills; a sleeve of his robe was missing. They had stealthily observed his movements, followed him, and seen him disappear into the dense growth among the hills, where he buried some large object that he apparently cherished. At the approach of the stonecutters, the creature had vanished like a bird into the depth of the forest on Takao.

"And what of it?" the abbot exclaimed. "Why trouble yourself with such a trifle? Are you thinking of pursuing the man?"

"N-no—not exactly, but the stonecutters are talking excitedly about capturing him. They think he's a brigand."

"Let him be, let him be. These are hard times and even a brigand must live. He will be fed when they get him to jail, but what of his wife and children? Isn't that so, Yoshikiyo?"

Yoshikiyo appeared to be struck by a thought and was gazing at the clouded crest of Takao with an abstracted look. He was about to reply, seemed to think better of it, and apologized instead for his long stay and quickly left the villa.

A persimmon that the birds had left uneaten hung golden red under the autumn sky, and the sound of stonecutters' chisels echoed icily among the clouds of the peak. . . .

An unending line of noblemen's carriages, processions of priests in their vestments, and crowds of inquisitive sightseers from all over the countryside made their way to the temple, where the destitute swarmed like flies to receive alms. Numberless Guards were posted along the route; and on the banks of the rivers, around the hamlet of Takeda, and wherever they camped, great bonfires lighted up the sky at night.

The ex-emperor's stay lasted two days. Toward evening of the second day a chill rain fell, and the scene, which had been alive with people, became strangely still. The Great Hall loomed through the darkness in all its magnificence, shimmering dreamlike in the reflected light of the many watchfires.

The Guards were settling at last to a late evening meal in their temporary shelters. An allotment of imperial wine had been distributed among them on the previous day, but they had all been too busy to taste it. Some Guards were drying their hunting cloaks at the fires; others had already taken off their armor and were passing around wine cups and attacking their food.

One Guard remarked: "It may be just gossip, but Wataru of the Genji didn't come for the dedication."

"Wataru? Oh, you mean Kesa-Gozen's husband. What's become of him?"

"Hmmm . . . just before we started, he quite suddenly went to take leave of the Minister of the Left, who, it appears, urged him to reconsider his decision, but Wataru handed in his resignation to the palace aide and hasn't been seen since in the capital."

"Oh, what did he mean by that?"

"Doubtless, consumed by hate for Morito, who murdered his wife, he's gone off to find him and take his revenge. He has been saying that he no longer can endure being pointed out as the husband of the murdered woman."

"There's no telling when Morito will be found. Wataru can hardly be blamed for feeling as he does. Seems to me, though, that Morito is fated to sin and to live out his span tortured with remorse."

"People have been saying that they've seen him in the hills of Takao or around Kumano. In fact, there have been any number of such stories, so he must be alive." . . .

In December 1141, though it surprised no one, the twenty-two-year-old Emperor Sutoku was suddenly dethroned, and the three-year-old son of ex-Emperor Toba and Lady Bifukumon was declared ruler and duly installed.

In mid-January, less than a month later, a young monk walked alone through the leafless woods of the Eastern Hills, gathering twigs broken off by the heavy fall of snow. Few would have recognized him as Yoshikiyo of the Guards, though his monk's robes sat ill on him.

"Ah, is it you?"

Saigyo stopped at the sound of someone hailing him. "You—Gengo?" . . .

They had now reached Saigyo's frail shelter, a comfortless hut behind the main temple. Saigyo gathered together some poems that lay scattered on a small table, put away his inkstone, and set about whittling kindling with a dagger, while Gengo washed at a nearby stream the provisions he had brought and set a pot of gruel to cook on the hearth. . . .

Their supper ready, Saigyo and Gengo, like fellow monks and equals, sat down beside the hearth. Even when they were through eating, they talked on. . . .

Gengo broke the silence. "Have you heard about Morito?"

Saigyo, who was dreamily contemplating the beauty of the white ashes and glowing embers, looked up suddenly. "Morito?" he asked, as though trying to recapture some faraway memory.

"His name was removed in December from the official list of criminals. A traveler lately from Kumano in Kishu told me that Morito is now a monk, the same Morito who killed Kesa-Gozen five years ago and disappeared. He has taken the name Mongaku and this past autumn vowed to do penance for one hundred days by bathing in the sacred waters of Nachi Falls."

"Ah, Morito! . . . There's nothing like the falls at Nachi for chastising the flesh, and no way to salvation except by good works."

"This traveler told me he went to the Nachi Falls to see what this mad monk was like and found Mongaku, all in white, a coarse rope about his waist, praying hoarsely as he bathed in the lashing waters—a sight to freeze anyone's blood! Mongaku, it seems, lost consciousness several times and would have drowned were it not for the caretaker at the falls. I was told that his hair and beard almost conceal his face and sunken eyes, and that he seems hardly human."

"So that's what happened to him." Plucking a burning brand from the fire, Saigyo began tracing some words in the ashes of the hearth.

A note of sympathy crept into Gengo's voice as he repeated the story of Morito's self-flagellations. Gengo had been one of those who most bitterly condemned Morito. . . .

In the ashes on the hearth, Saigyo traced and retraced the word "pity." He had yet to learn to accept life with all its good and evils, to love life in all its manifestations by becoming one with nature. . . .

Gifts he had none to preach salvation, the precepts of Buddha; all that he asked was to be left to exist humbly as the butterflies and birds.

Fuki Wooyenaka Uramatsu

Yasunari Kawabata[1]
(1899–1972)

A novelist, playwright, short-story writer, and film actor, Kawabata was awarded the Nobel Prize in 1968. He committed suicide in 1972.

The following section of Kawataba's novel *The Sound of the Mountain* carries the same title as the work from which it is selected.

THE SOUND OF THE MOUNTAIN

Yasuko, Shingo's wife, was sixty-three, a year older than he.

They had a son, a daughter, and two grandchildren, daughters of the girl, Fusako.

Yasuko was young for her age. One would not have taken her to be older than her husband. Not that Shingo

[1] Kawabata is his family name. I use the Western form here because that is the way readers are likely to know him.

himself seemed particularly old. They seemed natural together, he just enough older than she to make them a most ordinary couple. Though diminutive, she was in robust health.

Yasuko was no beauty. In their younger years she had looked older than he, and had disliked being seen in public with him.

Shingo could not have said at what age she had begun to look the younger of the two. Probably it had been somewhere toward their mid-fifties. Women generally age faster than men, but in their case the reverse had been true.

The year before, the year he had entered his second cycle of sixty years, Shingo had spat up blood—from his lungs, it had seemed. He had not had a medical examination, however, and presently the affliction had gone away. It had not come back.

Nor had it meant that he grew suddenly older. His skin had seemed firmer since, and in the two weeks or so that he had been in bed the color of his eyes and lips had improved.

Shingo had not detected symptoms of tuberculosis in himself, and to spit blood at his age gave him the darkest forebodings. Partly because of them he refused to be examined. To Shuichi such behavior was no more than the stubborn refusal of the aged to face facts. Shingo was not able to agree.

Yasuko was a good sleeper. Sometimes, in the middle of the night, Shingo would be tempted to blame her snoring for having awakened him. She had snored, it seemed, as a girl of fifteen or sixteen, and her parents had been at great pains to correct the habit; it had stopped when she married. Then, when she passed fifty, it had begun again.

When she snored, Shingo would twist her nose in an effort to stop her. If the twisting had no effect, he would take her by the throat and shake her. On nights when he was not in good spirits he would be repelled by the sight of the aged flesh with which he had lived for so long.

Tonight he was not in good spirits. Turning on the light, he looked at her profile and took her by the throat. She was a little sweaty.

Only when she snored did he reach out to touch her. The fact seemed to him infinitely saddening.

He took up a magazine lying at his pillow. Then, the

room being sultry, he got up, opened a shutter, and sat down beside it.

The moon was bright.

One of his daughter-in-law's dresses was hanging outside, unpleasantly gray. Perhaps she had forgotten to take in her laundry, or perhaps she had left a sweat-soaked garment to take the dew of the night.

A screeching of insects came from the garden. There were locusts on the trunk of the cherry tree to the left. He had not known that locusts could make such a rasping sound; but locusts indeed they were.

He wondered if locusts might sometimes be troubled with nightmares.

A locust flew in and lit on the skirt of the mosquito net. It made no sound as he picked it up.

"A mute." It would not be one of the locusts he had heard at the tree.

Lest it fly back in, attracted by the light, he threw it with all his strength toward the top of the tree. He felt nothing against his hand as he released it.

Gripping the shutter, he looked toward the tree. He could not tell whether the locust had lodged there or flown on. There was a vast depth to the moonlit night, stretching far on either side.

Though August had only begun, autumn insects were already singing.

He thought he could detect a dripping of dew from leaf to leaf.

Then he heard the sound of the mountain.

It was a windless night. The moon was near full, but in the moist, sultry air the fringe of trees that outlined the mountain was blurred. They were motionless, however.

Not a leaf on the fern by the verandah was stirring.

In these mountain recesses of Kama Kura the sea could sometimes be heard at night. Shingo wondered if he might have heard the sound of the sea. But no—it was the mountain.

It was like wind, far away, but with a depth like a rumbling of the earth. Thinking that it might be in himself, a ringing in his ears, Shingo shook his head.

The sound stopped, and he was suddenly afraid. A chill passed over him, as if he had been notified that death was approaching. He wanted to question himself, calmly and deliberately, to ask whether it had been the sound of the wind, the sound of the sea, or a sound in his ears. But he had heard no such sound, he was sure. He had heard the mountain.

It was as if a demon had passed, making the mountain sound out.

The steep slope, wrapped in the damp shades of night, was like a dark wall. So small a mound of a mountain, that it was all in Shingo's garden; it was like an egg cut in half.

There were other mountains behind it and around it, but the sound did seem to come from that particular mountain to the rear of Shingo's house.

Stars were shining through the trees at its crest.

As he closed the shutter, a strange memory came to him.

Some ten days before, he had been awaiting a guest at a newly built restaurant. A single geisha was with him. The guest was late, and so were the other geisha.

"Why don't you take off your tie?" she said. "You must be warm."

Shingo nodded, and let her take it off for him.

She was not a geisha with whom he was particularly familiar, but when she had folded the tie and put it into the pocket of his coat, which lay beside the alcove, the conversation moved on to personal matters.

Some two months before, she said, she had been on the point of committing suicide with the carpenter who had built the restaurant. But as they had prepared to take poison, doubts had overtaken her. Were the portions in fact lethal?

"He said there was plenty. The doses were all measured out, his and mine, he said, and that proved it."

But she could not believe him. Her doubts only grew.

"I asked him who did the measuring. Someone might have measured out just enough to make us sick and teach us a lesson. I asked him who the druggist or doctor was that gave it to him, but he wouldn't say. Isn't that strange? There we were, going to die together. Why wouldn't he answer me? After all, who was to know afterward?"

"A good yarn," Shingo had wanted to say.

And so she had insisted, she went on, that they try again after *she* had found someone to do the measuring.

"I have it here with me."

Shingo thought the story an odd one. All that had really

stayed with him was the fact that the man was a carpenter and had built the restaurant.

The geisha had taken two packets from her purse and opened them for him.

He had only glanced at them. He had had no way of knowing whether or not they were poison.

As he closed the shutter, he thought of the geisha.

He went back to bed. He did not wake his wife to tell her of the fear that had come over him on hearing the sound of the mountain.

Edward G. Seidensticker

Chapter 7
JAPANESE POEMS

Some of the best recent American scholarship in literature and the humanities has been devoted to Japanese poetry. Since I can't improve on it, I take the liberty of quoting Professor Earl Miner's characterization of that poetry.

> Philosophically dominated by a residual Shinto animism and imbued from early historical times with Buddhism, [Japanese poetry] tends: to mold its affective wealth into a poetry of states, often in harmonies of different states of awareness and perception; to explore feeling; to use images at once as concrete details and for metaphorical implications (rather than representation); and to excel on tonal rather than thematic complexity.[1]

In some ways, the history of Japanese poetry is a history of anthologies, at least until comparatively recently. The first great anthology of Japanese poetry is *Manyoshu,* or "Ten Thousand Leaves Collection." Compiled probably around A.D. 759, the *Manyoshu* includes poems by some of Japan's most famous poets, as well as by workmen, soldiers, prostitutes, beggars, and unknowns. Some readers may feel, as Hemingway did about anthologies of English poetry, that his favorite poems are by Anonymous, but the prevailing opinion is that the best poetry in the *Manyoshu* is by men in the middle ranks of court society—the society around the Japanese Emperor. Although most Japanese poetry is short, the *Manyoshu* includes a number of longer poems in a form called *choka,* which usually ends with one or more envoys. The second poetry anthology, *Kokinshu,*

[1] Alex Preminger *et al., Encyclopedia of Poetry and Poetics* (Princeton, N.J.: Princeton University Press, 1965), p. 423.

which was compiled around 905, was edited under imperial patronage (and sometimes with the emperor's personal assistance, or interference). By this time, the long poem, with an ambiguous exception to be discussed below, had disappeared from Japanese poetry, and even poems of medium length (the longest choka is, after all, only 149 lines) would not be seen again until modern times. The main form in Japanese poetry was now a form that is still used, the *tanka* (also known as the *waka* or *uta*), a poem of five lines, each line of which has a set number of syllables, as follows: 5, 7, 5, 7, 7. To appreciate the crucial juxtaposition and internal dynamic of the poem, it is important to know where the main internal division of the *tanka* comes. In *Manyoshu* times, the usual scheme was: 5, 7 (pause), 5, 7 (pause), 7, an arrangement that may derive from earlier forms in which the last line of a poem is simply spoken, or sung, twice. By *Kokinshu* times, the *tanka* normally divided 5 (pause), 7, 5 (pause), 7, 7. This kind of *tanka,* then, was composed of units of five syllables, twelve syllables, and fourteen syllables, so that the poem picked up speed as it went on. In later times the *tanka* was composed 5, 7, 5 (pause), 7, 7—and the *haiku* form (5, 7, 5) and the *renga* were born.[1]

In the early classical period, which may be taken to run to about A.D. 1100, three other important developments took place in Japanese poetry. The anthology itself was defined as a poetic genre; some writers experimented with mixed genres of poetry and prose; and finally, the poetry contest became a major court event.

Japanese poetry was still court poetry in 1206, when the next important anthology, the *Shinkokinshu,* was compiled. The two major figures of the age were the Emperor Go-Toba (1180–1239), at whose behest the *Shinkokinshu* was made, and the poet and critic Fujiwara Teika (1162–1242). According to modern opinion, the *Shinkokinshu*—the eighth of the imperial anthologies—marks the point at which the anthology truly became a literary form, a separate and independent form for aesthetic pleasure.

Working within a tradition, and with many previous discoveries to go on, Go-Toba, Fujiwara Teika, and Teika's committee on the anthology pulled these discoveries to-

[1] I am indebted to Lenore Mayhew for help with this material.

gether and added others of their own. Thus the individual short poems of the anthology, if read continuously, produced a flow rather like the coherent flow of a novel or a long poem—but more, perhaps, like the flow of a movie. In movies, the basic device producing this flow is called "montage." The individual poems are like a cinematographer's shots. The anthologist, like the film editor, builds them into scenes, then builds the scenes into sequences, and the sequences into an anthology (or film).

The techniques of montage—the relation between one poem and the next that causes the two poems intellectually or emotionally to collide and so to produce the forward flow of the book—are exceedingly subtle and complex, as subtle and complex as the minds of the artists who have made and remade them. To try to inventory them would, therefore, dizzy the arithmetic of analysis. Professor Earl Miner lists a few techniques: simple narrative development; seasonal unity; temporal progression; spatial progression. In his analysis he talks of "close view," "medium view," and "medium view nearer at hand." This terminology provides, I believe, the best clue for the modern Western reader who wants to respond to this form of Japanese literature. He or she should simply try to visualize clearly the scene being described in any particular poem, and then respond to the progression to the next poem spontaneously and non-intellectually, just as he or she would respond to the cuts and progressions in a movie.

In the twelfth century, the court's monopoly on poetry and taste began to weaken as a result of its loss of economic and political power. Zen priests from the Five Temples continued the tradition and culture of the older poetry, although by 1350 a new age, usually called the "Feudal Age," had begun. The main development in this era was probably the emergence of linked verse, or *renga,* a development from the poetry contests of the court period, as a prominent form. Each *renga* was composed by several poets, working together and taking turns. The trick, as with the anthology form, was to move (or cut) from short poem to poem in some artistic or effective way, by some identifiable—or at least feelable—principle of association, at the same time producing a harmonious whole. The standard *renga* had a hundred stanzas, alternating in 5, 7, 5, 7, 7 syllable lines.

Between the seventeenth and mid-nineteenth centuries, both the practice and control of Japanese poetry were greatly democratized. Samurai, successful farmers, and rich businessmen all wrote and appreciated the art. The major figure of this period was Matsuo Basho (1644–1694), known to many Americans for his *haiku*. It would scarcely be possible to overestimate Basho's influence: he brought together the humble, simple style of less serious forms with the philosophical and religious drift of the greatest earlier serious Japanese poetry. Basho also wrote travel diaries, a mixed verse-prose form. These diaries became, in Basho's hands, a kind of artistic fiction. The reader may, in fact, find them extremely modern. In their strong sense of life and their plotless plot, they are like the best nineteenth-century French novels or like Antonioni's films. Excerpts from Basho's famous *Oku no Hosomichi,* translated by the modern American poet Cid Corman, appear below.

Basho—with collaborators, of course—also left some exquisite examples of *haikai no renga,* or *renku.* This is a shortened sequence, like the *renga* but freer, with thirty-six stanzas or component poems instead of the renga's one hundred. A complete version of one of these, "Summer Moon," appears below in a new translation by Lenore Mayhew. Basho considerably refined the techniques of association which are so important to Japanese poetic sequences. He named five principles: *nioi* (smell), *hibiki* (echo), *utsuri* (change, or reflection), *kurai* (rank, that is, social status), and *omokage* (mental image, but perhaps better translated as allusion). These are impressionistic labels, like Dante's terms in his classification of words, by their sound, as "shaggy, glossy, combed-out and rumpled," and it is therefore sometimes difficult to associate the actual transition with the names as given by Basho. Some examples are discussed on p. 233.

Besides these principles of association, the game—if you like—of writing *renku,* or *haikai no renga,* is governed by certain other rules. The first stanza should contain a seasonal word to set the time of year. The second stanza should be closely related to the first, while the third stanza should differ completely in theme from the first and yet should be associated suitably with the second. Certain other specified stanzas were supposed to contain the word moon, or flower, or were supposed to deal with love, and the last stanza was supposed to deal with spring, so that the entire sequence would end on a note of peace and hope. The Japanese used to write these sequences on special papers, called *kaishi,* printed so that the writer would get the moon in the right stanza, the flower in the right stanza, and so on. *Kaishi,* that is, were an aid to the game. All this might seem to the Western reader like rigmarole, and no doubt many inferior poems were written to these prescriptions. But when Basho and Kyorai and their friends got together and wrote *renku* there was always the possibility that great poetry would emerge.

FROM THE "TEN THOUSAND LEAVES COLLECTION" OR MANYOSHU (CA. 759)

Kakinomoto Hitomaru

(fl. *ca.* 680–700)

Under the sea of Iwami,
Off the cape of Kara,
Miru clings to the deep rocks,
Sea-tangle grows on the shore.
And like sea-tangle
          my wife bends to me,
And deep as the deep sea-growing miru
                    is my love for her.

Too few nights
          we lay together.
Like tight-twined ivy
We were pulled apart.
It hurts to remember.
I look back toward the mountain,
But falling yellow leaves
Hide her waving sleeves
          as clouds
                above Yakami
                      hide the moon.
Now the sun drops,
          and I who thought myself a strong man
          have sleeves wet with tears.

Envoy I

My horse dark and fast
Gallops away—and she is left
Under that other sky.

Envoy II

Oh, yellow leaves
On the autumn mountain,
Stop the whirling curtain
of your fall,
So I can see my love.

Lenore Mayhew

Ishikawa Kimiko

(dates unknown)

And the fishing girls at Shika
Burn the salt,
Gather the seaweed,
Have no time
For the small combs
In their comb cases.

Lenore Mayhew

Anonymous poem from the "Hitomaru Collection" [1]

Like a silkworm
in a cocoon
That girl in her house
And her mother watching
watching.

Lenore Mayhew

[1] The "Hitomaru Collection" is thought to have been compiled by Kakinomoto Hitomaru and to include poems by him and others.

Owari
(dates unknown)

Blossoming
Spring hills
Dotted
With white-sashed girls
plucking spring herbs.

R. Steve Jackson

(End of poems from the "Ten Thousand Leaves Collection.")

Ariwara Narihara
(825–880)

Is this non-moon
            that same moon
This spring
            the spring of the past
And
            still the same
Only
            my own changing
                        unchanged
Soul? . . .

Lenore Mayhew

Lady Ise
(tenth century)

At a Time When She Was Unhappy in Love

My body is
As a dry winter field
Seared by fire—
But the burning
Brings no spring.

Lenore Mayhew

Lady Murasaki
(*ca.* 978 to after 1025)

To love the mountain-cherry
Is easy,
Why then
Regret life?

Lenore Mayhew

Priest Saigyo
(1118–1190)

I cannot take
The real as real,
How do I take
A dream as dream?

Lenore Mayhew

Fujiwara Teika
(1162–1242)

At Uji
The Lady of the Bridge
Spreads out moonlight
                    for a bed.
The night waits.
The autumn wind
                    grows dark.

Lenore Mayhew

Emperor Hanazono
(1297–1348)

Brightness of sun-slant
                    in the eaves,
Swallow-twitter
                    in shadow,
Around the willows in the garden
The green wind of spring.

Lenore Mayhew

Hideyoshi Toyotomi
(1536–1598)

Son of a farmer, Hideyoshi's military abilities made him the most powerful man in Japan in the age of civil wars. He rose to be kampaku, or regent, and *de facto* ruler of the country. Although he had no formal education, he studied poetry and Tea (see pp. 256–257). Naniwa (modern Osaka), mentioned in the poem below, was the site of Hideyoshi's tremendous castle and of his finest days of power and luxury.

Death-bed Verse

like dew
they fall

like dew
they vanish,

these tears:

and all the days
at Naniwa, too,

were dreams
of dreams.

William McNaughton

EARLIER HAIKU

Years of reading haiku, alone and with friends, have convinced me that a good clear pause at the end of the second line, to allow your mind to anticipate the poet's leap to line three, can greatly enhance your enjoyment of the poem.

Hattori Ransetsu
(1653–1707)

Death Verse

One leaf down
And another
And . . .

Lenore Mayhew

Matsuo Basho
(1644–1694)

The temple bell stops—
but the sound keeps coming
out of the flowers.

Robert Bly

There's a chirping
in the fisherman's hut
coming from among the dried shrimp.

Robert Bly

Autumn starting:
sea and rice fields
—one green.

Margrit von Braun

MATSUO BASHO'S TRAVEL DIARY OKU NO HOSOMICHI, OR BACK ROADS TO FAR TOWNS

Introduction

Early one spring morning in 1689, Basho, accompanied by his friend and disciple Sora, set forth from Edo (old Tokyo) on the long nine-month journey which was to take them through the backlands and highlands north of the capital and then west to the Japan Sea coast and along it until they turned inland again toward Lake Biwa (near Kyoto). Approximately the first half of this journey, the most arduous part, remains recorded in the *Oku no Hosomichi.*

Basho in his forty-sixth year and Sora in his forty-first had lived quietly near each other for some time. The journey was one both had looked forward to and realized would be difficult and even dangerous. And, indeed, one might *not* return. It was to be more a pilgrimage—and in the garb of pilgrims they went—than a case of wandering scholarship: a sight not uncommon even in modern Japan, visiting from temple to temple, seeing old acquaintances, places famed in history or poetry or legend, touchstones for the life lived, the dying to come, and what life continues. . . .

Sora also kept a journal of this trip, but it remains as a strictly factual "check," while Basho made his into (essentially) a poem (after some years)—a poem that has become a center of the Japanese mind/heart. . . .

Meanwhile a summer's journey awaits, two men are about to depart on foot, one of them already thinks of us.

(1689)
1

Moon and sun are passing figures of countless generations, and years coming or going wanderers, too. Drifting life away on a boat or meeting age leading a horse by the mouth, each day is a journey and the journey itself home. Amongst those of old were many that perished on the journey. So—when was it—I, drawn like blown cloud, couldn't stop dreaming of roaming, roving the coast up and down, back at the hut last fall by the river side, sweeping the cobwebs off, a year gone and misty skies of spring returning, yearning to go over the Shirakawa Barrier, possessed by the wanderlust. . . .

(March 27)
2

Yayoi: last seventh, slightly hazy dawn, "a waning moon, a failing light," summit of Fuji vague, crowns of blossoming cherry at Ueno and Yanaka, when would they—and would they—be seen again? Friends, gathering since nightfall, came along by boat to see us off. . . .

(March 30)
5

Thirtieth. Stayed at foot of Mount Nikko. Hosteler says: "They call me Hotoke Gozaemon.[1] Honesty's a habit with me, which is why the name, so feel right to home," he said. Impossible not to realize how Buddha appears upon this mean and muddled ground in just such guise to help shaman beggar pilgrims on, seeing our host's simple sincere manner, frank and down-to-earth. Firm-grained and unassuming, the very image of the man of *jen*,[2] worthy of all respect. . . .

(April 3)
8

Set out for a place called Kurobane in Nasu to see an acquaintance there and tried a shortcut through the fields. Caught sight of a village not too far off, made for it, rain started, evening coming on. Passed the night at a farmhouse and next morning tried crossing fields again. Horse pastured there. Asked the way of a fellow mowing nearby, who, plain as he was, wasn't without courtesy. "Let me see," he says, "you know this here field cuts off different ways and if you don't know which is which, worse luck, easy to get lost, so better let the horse there take you far as he can and when he stops, just send him back," and he lent us the horse. . . .

[1] Hotoke Gozaemon: like saying "Jack Buddha."
[2] *Jen:* the Confucian virtue, "natural human feeling for others, graded according to one's relationship to them." See p. 35.

(May 2)
17

Next day went around asking for *Shinobu-mojizuri* rock,[1] reaching Shinobu village. At a hamlet just the other side of the mountain, the rock, half buried in earth. Some village children tagged along and explained. In olden times, they said, it used to be up on top of the mountain, but villagers tired of people passing through tearing out their green grain to try on the rock, and bowled it over into the valley so its face is now hidden. Might well have been so.

seedlings pull
twist old
subtle rubbing

(May 9)
24

Then visited the Tamagawa at Noda and the Oki-no-ishi.[2] On Sue-no-Matsuyama[3] the temple known as Masshozan. Everywhere between pines graves, bringing home the fact that even vows of "wing and wing, branch and branch forever merging" must also come to such, sadness increasing, and at Shiogama Beach a bell sounded evening. . . . That night a blind minstrel played *biwa*[4] and chanted *Oku-joruri*.[5] Not like *The Tale of the Heike*[6] nor *mai*,[7] singing country tunes boisterously to our pillows, but

[1] *Shinobu-mojizuri* (*Davallia bullata*) is a local grass used for rubbing dye into cloth placed on a famous granitic rock. Favorite way of creating a fresh and natural design in the region. Word *shinobu* also, as a verb, means: "recalling times past." And it was believed that this particular rock, when rubbed with young plants, would reveal the image of one's beloved.

[2] A rock, in water, celebrated in poetry.

[3] Sue-no-Matsuyama: Pine Mountain Point. . . . Famous love poems related to it. Section full of images of fidelity.

[4] Japanese lute.

[5] Dramatic back-country balladry, accompanied by *biwa* or *shamisen* (Japanese mandolin).

[6] See pp. 174 and 193–211 .

[7] A sort of simplified dance based on the dance in Japanese Noh drama. The *mai* were much on the wane in Basho's time.

not unusual either, traditional in such out of the way places, and good that they're kept up. . . .

27

Ojima Beach, connected to mainland, projects into the sea. There, ruins of Ungozenji's[1] hut and *zazen*[2] rock and other things remain. And there, too, amongst pines still seen religious recluses, several here and there, by thatched huts where twigs drop off, living quietly, it seemed, as smoke of leaves and pine cones rose. . . .

30

Two temple halls we'd heard of, open. The *kyodo*[3] contains images of the Three Generals[4] and the *hikarido*[5] coffins of the three generations, and enshrines the three images of Buddha. The Seven Gems now gone, jeweled doors rent by winds, gilded pillars fretted by frost and snow, would have all been long since destroyed and back to grass but for reinforced walls on four sides and a cover over the tiled roof against wind and rain. So it still stands, memorial of a thousand years past.

May rains
falling may have left
hikarido

[1] Monk of famous probity and religious influence (1583–1659).
[2] Religious meditation.
[3] A library of sutras (Buddhist religious classics).
[4] The statues (of wood) are, in fact, of Buddhist deities, but not unusually configuring particular people. Here: Kiyohira, Motohira, and Hidehira, three famous members of the Fujiwara clan (1094–1189) of whom the last, Hidehira, had his seat at the place here visited by Basho.
[5] Second of the two temple halls just mentioned, *hikarido* means literally "Hall of Splendor" (built in 1124).

(May 15)

31

Seeing the Nambu road a good way off, stayed over at village of Iwade. Went on via Ogurozaki, Mitsu-no-kojima, and from Narugo Hot Springs made for the Shitomae Barrier and on over into province of Dewa. This route few travelers ever take, so the guards eyed us suspiciously and barely let us through. Climbed high mountain there, sun already down, and happening on a border-guard hut sought shelter there. For three days winds and rain fierce, forced to hang on in that dull retreat.

fleas lice
horse pishing
by the pillow

32

Man at the hut said, "From here to Dewa, with a high mountain to cross and the trail far from clear, better get a guide to take you over." So we hired a man, a strapping young fellow who looked like he could take care of himself, with a curved short sword at hip and oaken staff in hand, and on he took us. Felt like just the day to sort with danger and with some fear followed after. As the man said, the mountain was high and thickly wooded, beyond bird cry, in deep forest darkness like groping about at night. Felt as if dirt were tumbling from overloaded clouds, pushed, pushed on through *shino*[1] brush, waded water, stumbled rock, drenched in cold sweat, came out at last in region of Mogami. Our guide then said, "Generally it's not so easy along this trail. Glad we made it this time without any adventures." And contentedly left us. But we, even hearing this afterward, found our hearts beating faster. . . .

[1] Small bamboo.

(June 8)
37

Eighth, climbed Gassan. *Yushime*[1] hanging down from our necks, heads covered by *hokan*,[2] led by *goriki*[3] up into mountain air, clouds, mist, walking ice and snow, going some eight *li*[4] up until it seemed near the gateway to the clouds, sun and moon passing over, each breath a last one, numb, reached peak, sun down, moon out. Spread bamboo grass, used *shino*[5] as pillows, lay down, waited for daybreak. Sun up, clouds gone, headed down toward Yudono. . . . Perched on a rock resting awhile, saw half-opened buds of three-foot cherry trees. Buried under piled-up reluctant snow, slow blossoms don't forget spring, remarkable stubbornness. . . .

44

Visited Tada Shrine here. Sanemori's[6] helmet and part of its *nishiki*[7] there. In days of old, presented to him, as a member of the Genji, by his commander Yoshitomo, it is said. Clearly not designed for a common soldier. From eye-cover to ear-flap engraved with chrysanthemums interlaced by ivy scrollwork, a dragon headpiece with hoe-shaped frontlets attached. After Sanemori's death in battle, Kiso Yoshinaka with message of prayer donated it to the shrine, Higuchi Jiro his emissary: can see them there even now as the annals of the shrine describe.

[1] Paper garland often worn by mountain priests.
[2] Cotton headgear with pointed ends.
[3] Literally "strong power": mountain guide.
[4] One *li* = approximately one-third mile.
[5] Small bamboo.
[6] The oldest warrior killed fighting for the Taira clan against the Genji: he had dyed his hair black so as not to be spared. Originally, as a young man, he had fought for the Genji. His story appears in the *Tale of the Heike* and was made the subject of a Noh play. The word "cruel" in the haiku is drawn from the Noh.
[7] Imperial brocade.

cruel!
under the helmet
cricket

Introduction and translation by Cid Corman

BASHO, KYORAI, AND BONCHO: THE RENGA, OR POETIC SEQUENCE

The introduction to this chapter contains some discussion of sequences, with suggestions as to how the Western reader might approach them. In "Summer Moon," below, Bonsho's second poem is said to be linked to Kyorai's first poem by *hibiki,* "urgency echoing urgency"; Basho's fifth poem to Boncho's fifth poem by rank, the degree of dignity being determined by servants in Boncho's three lines. Kyorai's tenth poem is said to be linked to Basho's tenth poem by *omokage:* Basho's lines make Kyorai think of the poet-priest and hermit Saigyo, and then Kyorai writes of another character suggested by the image of Saigyo. Basho's twelfth poem is linked to Boncho's twelfth poem by *utsuri*: "illusion reflects illusion."[1]

Summer Moon

In the town
smells of things
under a summer moon.

Boncho

"It's hot, it's hot":
At every gate the same sigh.

Basho

[1] See Maeda Cana, *Monkey's Raincoat* (New York: Mushinsha/Grossman, 1973), pp. xvi–xxi. The book is an excellent study of *renku* and gives invaluable material on specific works.

Only the second
batch of weeds . . .
and ears on the rice.

Kyorai

Shake the ashes
from the dried sardine.

Boncho

Around here
silver coins are oddities.
Damned inconvenient.

Basho

Fantastic,
swagger sword.

Kyorai

Walking through
the wet thicket—
frightened of a frog.

Boncho

Picking butterburr sprouts . . .
the light goes out.

Basho

The Buddha mind—
with the first flowers
wakes up.

Kyorai

Nanao in Noto—[1]
a grim winter.

Boncho

Old age
sucking on
fish bones.

Basho

[1] Nanao in Noto: a place in Ishikawa Prefecture (central Honshu). Religious hermits liked it because it was cold and desolate.

He lets the lover in
at the small gate.[1]

Kyorai

A leaned-on screen
always falls.
Servants!

Boncho

Bamboo grating on the bathroom floor—
not too cheerful.

Basho

Fennel seeds
carried off
by the night wind.

Kyorai

It's so chilly!
And the priests sets out for the temple.

Boncho

The monkey master
leads his monkey through the world . . .
autumn moon.

Basho

He pays out
the one *to* tithes.[2]

Kyorai

[1] He lets the lover in: an allusion to *The Tale of Genji,* Part I, Chapter VI: "The gate through which his carriage had to pass . . . was . . . locked. When at last the man who kept the key had been discovered, he turned out to be immensely old and feeble. With him was a big awkward girl who seemed to be his daughter or granddaughter. . . . She seemed to be suffering very much from the cold, for she was hugging a little brazier of some kind with a stick or two of charcoal burning none too brightly in it. The old man had not the strength to push back the door, and the girl was dragging at it as well. Taking pity on them, one of Genji's servants went to their assistance. . . . Genji remembered the poem in which Po Chü-i describes the sufferings of villagers in wintry weather and he murmured the lines: 'The little children run naked in the cold; the aged shiver for lack of winter clothes'" (Waley's translation). To be effective here, Kyorai's cryptic reference would have to stimulate in the reader's memory a recollection of a good part of this scene.

[2] One *to:* roughly ten kilograms.

Six pieces
of green wood
laid across the puddle.

Boncho

Dreaming, he spoils his tabi[1]
in the black mud.

Basho

Not as fast
as the horse:
the sword-bearer.

Kyorai

The apprentice
spills the water he carries.

Boncho

Shoji doors,[2]
a straw-mat fence:
the large house is for sale.

Basho

Peppers in the garden
will be green, then red.

Kyorai

Quietly with no fuss
making sandals
in the moonlight.

Boncho

Early morning in the fall:
shaking out fleas in private.

Basho

The mousetrap
overturned
and empty.

Kyorai

[1] Tabi: Japanese-style socks, split between the great and second toe so that the wearer can put on Japanese footwear (*geta* or *zori*).
[2] Shoji: Japanese-style sliding "doors," or walls (they are light and are made of translucent paper).

Clothes chest
so bent the lid won't fit.

Boncho

Without one backward look
he leaves one hermitage
for the next.[1]

Basho

Glad to be alive!
My poems have been anthologized.

Kyorai

Love.
So many different ways
to have been in love.

Boncho

At the end of life—
all Komachis.[2]

Basho

"Why?"
She sips gruel
and can't stop the tears.

Kyorai

This huge wooden floor—
when he's away from home.

Boncho

He lets the lice
crawl on his hand
shaded by cherry flowers.

Basho

[1] This poem probably refers to some unknown person living by the Buddhist doctrine *issho fuzai*—"Stay not in one place."

[2] Komachi: reference to Ono no Komachi (mid-tenth century), poetess and great beauty. In her youth she is said to have been cruel to suitors, and to have had an obscure and miserable old age.

Immobile haze
moon, spring, sleep.

Kyorai

Lenore Mayhew

LATER HAIKU

Taniguchi Buson
(1715–1783)

Spring rains:
a child's rag ball
soaks on a roof.

Cynthia Hogue

I go
You stay:
Two autumns.

Lenore Mayhew

Teiji
(mid-eighteenth century)

A flowering weed—
Hearing its name
I looked again.

Lenore Mayhew

Kobayashi Issa
(1762–1826)

A much-loved haiku poet, Issa spent his life in extreme poverty, a fact about which he is often—though not always—cheerful in his poems. Robert Bly calls Issa "the greatest frog poet, the greatest fly poet, and maybe the greatest child poet in the world."

Now listen, you watermelons—
if any thieves come—
turn into frogs!

Robert Bly

The Unlocked Gate

A brushwood gate:
Where the lock should be—
This snail.

John Levy

Masaoka Shiki
(1867–1902)

Shiki was probably the major modern haiku poet. He also wrote *tanka.*

Summer Night

Lightning:
A glimpse of water
Between the trees.

John Levy

KO-UTA: "SHORT SONGS," OR "GEISHA SONGS"
(nineteenth to twentieth centuries)

A folk form, the *ko-uta* came into being entirely in the popular quarters, outside the aristocratic and scholarly milieu of traditional Japanese poetry. Much-loved and often written by geisha, *ko-uta* are now being taught in Tokyo by former geisha.

Trouble? No more.
I hide in my happiness
As the firefly
When it hides,
Hides
In a shaft of moonlight.

William McNaughton

Yosano Akiko
(1878–1942)

She fell in love with and married her poetry teacher, Yosano Hiroshi, and came to write better than he. Many consider Akiko to be one of Japan's very best twentieth-century poets.

The orange poppy
In the evening
Shuts away her blossoming
Is again young.
It is evening
And I would be
The orange poppy.

Lenore Mayhew

Five piles standing in the river,
Five crows sitting on the piles—
It is maddening!

Glenn Hughes and Yozan T. Iwasaki

The Day

The day for moving mountains is coming.
You don't think so?
It is coming: for a while
the mountain sleeps,
but in other times
mountains all moved in fire. If you do not believe that,
oh man, this at least believe:
all sleeping women
will awake now and move.

William McNaughton

The Grass

However the wind
blows over the grass,
grass leans aside.

But we are not so,
for as the heart
twists and turns,
the self leans.

Not knowing
what's good, what's bad
we alone
turn and twist.

William McNaughton

Yanagiwara Akiko
(early twentieth century)

She married into a noble family and scandalized conservative Japanese society by leaving her husband. An early "liberated woman," her pseudonym was "White Lotus."

Two Poems

If a woman be loved, hated, and envied
Her life is worth the living.

When the rain falls,
You, toad,
Go dragging yourself slowly about.
You are one of the riddles of the universe.

Glenn Hughes and Yozan T. Iwasaki

A Modern Senryu[1]

European food—
Every blasted plate
Is round.[2]

Geoffrey Bownas and Anthony Thwaite

[1] Though like haiku in form, senryu use colloquial language more freely; dispense with the season word of haiku; and tend to be satirical, dealing in shortcoming and failure. The author of this modern senryu is unknown.

[2] As visitors to Japan may know, the layout of a meal on the table can be an aesthetic matter for the Japanese. It includes the relation of a dish (shape and size) to the food served on it.

Hagiwara Sakutaro
(1886–1942)

Sakutaro was important as the first Japanese poet to unite Western ideas with the Japanese cultural tradition, developing a modern quasi-Western style resembling Baudelaire and Rimbaud.

At the Subway

I came alone to the subway
I wander along the blue platform
I cannot stand waiting for you—
Even in dreams, you do not come.
The phantom taillights
Disappearing down the dark tunnel
wall
A melting reflection
Down the wall a fading reflection
"The phantom taillights" "phantom love"
Secret messages
Beginning . . . words . . . leaves

Suzanne S. Olton

Kitahara Hakushu
(1885–1942)

Spring Birds

The singing of spring birds
Is woven into the folds
Of ancient robes.
They sing
Into the dark
Blue and silver
Of chrysanthemums.

The singing of spring birds
Singing a summer of *utazawa*[1]
In the gold and green dusk
Of this river.

The singing
Singing of spring birds.

Richard Kent

Sato Haruo
(1892–1964)

Autumn Persimmon Leaves

In the frost
of a night,
autumn leaves

are memories, spreading

dust on the
ground, and in
the tree, they

leave invisible fruit

and the autumn
sky
seems to be steel.

William McNaughton

[1] A kind of Japanese popular ballad.

Murano Shiro
(b. 1901)

Bird-Nest

out of eyes', hands',
memories' reach always,

always unseen
in shadow, depth, and thicket

out of which the sounds,
sharp, affectionate

of nurturing with love,
out of quiet spots . . .

William McNaughton

Zoo

From the thick trees
the sounds of many beasts crying for food,
and sound of birds—

to this sunlit place
that smells of animals gathered in,
men who are tired of Man
bring their children, high-spirited and gay.

William McNaughton

Horiguchi Daigaku
(b. 1892)

Poems

Poems are the sex of words,
That's why words hide their poems.

William McNaughton

Miyazawa Kenji
(1896–1933)

The Politicians

Running around here and there
stirring up trouble and bothering people
a bunch of lushes—
fern leaves and cloud:
the world was so chilly and dark—

Before long that sort
will up and rot all by themselves
and be washed away by the rain
and afterward, only green fern.

And when humanity is laid out like coal
somewhere some earnest geologist
will note them in his notebook.

Gary Snyder

Nishiwaki Junzaburo
(b. 1896)

Ann Veronica

Before eloping
to the Alps with the man—
he was a professor of biology—
she was back in her hometown for a week
to savor the separation.
In the garden that hadn't changed
she with her secret pouted for love.
She sucked on a tiger lily.
"By the wall when a little girl
despite the anger of
God
wasps
and Dad
I stole the plums and ate them."
I met her in the village.
At a village inn, over gooseberry, brandy, and crabs,
she talked in the lamplight like a ruby
brushing back her hair with slim fingers
"The body and the flowers are the same to me."

Hiroaki Sato

Chapter 8
JAPANESE RELIGIOUS AND PHILOSOPHICAL WRITINGS

The Meiji emperor Mutsuhito (1852–1912) once wrote a poem which, on the surface, was about his garden in the imperial palace. "Look," he said, "at the great variety of flowers, native and exotic, that flourish here!" The emperor, in fact, was writing about the energetic (one might say passionate) eclecticism of Japanese culture. He knew his culture well.

The native vision is Shintoism, a complex, subtle, and completely indigenous belief—animism, if you wish—which includes the belief that the Japanese emperor is descended from the Sun God. When you see, for the first time, a little shrine at the entrance to a side street, and in the shrine a pair of stones wearing bibs, the stones themselves looking vaguely like two-foot-high dolls, and fresh flowers in front of the stones; when you encounter a rope girdle on an enormous old tree, with hundreds of little prayer papers tied to the rope—you have begun to study Shinto the only way (in my opinion) you can study it: by breathing in a Japanese ethos.

Confucianism; Taoism; Buddhism (in a multitude of forms); neo-Confucianism; Christianity (Catholic and Protestant); the strange new religions—all these, as the Meiji emperor's poem suggests, have taken life and flourished in Japan. The emperor's poem states the case. The best I can do in this chapter is to try to select works that present the Japanese mind in something like its true tone, complexity, and eclecticism. For this purpose I have chosen from two works which the Japanese have read and loved through centuries, finding in them a fair image of themselves. They are Kenko's *Tsurezure-gusa,* or *Essays in Idleness*; and Chomei's *Hojoki,* or *My Ten-by-Ten Hut.* And I have chosen from certain writings on "the philosophy of Tea." Perhaps nowhere does one see so clearly, as in the theory and practice of Teaism, the Japanese state of mind, the quintessentially and exquisitely Japanese vision of things. Much influenced by Zen, Tea also brings in—and holds in balance—elements of Taoism, Shingon Buddhism, and Shinto.[1]

Kamo no Chomei
(1154–1216)

HOJOKI: MY TEN-BY-TEN HUT

The river's waters are always changing. The foam on the pond appears, disappears. So is it in this world with men and their houses.

In Kyoto, beam lies beside beam, roof rises beyond roof. You would think the estates and ordinary houses were built to last forever. How many of them have been there for any long time? This year a house burns down; next year it's built again. An estate falls apart, a hut rises on the land.

The men that live in them are like this, too. Many people live there still. You used to know twenty or thirty. Now? You know maybe two or three. In the morning death, birth in the evening. Man's life is like foam on a pond. . . .

Since I first started watching things, I have lived for forty years. I have seen many unthinkable things take place. On May 28, 1177, during a bad storm, fire broke out around 7 P.M. in Kyoto's southeast quarter. It burned all the way to the Gate of the Red Sparrow in the northwest. . . .

In front of the wind the flames spread like a fan. Smoke smothered houses farther off; nearer places were caught in loops of flame. The air filled with ash; you could see fire re-

[1] At least two other blocks of material in this anthology bear directly on Japanese religion and philosophy: the Zen (Ch'an) writings in Chapter 4, and the Buddhist writings—especially the excerpt from *The Lotus Sutra*—in Chapter 17.

flected in the sky. The neighborhood was lit red, and wind-blown flames leaped over the nearby streets.

What does a man's mind think of in things like this?

Some collapsed from smoke. Some were burned in the flames and died at once. There were those who ran back to save their belongings and did not come out again. The property damage was impossible to estimate. . . .

The tradition is, emperors used to rule with feeling for the common people—lived in a simple thatched palace without big porches. And when they saw the smoke from people's cooking fires thin out, the emperors remitted taxes. If you want to understand what's going on today, compare it with the past.

Then there was a great food shortage, in 1181 I think it was . . . too long ago to be sure of the date. The famine lasted for two years. All spring, all summer, there was no rain; and in fall and winter, bad winds and floods. . . . Many common people left the land and crossed the frontiers; others went up into the hills. Prayers were offered; religious ceremonies were observed. It didn't help. . . .

The following year plague was added to famine. . . . the dead were so thick you couldn't drive a horse and car along the river. . . . The priest Okurakyo Ryugyo, of the Jison Church of the Ninwa Temple, and other holy men went among the dead, writing *A, Amida,*[1] on their foreheads. Ryugyo counted the dead in the inner city, between First and Ninth Avenues and between Kyogoku and the Gate of the Red Sparrow. In all he counted forty-three thousand two hundred. . . .

In 1185 there was a bad earthquake—one like we don't often have. Mountains fell, rivers were reversed. . . . I saw a boy, six or seven years old, playing in a hut he had built against a wall. The wall fell on him. His eyes hung from their sockets. I saw the parents pick him up. The father was a samurai, and even so he cried.

The worst shocks did not last long, but for many days there were twenty or thirty aftershocks a day, big enough to be upsetting under ordinary circumstances. Then the

[1] Japanese name of the Buddha Amitabha, who in Mahayana Buddhism became the great savior as God of the Western Paradise.

shocks diminished to four or five a day . . . then to two or three . . . then to one a day, and sometimes there were quiet days. These disturbances lasted for three months. . . . For a long time people talked about the world's miseries and about mankind's meanness and frivolity. Now nobody mentions the great earthquake of 1185.

Our life in the world is empty and unimportant. We are unimportant and empty in it, and so are our houses. A weak man with a powerful friend may have moments of happiness; they do not last. He is afraid to weep, afraid to show his emotions. . . . A poor man living next door to a rich man is ashamed of the way he looks. The temptation is there, to flatter and play up. . . . He envies his neighbor, and knows what his neighbor thinks of him.

If a man lives downtown, he is in danger from fire. If he lives in the suburbs, he loses his time in travel, and he must be afraid of thieves. . . .

If you work for the other man, you are his slave. If other men work for you, your emotions enslave you. To go with the world is a pain; not to go with it is "insanity." . . .

When I reached sixty—a year that is now drying up like dew—I made another place, like a traveler's lean-to, an old silkworm's last cocoon. This place is smaller than before . . . my age increases, my house diminishes. But this is no ordinary hut . . . ten by ten, ceiling less than seven feet. I didn't set it firm in the ground. What if I want to move? I built a little foundation, set up a framework, and thatched it over. I can take it down easily if I want, pay somebody to push two wheelbarrow loads to my next address. . . .

I play my lute. I listen to the wind in the pines, it sounds like the song "Autumn Wind." The running stream sounds like the song "Flowing Fountains." I don't sing very well, or play . . . so what? Who's going to hear it? I play to feed my heart up here alone. . . .

When the night is calm, I sit at the window and watch the moon. I think of ancient men of unusual genius or listen to the monkeys calling in the brush nearby, and I weep. In the trees there are fireflies, and far off I can see . . . is it the fisher's fires at Maki Island?

Daybreak . . . a light rain. I think of a storm and of the woods.

A copper pheasant calls, "Horohoro!" Is it my father calling? My mother?

Below the peak the deer run. They are not afraid of me anymore. How far away the world is now.

When the night is cold, I stir up the fire . . . comfort for an old man waking up from his nap. This wild hill is not a spooky place, and yet . . . owls make their melancholy sounds, and like the mountainous land—well, a mountainscape is various. Learned and thoughtful men have written of this before . . .

I came here for a few days . . . five years ago. The hut has weathered. The eaves are full of leaves; the ground around is green with moss. From time to time I hear what's been going on in Kyoto. Important people have died. Unimportant people have died, thousands of them. . . .

I have two servants: my hands work for me, my feet carry me around. I don't have to keep an eye on them. . . . I know when they are tired, so I let them rest. I do not overwork them. If they "don't feel like it," I leave them alone. They work hard, generally, and seem to be in good shape. Too much idleness is bad. . . .

Why should I make another man work? What right does any man have to another man's energies?

I choose the food, I select the clothes. My clothes are wisteria cloth and hempen stuff. I eat wild plants and nuts I find on the slope. . . .

I am not preaching a message for rich people. I am just comparing my old life with the new one. . . .

What should I regret? Why should I be anxious?

My body seems like a cloud in the sky; I look at it without confidence and without reproach. My life has a center of joy in the pillow I sleep on at night. My days have a focus of hope in the beauties of nature I see all the time. . . .

When I go into Kyoto, sometimes I feel a little ashamed of the way I look—like a beggar. Then when I come back to the hut, I feel sorry for the men who squirm and struggle in the world of dust. . . .

Does the fish get tired of his water? We are not fish, so we can't say. Isn't the bird always trying to get back to his old woods? We are not birds, so we can't say. A recluse's life is like that. . . .

My life is like a setting moon, hanging just above a hill. Pretty soon I will be in the Three Realms of Darkness. What have I done in the past that I will have to answer for? Buddha says, "Do not be attached to anything in the world." I like my hut. . . .

William McNaughton

Kenko

(Urabe no Kaneyoshi—1283–1350)

ESSAYS IN IDLENESS

If man were never to fade away like the dews of Adashino, never to vanish like the smoke over Toribeyama, but lingered on forever in the world, how things would lose their power to move us! . . . If that is not enough for you, you might live a thousand years and still feel it was but a single night's dream.

Beautiful hair, of all things in a woman, is most likely to catch a man's eye. Her character and temperament may be guessed from the first words she utters, even if she is hidden behind a screen. When a woman somehow—perhaps unintentionally—has captured a man's heart, she is generally able to sleep peacefully. She will not hesitate to subject herself to hardships, and will even endure cheerfully what she would normally find intolerable, all because love means so much to her.

The pleasantest of all diversions is to sit alone under the lamp, a book spread out before you, and to make friends with people of a distant past you have never known. The books I would choose are the moving volumes of *Wen Hsuan,* the collected works of Po Chü-i, the sayings of Lao-tzu, and the chapters of Chuang-tzu.

Kin'yo, an officer of the second rank, had a brother called the High Priest Ryogaku, an extremely bad-tempered man. Next to his monastery grew a large nettle tree, which occasioned the nickname people gave him, the Nettle Tree High Priest. "That name is outrageous," said the high priest, and cut down the tree. The stump still being left, people referred to him now as the Stump High Priest. More furious than ever, Ryogaku had the stump dug up and thrown away, but this left a big ditch. People now called him the Ditch High Priest.

There are innumerable instances of things which attach themselves to something else, then waste and destroy it. The body has lice; a house has mice; a country has robbers; inferior men have riches; superior men have benevolence and righteousness; priests have the Buddhist law.

A man who is trying to learn some art is likely to say, "I won't rush things and tell people I am practicing while I am still a beginner. I'll study the art myself, and only when I have mastered the art will I perform before people. How impressed they'll be then!"

People who speak in this fashion will never learn any art. The man who, even while still a novice, mixes with the experts, not ashamed of their harsh comments or ridicule, and who devotedly persists at his practice, unruffled by criticism, will neither become stultified in his art nor careless with it. Though he may lack natural gifts, he will with the passage of the years outstrip the man who coasts on his endowments, and in the end will attain the highest degree of skill, acquire authority in his art and the recognition of the public, and win an unequaled reputation.

The performers who now rank as the most skilled in the whole country were at the beginning considered incompetent, and, indeed, had shocking faults. However, by faithfully maintaining the principles of their art and holding them in honor, rather than indulging in their own fancies, they have become paragons of the age and teachers for all. This surely holds true for every art.

Donald Keene

CHA NO YU: "THE WAY OF TEA"

IT'S SILLY TO WRITE YOUR NAME WITH
A CHARACTER NOBODY'S EVER SEEN BEFORE.

IF YOU WOULD FOLLOW BUDDHA'S WAY,
IT IS ONLY THIS: LIVE A LIFE OF LEISURE
AND DON'T TAKE THINGS SERIOUSLY. THESE
ARE THE MAIN THINGS.

—Kenko[1]

Sen no Rikyu
(1521–1591)

The First Tea-Master of his own age, and founder of the influential Ura Senge School of Tea, Sen no Rikyu virtually fixed the form and philosophy of Tea Ceremony for all time. Once a friend of Hideyoshi Toyotomi (1536–1598), the *de facto* ruler of Japan, Rikyu finally fell out with him, either because he would not "sell" his widowed daughter to Hideyoshi, or because his power was a threat to Hideyoshi, who forced him to commit suicide.

Practice harmony, practice respect, practice purity, and practice calm, *Wa Kei Sei Jaku*—these are the principles of tea.[2]

A man came and asked Rikyu, "What are the mysteries of tea?"

[1] "Kenko": see pp. 253–254.

[2] Purity (*Sei*) is also required by Shinto. You perform an ablution before you go into a Shinto shrine, just as you wash your hands before entering a teahouse. The simplicity and style of tea utensils is like the simplicity and style of utensils used for offerings to the *Kami* (spirits, gods).

Respect (*Kei*) is like the respect the Zen monk is taught to have for his food.

"You put the charcoal," said Rikyu, "so that the water will boil properly. You make the tea to bring out its best taste. Arrange the flowers to look as though they're growing. In summer try to create a feeling of 'cool,' and in winter a feeling of 'warm.' These are the mysteries of tea."

"I already know all that," said the man.

"Well," said Rikyu, "if there is anyone who already knows it, I will be happy to be his student."

"The Hundred Rules of Rikyu"

If anyone wishes to enter the Way of Tea, he must be his own teacher.

Ashamed to show ignorance, he will never be any good.

To become expert: love and then perseverance; dexterity and then perseverance; perseverance and then perseverance.

If you give somebody flowers, they shouldn't be completely open, for that would be impolite.

If you give a tea for people who have been to a flower viewing, don't hang in the *tokonoma*[1] any picture of birds or flowers, and don't put any real flowers there, either.

Kettles have all sorts of names and shapes, but after all they are all kettles.

When Rikyu went to see Somu, Somu said, "I've got some fine water." And so he took the kettle off and went out. Rikyu put on some charcoal, and then Somu came back with the dripping kettle . . . Sen no Rikyu, author of "The Hundred Rules of Tea."

Rules are rules, yes, but only a fool will glue down the capo on a guitar.

The evening before Hideyoshi came, it began to snow. Rikyu set out covers on all the steppingstones and took them off in the morning.

One day Hideyoshi said to Rikyu, "Seen any good teakettles lately?"

[1] *Tokonoma:* the alcove in a Japanese room where calligraphy or a painting, and perhaps arranged flowers, are set as the primary decoration of the room that day.

"The other day," replied Rikyu, "out in Awataguchi, I saw a beggar fixing his meal. He was boiling water in a beautiful kettle, a really rare and splendid thing."

"Go get it from him," said Hideyoshi. "Pay him whatever he wants—fief, money, or anything."

So Rikyu went to Awataguchi and told the beggar: "His Excellency will give you whatever you want for that kettle—fief, money, or anything . . ."

"I'm poor," cut in the beggar, "and I don't own anything at all. If I give away my kettle, how will I boil water for tea? I have a good kettle, so what happens? People come and pester me about it."

And the beggar took the kettle and threw it against a stone so that it broke. Then he ran away.

Rikyu took the broken kettle back to Hideyoshi, who had it repaired.

Hideyoshi said, "He must be from some province where an enemy of mine is lord. I may have killed his lord. This kettle belonged to a loyal man."[1]

But the beggar was, in fact, a retired Imperial bodyguard named Tanaka. He lived in a hut. He made tea or boiled rice and talked to men of the place, grooms and palanquin bearers, as they passed by, and sometimes they took tea with him.

William McNaughton

Matsudaira Naritada
(nineteenth century)

"Tea Maxim"

Natural elegance is the real elegance.

William McNaughton

[1] We see Hideyoshi here thinking in terms of Bushido, the warrior's way, rather than in terms of Tea or of the Zen Buddhism which so influenced Tea.

PART THREE: KOREA

Chapter 9

KOREAN TALES

Around the middle of the first century B.C., there were three separate kingdoms in Korea: Koguryo (37 B.C.–A.D. 668) in the Yalu River valley; Paekche (18 B.C.–A.D. 660) south of the Han; and Silla (57 B.C.–A.D. 668) in the southeast corner of the peninsula.[1]

In the sixth century A.D. the scholar Solch'ong worked out a writing system for Korea called "Idu," based on Chinese characters. In the same century, Korea introduced writing, Buddhist imagery and astronomy, geography, medical arts, agricultural techniques, metallurgy, and music to the Japanese. Over the next few hundred years, Korean scholars, priests, artists, and artisans traveled to Japan, educating the Japanese in technique and doctrine. At the same time young Korean aristocrats were traveling to China to study Chinese civilization. As a consequence, Korea became a bridge across which Chinese culture passed to Japan.

When Emperor Yang, of the Sui (Chinese) dynasty, sent a 200,000-man army into Korea, General Uljimunduk (late sixth to seventh century) met the invaders in a valley near P'yongyang. Uljimunduk composed a poem in classical Chinese warning the invaders to surrender or be annihilated.

Heaven's wisdom,
The arts of war, and geography
Favor us. Think
Of your weakness now.

[1] This brief introductory sketch on Korean cultural history is included because the editor believes it will help the reader understand Korean tales and poetry—and especially to understand the great influence of Chinese culture on Korea. A similar sketch of cultural history appears in Chapter 11 for Vietnam.

We are proud. We will win.
I ask you to weigh these words.

Instead of surrendering, the Chinese army tried to retreat. Only 2700 of them ever reached China again.

In 918 the Koryo dynasty (918–1392) was founded, and by 935 its first ruler, Wang Kon, had unified Korea and had brought it all under his sway. Devoutly Buddhist, Wang Kon built many temples. Soon princes and nobles in great numbers had become priests, and the country was run by a hierarchy (in its original sense of government by priests).

In 958 King Kwanghong set up an examination system for the government service, modeled on the Chinese system of civil service. This led to a renaissance in Korea of the study of Chinese culture. Candidates were expected to be knowledgeable in Chinese literature and philosophy, and were required to write poetry in Chinese. Since one of the four parts of the examination was a test in the Chinese language, the "Idu" writing system fell out of favor.

Early in the eleventh century, during the Tartar invasion of Korea, King Hyonjong began to publish the *Taejang-gyong,* or *Stories of the Great Deeds* (of Buddha), and by the end of the century six thousand volumes of the work were in print. In 1236, during the Mongol invasion of Korea, all six thousand volumes were burned. But republication was begun almost immediately, and the entire set is still extant.

In 1145, King Injong set a group of scholars to work to compose the first history of Korea. The group, under the direction of Kim Pu-sik (1075–1151), took as a model the great histories of China. Its work, *History of the Three Kingdoms,* which was compiled in Chinese, included chronologies, monographs, and biographies on Koryo (Koguryo), Paekche, and Silla.

Subsequently, the monk Ilyon (1206–1289) edited a history called *Materials for the Study of the History of the Three Kingdoms,* which focused entirely on ordinary people—their lives, arts, legends—and on the oral tradition, including poetry. Ilyon's work was published shortly after the introduction of the printing press to Korea in 1234—about 220 years before Gutenberg (and about 200 years later than the first movable-type printing in China).

From 1096 on, the Korean aristocracy had fostered ceramic art, and Korean porcelain soon became famous throughout Asia, and eventually in the West as well. The art probably reached its finest development in the thirteenth century.

Japan invaded Korea in 1380, but her troops were defeated by the Korean army under general Yi Song-gye, who thereupon became a national hero. In 1392, he established the Yi dynasty, of which he was first ruler. Yi Song-gye undertook far-reaching reforms. He seized the great estates belonging to the Buddhist hierarchy and the nobility, disbanded their armies, and carried out a revolutionary program of agrarian reform.

Early in the fifteenth century, King Sejong (1418–1450) brought about a reform in the writing system, forming a national committee of scholars which, after four years of research, published a new national alphabet with twenty-eight letters, considerably more simple than the Chinese and Japanese writing systems.

In 1469 the Yi dynasty promulgated a set of laws and constitutional principles, *Rules of Good Government*. Both Confucian and Taoist in inspiration, these *Rules* were, in effect, the Constitution of Korea during the five centuries of Yi rule.

The Yi dynasty disintegrated early in the twentieth century, and in 1910, Korea was annexed by Japan. In 1945, at the close of the Second World War, the country was partitioned into North and South Korea by foreign powers and politicians, and the Koreans claim still to be waiting for "freedom and independence."[1]

If we restrict our definition of literature to what gets written down, the earliest Korean literature is probably the *Taejanggyong*, or *Stories of the Great Deeds*. Since the *Taejanggyong* is also religious literature, its classification as prose fiction is somewhat ambiguous. But then, Homer and Ovid, too, were once religious literature.

The next story literature after the *Taejanggyong* may be found in Ilyon's *Materials for the Study of the History of the Three Kingdoms*. Ilyon's interest in folklore, stories, poetry, and the people's lives and arts, gives *Materials* a

[1] Peter Hyun and Hisik Mine, *Anthologie de la Poésie Coréenne* (N.p.: Librairie St.-Germain-des-Prés, 1972), p. 32.

more modern feel than its more orthodox and classical predecessor.

The following stories, whatever their original sources and form, were collected and put into the form on which the translations are based by the scholar Im Bang (1640–1722, or after). Im served as governor of Seoul and as cabinet secretary. In 1722, in a fight over the choice of an heir apparent, he was exiled to northern Korea.

In the stories, the reader familiar with Chinese literature will see further evidence of the influence and impact of Chinese culture on Asia. Alter a place name here and there, or a local detail, and the stories easily could all have been written in China. In fairness to their author, however, it should be said that Im Bang was a man of enormous and eclectic erudition, and in another story (which he did not set in Korea) he gives a version of Odysseus's escape from the Cyclops.

FOLK TALES
FROM THE KOREAN OF IM BANG AND YI RYUK

THE STORY OF CHANG TO-RYONG

Taoism has been one of the great religions of Korea. Its main thought is expressed in the phrase *su-sim yon-song,* "to correct the mind and reform the nature"; while Buddhism's is *myong-sim kyon-song,* "to enlighten the heart and see the soul."

The desire of all Taoists is "eternal life," *chang-saing pul-sa*; that of the Buddhists, to rid oneself of fleshly being. In the Taoist world of the genii, there are three great divisions; the upper genii, who live with God; the midway genii, who have to do with the world of angels and spirits; and the lower genii, who rule in sacred places on the earth, among the hills, just as we find in the story of Chang To-ryong.

In the days of King Chung-jong (1507–1526) there lived a beggar in Seoul, whose face was extremely ugly and always dirty. He was forty years of age or so, but still wore his hair down his back like an unmarried boy. He carried a bag over his shoulder, and went about the streets begging. During the day he went from one part of the city to another, visiting each section, and when night came on he would huddle up beside someone's gate and go to sleep. He was frequently seen in Chong-no (Bell Street) in company with the servants and underlings of the rich. They were great friends, he and they, joking and bantering as they met. He used to say that his name was Chang, and so they called him Chang To-ryong, To-ryong meaning an unmarried boy, son of the gentry. At that time the magician Chon U-chi, who was far-famed for his pride and arrogance, whenever he met Chang, in passing along the street, would dismount and prostrate himself most humbly. Not only did he bow, but he seemed to regard Chang with the greatest of fear, so that he dared not look him in the face. Chang, sometimes without even inclining his head, would say, "Well, how goes it with you, eh?" Chon, with his hands in his sleeves, most respectfully would reply, "Very well, sir, thank you, very well." He had fear written on all his features when he faced Chang.

Sometimes, too, when Chon would bow, Chang would refuse to notice him at all, and go by without a word. Those who saw it were astonished, and asked Chon the reason. Chon said in reply, "There are only three spirit-men at present in Cho-sen, of whom the greatest is Chang To-ryong; the second is Cheung Puk-chang; and the third is Yun Se-pyong. People of the world do not know it, but I do. Such being the case, should I not bow before him and show him reverence?"

Those who heard this explanation, knowing that Chon himself was a strange being, paid no attention to it.

At that time in Seoul there was a certain literary undergraduate in office whose house joined hard on the street. This man used to see Chang frequently going about begging, and one day he called him and asked who he was, and why he begged. Chang made answer, "I was originally of a cultured family of Chulla Province, but my parents died of typhus fever, and I had no brothers or relations left to share my lot. I alone remained of all my clan, and having no home of my own I have gone about begging, and have at last reached Seoul. As I am not skilled in any handicraft, and do not know Chinese letters, what else can I do?" The undergraduate, hearing that he was a scholar, felt very sorry for him, gave him food and drink, and refreshed him.

From this time on, whenever there was any special celebration at his home, he used to call Chang in and have him share it.

On a certain day when the master was on his way to office, he saw a dead body being carried on a stretcher off toward the Water Gate. Looking at it closely from the horse on which he rode, he recognized it as the corpse of Chang To-ryong. He felt so sad that he turned back to his house and cried over it, saying, "There are lots of miserable people on earth, but who ever saw one as miserable as poor Chang? As I reckon the time over on my fingers, he has been begging in Bell Street for fifteen years, and now he passes out of the city a dead body."

Twenty years and more afterward, the master had to make a journey through South Chulla Province. As he was passing Chi-i Mountain, he lost his way and got into a maze among the hills. The day began to wane, and he could neither return nor go forward. He saw a narrow footpath, such as woodmen take, and turned into it to see if it led to any habitation. As he went along there were rocks and deep ravines. Little by little, as he advanced farther, the scene changed and seemed to become strangely transfigured. The farther he went the more wonderful it became. After he had gone some miles he discovered himself to be in another world entirely, no longer a world of earth and dust. He saw someone coming toward him dressed in ethereal green, mounted and carrying a shade, with servants accompanying. He seemed to sweep toward him with swiftness and without effort. He thought to himself, "Here is some high lord or other coming to meet me, but," he added, "how among these deeps and solitudes could a gentleman come riding so?" He led his horse aside and tried to withdraw into one of the groves by the side of the way, but before he could think to turn the man had reached him. The mysterious stranger lifted his two hands in salutation and inquired respectfully as to how he had been all this time. The master was speechless, and so astonished that he could make no reply. But the stranger smilingly said, "My house is quite near here; come with me and rest."

He turned, and leading the way, seemed to glide and not to walk, while the master followed. At last they reached the place indicated. He suddenly saw before him great palace halls filling whole squares of space. Beautiful buildings they were, richly ornamented. Before the door, attendants in official robes awaited them. They bowed to the master and led him into the hall. After passing a number of gorgeous, palacelike rooms, he arrived at a special one and ascended to the upper story, where he met a very wonderful person. He was dressed in shining garments, and the servants that waited on him were exceedingly fair. There were, too, children about, so exquisitely beautiful that it seemed none other than a celestial palace. The master, alarmed at finding himself in such a place, hurried forward and made a low obeisance, not daring to lift his eyes. But the host smiled upon him, raised his hands and asked, "Do you not know me? Look now." Lifting his eyes, he then saw that it was the same person who had come riding out to meet him, but he could not tell who he was. "I see you," said he, "but as to who you are I cannot tell."

The kingly host then said, "I am Chang To-ryong. Do you not know me?" Then as the master looked more closely at him he could see the same features. The outlines of the face were there, but all the imperfections had gone, and only beauty remained. So wonderful was it that he was quite overcome.

A great feast was prepared, and the honored guest was entertained. Such food, too, was placed before him as was never seen on earth. Angelic beings played on beautiful instruments and danced as no mortal eye ever looked upon. Their faces, too, were like pearls and precious stones.

Chang To-ryong said to his guest, "There are four famous mountains in Korea in which the genii reside. This hill is one. In days gone by, for a fault of mine, I was exiled to earth, and in the time of my exile you treated me with marked kindness, a favor that I have never forgotten. When you saw my dead body your pity went out to me; this, too, I remember. I was not dead then, it was simply that my days of exile were ended and I was returning home. I knew that you were passing this hill, and I desired to meet you and to thank you for all your kindness. Your treatment of me in another world is sufficient to bring about our meeting in this one." And so they met and feasted in joy and great delight.

When night came he was escorted to a special pavilion, where he was to sleep. The windows were made of jade and precious stones, and soft lights came streaming through them, so that there was no night. "My body was so rested and my soul so refreshed," said he, "that I felt no need of sleep."

When the day dawned a new feast was spread, and then farewells were spoken. Chang said, "This is not a place for you to stay long in; you must go. The ways differ of us genii and you men of the world. It will be difficult for us ever to meet again. Take good care of yourself and go in peace." He then called a servant to accompany him and show the way. The master made a low bow and withdrew. When he had gone but a short distance he suddenly found himself in the old world with its dusty accompaniments. The path by which he came out was not the way by which he had entered. In order to mark the entrance he planted a stake, and then the servant withdrew and disappeared.

The year following the master went again and tried to find the citadel of the genii, but there were only mountain peaks and impassable ravines, and where it was he never could discover.

As the years went by the master seemed to grow younger in spirit, and at last at the age of ninety he passed away without suffering. "When Chang was here on earth and I saw him for fifteen years," said the master, "I remember but one peculiarity about him, namely, that his face never grew older nor did his dirty clothing ever wear out. He never changed his garb, and yet it never varied in appearance in all the fifteen years. This alone would have marked him as a strange being, but our fleshly eyes did not recognize it."

THE GRATEFUL GHOST

It is often told that in the days of the Koryo Dynasty (918–1392), when an examination was to be held, a certain scholar came from a far-distant part of the country to take part. Once, on his journey, the day was drawing to a close, and he found himself among the mountains. Suddenly he heard a sneezing from among the creepers and bushes by the roadside, but could see no one. Thinking it strange, he dismounted from his horse, went into the brake and listened. He heard it again, and it seemed to come from the roots of the creeper close beside him, so he ordered his servant to dig around it and see. He dug and found a dead man's skull. It was full of earth, and the roots of the creeper had passed through the nostrils. The sneezing was caused by the annoyance felt by the spirit from having the nose so discommoded.

The candidate felt sorry, washed the skull in clean water, wrapped it in paper, and reburied it in its former place on the hillside. He also brought a table of food and offered sacrifice, and said a prayer.

That night, in a dream, a scholar came to him, an old man with white hair, who bowed, thanked him, and said, "On account of sin committed in a former life, I died out of season before I had fulfilled my days. My posterity, too, were all destroyed, my body crumpled back into the dust, my skull alone remaining, and that is what you found below the creeper. On account of the root passing through it the annoyance was great, and I could not help but sneeze. By good luck you and your kind heart, blessed of Heaven, took pity on me, buried me in a clean place, and gave me food. Your kindness is greater than the mountains, and like the blessing that first brought me into life. Though my soul is by no means perfect, yet I long for some way by which to requite your favor, and so I have exercised my powers in your behalf. Your present journey is for the purpose of trying the official examination, so I shall tell you beforehand what the form is to be, and the subject. It is to be character groups of fives, in couplets; the rhyme sound is 'pong,' and the subject 'Peaks and Spires of the Summer Clouds.' I have already composed one for you, which, if you care to use it, will undoubtedly win you the first place. It is this:

'The white sun rode high up in the heavens,
And the floating clouds formed a lofty peak;
The priest who saw them asked if there was a temple
there,

And the crane lamented the fact that no pines were
visible;
But the lightnings from the cloud were the flashings of
the woodman's ax,
And the muffled thunders were the bell calls of the holy
temple.
Will any say that the hills do not move?
On the sunset breezes they sailed away.' "

After thus stating it, he bowed and took his departure. The man, in wonder, awakened from his dream, came up to Seoul; and behold, the subject was as foretold by the spirit. He wrote what had been given him, and became first in the honors of the occasion.

James S. Gale

Chapter 10
KOREAN POETRY

If native traditions are to be followed, the first Korean poetry was in a genre called "Si-ka,"[1] which is defined as "song mixed with poetry." Early Korea also had a form of danced ballad called the *minyo.* Although the oral tradition preserved no *minyo,* the *Chinese History of the Later Han Dynasty* (A.D. 25–222) says that the early art of Korea dealt with religion, great men, and rites for the dead.

The first identifiable form of Korean poetry is the *hyangga,* or native song, which usually deals with Buddhist themes or popular legends. *Hyangga* are still extant, dating from the sixth century A.D., when the "Idu" writing system was invented. The strophes of *hyangga* are either four, eight, or ten lines long, and each line may run from four to fifteen syllables.

According to one modern authority, at least,[2] the northerners in Korea saw life and nature (and wrote about them) with a somewhat more abstract vision, Confucian in its strictness, whereas the southerners—the poets and philosophers of Silla—had a more imaginative and intimate vision of nature and a Taoist sense of the mystical arts. Some of them resigned jobs and rejected official honors to retire to the mountains and to become, in the good old Taoist tradition, sennin. The common people called them winged divinities, and described them as living on fruit and dew and enjoying eternal youth and eternal life.

I have written in the preceding chapter of the Chinese examination system, its imitation in Korea in 958, and of the renaissance of Chinese literature and philosophy in Korea that followed. One upshot of this renaissance was a new poetic form, the *changga,* or long poem. Long, divided into

[1] Hyun and Mine, *op. cit.,* p. 15.
[2] *Ibid.*

strophes, and punctuated by a refrain, the *changga* probably owe a great deal to the *minyo* tradition. They were sung by entertaining girls and by the common people; with a few exceptions, the poets of this period did not come from a privileged elite.[1]

Late in the twelfth century there appeared a new poetic form, the *sijo,* which became in time the most important in Korean poetry. It assumed a place analogous to the Japanese *tanka,* the Chinese *lü-shih,* or the sonnet in English. The *sijo* proved itself very adaptable. Though formalistic and requiring discipline and long practice, it could be—and was—written by such diverse groups as entertaining girls, military men, politicians, and scholars, and with such diverse approaches as the didactic, dramatic, heroic, and metaphysical. The word *sijo* means "melody of the times," and *sijo* have been written on subjects that run from visions of the divine or permanent world to simple love affairs.

The classic form of *sijo* has three lines, each of which is subdivided into smaller groups of syllables. The poems are not required to rhyme, though rhyme is not avoided, and head rhymes are often used.

Around the middle of the fifteenth century, a form of poem in prose, called *kasa,* appeared. Not musicalized in strophes, the *kasa* nevertheless have strong independent rhythms, marked caesuras more regular than in ordinary prose, and the fancy and the metaphorical language of poetry.

Currently, Korean poetry is what we could call "international poetry," a poetry with freer rhetoric and form, jazz rhythm, new (and sometimes, perhaps, farfetched) imagery, and so forth. It also shows many of the ideological characteristics of modern poetry. It repudiates what Santayana called the bourgeois tradition, and it believes in individual experience and individual freedom while claiming a commitment to social justice and social revolution. It owes a great deal to the French *symbolistes* of the nineteenth century, most notably Laforgue and Baudelaire. Like the modern poets of many other nations, Korean poets learned from the French *symbolistes* what modernism means.

[1] The anonymous poem, "The Bakery," pp. 275–276, is a good example of the *changga.* Very popular during the Koryo dynasty, "The Bakery" was suppressed by later anthologists as being obscene.

Modern Korean poetry was born under the most adverse of circumstances: foreign occupation. From 1910 to 1945, Korea was occupied by the Japanese, who set up a military government and a psychological police whose function it was to control and suppress subversive ideas and ideals—which meant, of course, anything tending to promote Korean national pride, independence, or nationalism. Some of the makers of modern Korean literature were martyred by the occupation and the psychological police.

Ch'o Yong
(eighth century)

Song (Hyangga)

I went downtown tonight
To the capital under the clear moon.
I came home: what did I see?
Four legs under my quilt.

Used to be two of them were mine—
But what about the other two?
Tonight, I'm sure of this,
The other two are not mine.[1]

William McNaughton

[1] According to the story, Ch'o's wife was so beautiful that one night a demon disguised himself as a human being and got into the lady's room while Ch'o was out drinking with friends. Ch'o composed this poem when he came home that night. The demon was so moved by Ch'o's calm that he disappeared and never returned.

Yi In-ro
(1152–1220)

Thoughts at the Beginning of a New Era

The candle burns: the flame is like jade.
I run a peach-wood comb through my hair,
Hairs fall to the paper floor;
My head looks all right. I tie my hair up in a
    tight new knot,
But the country, given over
To corruption and counterplots,
Is not in any shape to face its enemies.
The jade flame suffocates
In the candle's cooling wax,
And sleep drowns my hopes.

William McNaughton

Yi Kyu-bo
(1168–1241)

Cock Crow

Cock crow
and over the thatched hut on the river
                the moon turning white—
in the water
        one by one
            dark ripples slip past
black as shadows
            on the white bridge of the moon.
The east wind moves in the willows . . .
In circles of moonlight
                    the fishermen come home.
In the distance
            they look like white flowers . . .
their singing comes nearer and nearer . . .

are they fishermen . . .
or ghosts?

Lenore Mayhew

Unknown Woman
(1275)

The Bakery

I went to the bakery to buy a roll,
The baker took me by the hand.
If they tell this story in the street,
You'll be to blame, little flower.
Yes, yes, we went into the bushes
Hidden and not far,
Wi wi Doron dung sung darero diro darero diro.

I went to Sam-ang Temple to light the lamp,
The bonze took me by the hand.
If they tell this story on the street,
You'll be to blame, little nun.
Yes, yes, we went into the bushes
Hidden and not far,
Wi wi Doron dung sung darero diro darero diro.

I went to the well to draw some water,
The soldier took me by the hand.
If they tell this story in the street,
You'll be to blame, little dipper.
Yes, yes, we went into the bushes
Hidden and not far,
Wi wi Doron dung sung darero diro darero diro.

I went to the inn to get a glass of water,
The innkeeper took me by the hand.
If they tell this story on the street,
You'll be to blame, little cup.
Yes, yes, we went into the bushes

Hidden and not far,
Wi wi Doron dung sung darero diro darero diro.

William McNaughton

Yi Sung-in
(1327–1392)

Lament for My Master

Sorrow for my heart:
the sound of crickets in the rain
like his smile.

Sorrow to my eye:
the jade hill on the red tapestry
like his brocade robe.

Sorrow in my house:
the sound of flowers in the garden
like his voice—
a dream.

Lenore Mayhew

Yu Ung-bu
(fifteenth century)

Last Night the Wind

Last night the wind
soughed: it carried snow.
The pines bend down.

Why worry the flowers
That the wind is going to break?

William McNaughton

Song Sun
(1493–1583)

Sleepy Birds

Birds settle in
and a priest
crosses a one-log bridge.
In the distances
a bell is ringing
"How far away is your temple?"

Lenore Mayhew

Hwang Jin-i
(1506–1544)

Hwang Jin-i, a courtesan in the sixteenth century, was famous throughout the country for her beauty and for her talents as poetess and singer.

This Long Winter Night

I'll take this long winter night,
I'll fold it once
and roll it up
And store it under my down quilt.

I'll unfold and roll it out
the night my lover comes.

William McNaughton

Blue Stream

Blue stream between the blue cliffs,
Do not be proud of the course you cut.

When you reach the ocean
You'll see how difficult it is,
To come back. The moon falls on the naked peaks
And you, you should think a little of rest.[1]

William McNaughton

When It's All Over

As petals

As petals of flowers fall in the wind
My soul turns in the sky.
As a shadow of pallid moon
As the moon behind black clouds
My body drops into the earth
Into the shadows of a steep valley.
Dig my grave and let me sleep.
Let happy young women come to the hill
And sing in the happiness of their youth.
Let them have a place on my mound
And if they like, cry over a bad woman's life.

William McNaughton

Yu Ja-sin
(1533–1612)

The Setting Sun

The river
goes silver in the setting

[1] Hwang Jin-i wrote this poem for the famous scholar Pyok Kye-su, whose name means "blue water." Pyok was well-known for his dis-esteem of women and of their pleasures. Going to see him, Hwang was turned away at the door. So she enlisted a mutual friend (male) to arrange to meet Pyok in the mountains. When Pyok arrived, riding on a mule, the friend was not there, and Hwang Jin-i was. She recited this poem, with its play on his name. He stayed to have a cup of wine with her, to praise her verses, and . . .

sun; in the wind
I sleep, my line in my hand.

The moonlight fills up my boat.

William McNaughton

Chong Ch'ol
(1536–1593)

Drinking Song

Empty your glass! And every glass
We'll pick a flower . . .

When you die, whether they
Roll you in a mat of straw
And drag you away with a rope,
Or lay you on a gaudy funeral cart

And a thousand weeping friends walk behind,
The wild ferns
Will grow over you,

And chestnut trees, and poplars.
The sun will come up, the moon will shine,
And when the cold wind shrieks . . .

When the last friend has left your grave
And only the monkey
Cries in the woods,

Who'll ask you to have a glass then?
Then what good will it do
To be sorry
You didn't drink with me now?

William McNaughton

Im Je
(1549–1587)

Sijo

Are you asleep? Or
lying down? in this wild grass.
White bones! Why, why?
                    Where is the red of your cheeks?
Now you will never fill my cup.
My heart swells with sadness.[1]

William McNaughton

Yi Chung-kai
(1556–?)

Travel Sketch

On the riverbank
                    the inn is silent,
green willows dance above the reeds,
a cloud of flowers
                    touches the morning haze.
And when the night comes
a flag of light
                    flutters like silk
over the wall of mountains.

So tired from travel
                         even my face hurts—
but this place rests me,
my thoughts are like willow boughs
                         moving over the river,

[1] This poem was composed after a visit to the grave of Hwang Jin-i. The poem cost the poet his job in the Department of Education.

the ripples in the water
are the rhythms of my dreams.

Lenore Mayhew

Hong Nang
(1568–?)

A famous entertaining girl, Hong Nang wrote the poem below for her friend, Ch'oe Kyong-ch'ang, known as one of the "Three Great Poets" of the age. He is supposed to have wept when he received it.

I send you these willow branches
cut in the mountain.
Plant them
In your garden

And if they bloom: think of me.

William McNaughton

Yun Son-do
(1587–1671)

Often called Korea's greatest poet, Yun Son-do excelled in the *sijo* form. His "Fisherman's Calendar" (of which two stanzas are given below) is said to be "the highest peak of classical *sijo* composition." The onomatopoetic line ("*chigukch'ong,*" etc.) gives the rhythm of the act of rowing, and the poem is very effective when read aloud.

The Fisherman's Calendar

The day is warming:
the fish rise in the water.
Hoist the anchor! Hoist the anchor!
Two or three seagulls flying,
rising and swooping, hover around.
Chigukch'ong, chigukch'ong, oshwa!
The rods are all ready;
has the wine flask been put in?

Jade and silver scales—
how many fish have I caught?
Row away, row away!
Make a fire of reed stems,
choose some fish, then broil them.
Chigukch'ong, chigukch'ong, oshwa!
Turn that earthenware jar upside down
and fill the gourd with wine.

Richard Rutt

Han Yong-un
(1879–1940)

Poem

Is your voice
silence?
When you do not sing
I hear your voice quite clear—
Your voice is silence.

Is your face
shadows?
I close my eyes,
I see your face quite clear—
Your face is shadows.

Is your shadow
light?
On the dark glass
Shines your shadow.
Your shadow is light.

William McNaughton

Yi Sang-hwa
(1900–1943)

Does Spring Come to Stolen Fields?

The land is no longer our own.
Does spring come just the same
to the stolen fields?
On the narrow path between the rice fields
where blue sky and green fields meet and touch,
winds whisper to me, urging me forward.
A lark trills in the clouds
like a young girl singing behind the hedge.
O ripening barley fields, your long hair is heavy after the night's rain.
Light-headed, I walk
lightly, shrugging my shoulders, almost
dancing to music the fields are humming—
the field where violets grow, the field
where once I watched a girl planting rice, her hair
blue-black and shining—
I want
a scythe in my hands, I want
to stamp on this soil, soft as a plump breast,
I want to be working the earth and steaming with sweat.

What am I looking for? Soul,
my blind soul, endlessly darting
like children at play on the river,
answer me: where am I going?
Filled with the odor of grass, compounded
of green laughter and green sorrow,

I walk all day, lamely, as if possessed
by the spring devil:
for these are stolen fields, and our spring is stolen.

Peter H. Lee

Yi Kwang-su
(1892–?)

A Wind Flower

Near the hut
in the barley field—
a grave
        and a windflower
with a bent neck.

The man in the grave
once lived in the barley field
spring after spring
loved the new green and yellow
                                of barley thrust,

And this spring
                the barley field is green again,
and the windflower opens.
The man's children
carry mud-spattered
vegetable knives—
spring in country villages
over and over,
life
        going on and on . . .

Lenore Mayhew

Ju Yo-han

(b. 1900)

Poem

I still remember this:
A boat adrift in the morning fog
Running up its sail.

A boat adrift, noiseless
On the waves a morning without wind.

The boat's vanished, time has gone by,
And what I dreamed of in my youth,

Like the boat adrift in morning fog
Running up its sail,
Is gone for good.

William McNaughton

Kim P'albong

(b. 1903)

Lamentation of the White Hands

Easy at chairs in a café, boasting
of the white arms, here are the young
Russians of sixty years past,
shouting "V NAROD!"[1]

Café-chair revolutionists,
your hands are too white.

[1] V NAROD (Russian): Into the People! There was a V NAROD Movement in late-nineteenth-century Russia made up of intellectuals trying, for Romantic Marxist reasons, to amalgamate themselves into the common people. The movement was imitated in Korea in the thirties.

Only in a saying, "V NAROD!" . . .
proud of the white arms, the useless
lamentation of the young Russians
of sixty years past is still with us.
Café-chair revolutionists,
your hands are too white.

You are the "white hands"—
meaningless to those farmers
who want to advance
and who have little "gustration."
You are the café-chair revolutionists.

"The lamentation of the white hands"
of the young Russians, sixty years ago,
must have been a hard sign of wishing
to go out for their commitment,
forgetting about the taste of good food.

Café-chair revolutionists,
your hands are too white.

Ko Won

Mo Yun-suk
(b. 1909)

Young Girl in a Wheat Field

The setting sun diffuses no melancholy,
And to the south the village
Smiles in the soft light.

A young girl walks slowly in the dusk,
A basket in her hand;
She keeps her love
On through the field of red wheat.

The shadows embrace
the stars

Shining in the sky.
The calf gets his milk. The young girl's dream
never ends.

The young girl's eyes
Move slowly back and forth
Across the field. She amuses herself
With this celestial meditation.
A rose spreads across her face.

She will not perfume
Her olive hair.
She draws energy
from the evening dew.
There's no one as beautiful.

I hear her heart beat like an echo of prayers.
Sad, she leans against
A tree.

William McNaughton

Pak Mogwol
(b. 1917)

April

On a lonely peak,
feathery crests of pine needles.

When a cuckoo laments
a long day in the leap month,

in a woodman's hut,
behind the half door,

a blind girl gives ear,
pressed to the gate pillar.

Peter H. Lee

Jo Pyong-hwa
(b. 1921)

Crushed Between City and Civilization

Crushed between city and civilization
We're a battered people.
Our happiness we seek with bribes.

I say to my heart: Put out this fire.
I pass silent, sleepless night
After night

But I hope, I hope—
A promise is something too precious . . .

When dead leaves shine
In the bright autumn air, we stand
On street corners, we tell over
And over our old stories.

In the blazing summer
We grin.
We bear the long, bone-crushing days.

William McNaughton

Ku Ja-un
(1926–1972)

Epitaph

My father lies in the earth.
My mother, then, loved him so much.
When he was young he went abroad to study.
Later he came back
To his little hut to live out his life.
Who, really, hasn't sometime left his native land behind?

The dead leaves whirl
Under the trees.

Weep, weep, people of my country!
What my father remembered
Was the flower of his young youth.

William McNaughton

Yi Byong-bok
(b. 1927)

Jazz Dance

Like a wounded buck
spitting blood? No, like
A mad woman's
neglected skirts,
the jazz shakes unhappily:
Unoccupied space
is real as a flame
when our lighted eyes,
Deceived by unreal things,
struggle each with each;
sin is made clean,
The shadows
grow soft
Like a breath.
Not of things past,
Not of things to come,
The night is promised to today's sun,
The night
is silent
Like a suffocation.
The night keeps no accounts.
It's not "fever" I have—this battle
makes me insane,
Held against your skin, I—my throat burns.
This is not love.
What would you call it?

Masochism? Or some rage without name?
My liberated breasts! You are prouder
                    than any hero!
Your smiles
        your teeth—
The juice and seeds of a pomegranate.

What did my worn-out eyes want?
        My body, let go, drifts with the seaweed.
My heart! my heart
        ragged and ripped . . .

William McNaughton

PART FOUR: VIETNAM

Chapter 11
VIETNAMESE TALES

According to Vietnamese history an organized ethnic community, known as the kingdom of Van Lang, existed in Vietnam almost 4,000 years ago.[1] At present, however, there are about sixty distinct ethnic groups in Vietnam, each with its own language, belonging to one of three major language families: the Sino-Tibetan, the Mon-Khmer, and the Malayo-Polynesian. The dominant cultural group, the Viets, comprise more than 60 percent of the population, and their language—*Kinh*, or Vietnamese, adopted after a long struggle first with Chinese, then with French—is now the official language of the country and the medium of their modern literature.

The Vietnamese themselves refer with pride to the originality and strength of their early civilization during the first millennium B.C., and for them the best proof of its strength was its ability to resist assimilation by the Chinese. In 111 B.C., however, the Han Dynasty of China conquered Vietnam, and the Chinese remained in the country for the next ten centuries, leaving their imprint on Vietnamese culture and institutions. But the forceful Chinese policy of assimilation was met by frequent insurrections and revolts, and in the end the distinct and original culture of the Viets survived.

The Han invasion of 111 B.C. can be used conveniently to mark the beginning of the great drama of Viet national life: its need and stubborn determination to maintain itself and to preserve its identity against invasion and domination by powerful alien cultures, and somehow to survive the long and bitter wars it fought on its own soil against these

[1] Nguyen Khac Vien, *et al.*, *Anthologie de la Littérature Vietnamienne*, 2 vols. (Hanoi: Édition en Langues Étrangères, 1972–73), Vol. I, pp. 11–12.

cultures. In the twelfth century the Viets had to fight against armies of the Chinese Sung dynasty; in the thirteenth century against the Mongols; and in 1407 the Ming dynasty was able to take advantage of Vietnam's internal troubles and to occupy the country until 1427. In the eighteenth century the king Le Chieu Thong asked the Ch'ing emperor for military assistance in a civil war, and the Chinese instead sent a huge army of invasion—two hundred thousand men. It was wiped out near Hanoi in 1789.

European missionaries came to Vietnam in the seventeenth century, bringing the Roman alphabet with them. In 1802 the French government aided the south Vietnamese aristocracy in putting down a popular insurrection, and a new monarchy was set up in Hue with French support. In 1858 the French determined to conquer Vietnam, and a long struggle, from 1860 to 1900, began. The resistance was led by educated men and men of letters and supported by the peasants. By 1900, however, the resistance was virtually exhausted, and no movement arose to challenge French rule until around 1930, when Nguyen Ai Quoc (Ho Chi Minh) began to organize and to work for Vietnamese independence.

Naturally this great drama of Vietnam's national life is reflected in its literature, which includes many fine works inspired by national pride, by determination to resist invaders and conquerors, and by exultation over their defeat.

In the tenth century, when the Vietnamese finally freed themselves from Chinese rule, four powerful systems of belief flourished side by side in Vietnam. There were various local beliefs, some of which the modern student would probably characterize as animism, others of which were dedicated to scholars and/or patriots. Even today you can find people who have altars in their homes and make offerings to the spirit of Joan of Arc, or of Victor Hugo, as well as to Vietnamese heroes.

Like the Chinese, the Vietnamese speak of the three teachings—Confucianism, Taoism, and Buddhism—and these were also powerful in tenth-century Vietnam. As in China, the beliefs and practices of Taoism—cultistic Taoism—got mixed up with local cults and produced a complex and rather disorderly pantheon. Philosophical

Taoism—the doctrines of Lao-tzu and Chuang-tzu—was known only to an educated minority.

And finally, there was Buddhism, introduced by Indian missionaries before the second century A.D., and, by the tenth century, Vietnam's dominant religion. In Vietnamese Buddhism, the most important sect was the *dhyana* sect, whose point of view is summarized rather well in the work *Khoa Hu Luc,* written during the Tran dynasty (1225–1400):

> Until you've achieved the Buddha mind, abstain and pray! But the day you achieve it, you'll see that Buddha doesn't exist, and Bodhisattvas don't exist. Then you won't need to pray or abstain anymore.
>
> Nothing is born,
> Nothing dies.
> When you understand this,
> Buddha appears, the round of avatars is ended.

Besides a popular religion, Buddhism became a state religion as well.

While the Viets were under Han (Chinese) rule, they naturally were exposed to Confucianism, its doctrines and practice. In 1070 the Ly kings, imitating Chinese emperors, made the cult of Confucius a state religion. In 1075 the Vietnamese government set up a system, similar to the Chinese system of civil-service examinations, to recruit mandarins for the government, and Confucianism became even more important.

Some competition developed in Vietnam, as in China, between Buddhism and Confucianism. The Confucian scholar Le Quat (fourteenth century) deplored the Buddhist influence in Vietnamese national life:

> Ask Buddha's blessing, be afraid of his curse—why do such beliefs grow so firmly in people's hearts? Princes of the blood and common people alike waste their resources, go off and give them to the pagodas, and are as happy as if they brought back in their hands a contract guaranteeing their deal in the other world. Wherever you find a house, you find a pagoda, and when one of 'em falls, they build it up again. Bells,

> towers, pagodas, drums—half the population is wasting its time and energy on this stuff.

But there were no "religious wars," and tolerance seems to have been characteristic of Vietnamese life from a very early period.

Two important early collections of Vietnamese tales exist: the *Viet Dien U Linh,* or *Invisible Powers of the Viet Nation,* by Ly Te Xuyen (fourteenth century), and the *Linh Nam Chich Quai,* or *Collection of Weird Tales of Linh Nam,* by Vu Quynh (1452–1497) and Kieu Phu (fifteenth century). *The Viet Dien U Linh* is divided into three parts: biographies of kings and noblemen, stories about mandarins and faithful vassals, and legends about spirits. The *Linh Nam Chich Quai,* with its twenty-three legends and folktales, is one of the oldest written works of Vietnamese folklore. The Vietnamese prize it for its sociological and historical value.

But for literary value, Nguyen Du's *Truyen Ky Man Luc,* or *Great Collection of Astonishing Tales,* must take first place. Nguyen Du, who lived in the sixteenth century, is supposed to have been the favorite student of the famous man of letters, poet, and patron Nguyen Binh Khiem. Successful in the civil-service exams, Nguyen Du served a year in the mandarinate; then he resigned. "To take care of his old mother," was the official reason, but students now believe that, like the Chinese poet T'ao Ch'ien, he preferred his farm and garden to public life. In retirement Nguyen Du composed the *Truyen Ky Man Luc* in imitation of a work by the Chinese writer Ch'u Chung-chi (1341–1427). Nguyen's own work is in classical Chinese. The *Truyen Ky Man Luc* may have been polished or touched up by Nguyen Binh Khiem.

Modern students in Hanoi praise *Truyen Ky Man Luc* because it "brings social criticism to its highest level" and it "severely criticized kings, mandarins and all kinds of bureaucrats, at the same time revealing the common people's misery."[1] I do not find any of these characteristics in "The Kapok Tree."

It is here simply because it is one of the best ghost sto-

[1] Nguyen Khac Vien, *ibid.,* p. 49.

ries I know. It is also an excellent example of a kind of tale very popular in China and can serve further to illustrate the enormous influence Chinese culture has had all over East and Southeast Asia. The reader will also notice the presence of a Taoist miracle worker—a reflection of popular belief in cultistic Taoism and its "priests."

Nguyen Du
(sixteenth century)

THE KAPOK TREE
(FROM THE TRUYEN KY MAN LUC)

In Bac-ha there was a good-looking young man named Trinh Trung Ngo. Trinh Trung Ngo came from a wealthy family. He himself was a river merchant—rented a boat and traveled south in his business.

Sometimes Trinh tied up his boat at the Lieu-khe Bridge and went to the markets at Nam Xuong. Whenever he made this trip, a beautiful young woman always came out from East Village, with a little servant woman following her. Trinh sneaked looks at the young woman, and it struck him that she was extraordinarily beautiful. But since it was not his country, he didn't know exactly how to find out about her. All he could do was hide his feelings.

Then one day, seeing her again, Trinh tried to say a word or two to her, and get acquainted. But she took her skirt in her hands and walked quickly away, saying to the servant woman: "Oh, spring! I've been drunk with it these many days now. I've been staying in bed and not getting up. It's been six months since I went to the Lieu-khe Bridge. I wonder what the countryside is like this morning. Wouldn't it be nice to go see the old place again tonight? It may make me feel a little better. Would you like to come?"

That evening Trung Ngo went to the Lieu-khe Bridge and waited around. It got very late, past the hour when everyone was in bed. But then the beautiful young woman, in fact, came to the bridge. The servant woman walked behind her carrying a small violin. Coming to the bridgehead, the young woman sighed. She said: "The rivers and hills are like they always were. Oh, but the lady has lost the lover she had. It makes you think of times gone by . . ."

The young woman sat on the bridge parapet. She took the violin and played a few southern songs, or some measures of "Autumn Thoughts." She played and played. Then putting down the violin, she said, "How I feel, how I *really* feel—I try to say that with my violin. There's nobody here to understand the music, or understand me. I'm going home."

Hearing what she said, Trung Ngo stepped in front of her and said: "I'm a person who can understand the music. Try me."

The young lady was very surprised. She said: "You're here, too? The other day you gave me a look . . . I still remember it. But I had something to do then, and I couldn't tell you what I felt. Tonight it's so quiet, I thought I'd take a walk. I didn't expect to see you here. If Heaven hadn't intended it, how could it have happened that we met? But you—you are jade, you're pearls and . . . and with you, I feel embarrassed, I feel . . . impure."

Trung Ngo asked her what her name was and where she lived. The young woman frowned and said, "I'm Nhi-Khanh. My grandfather is Mister Hoi. We're well-known in the village. My parents died; it was quite unexpected. It's not too easy for the rest of us now. My . . . husband left me not very long ago, and so I moved out of our house. We moved out to the country.

"Sometimes I think . . . how human life is just a dream, and then I try my best to enjoy the fading pleasures that there are. Once we're buried, we belong to the Land of the Springs, and then if we want to catch some happiness, or look for love, well, it's too late then."

Trung Ngo and Nhi-Khanh, with a single will, went on board the junk. Nhi-Khanh, speaking softly, said: "I . . . I know I'm going to die soon. The days go by like years, and nobody even knows I'm there. If, my beautiful friend—if you could make showers of sunlight fall on the dark valley, if you could strike the dull bud with warm air, so that the withered roses and the faded violets would live in the radiance of spring: if you could do that, my hopes in life would become real."

She took off her dress, and together they enjoyed love's delights. As remembrance of this night of happiness, Nhi-Khanh wrote two poems.

Her first poem goes like this:

At the far end of the village, a long time asleep—the
 sleep of noon lasts on,
Speaking of separation, I blush in front of my love.
The young shoots of jade[1] rearrange the bracelet of
 pearls,
The silk belt is untied, the embroidered sandals
 removed.
One man dreamed he was a butterfly; he woke up and
wondered
 what he was.[2]
Spring came at the third watch—cry, cry! for him
 who, leaving with a constant heart, will be changed
 into a cuckoo!
I leave now, the oath—to be buried in the same tomb
 —not yet fulfilled,
But one day I will die of happiness to show my love.

Nhi-Khanh's second poem ran like this:

Rendezvous of beauty, what could spoil such a night?
Drunk, I take my guitar and pluck a few notes.
The pin of jade, like that that changed into a swallow,
 carelessly fastened to the undone hair knot,
The wasp's waist of gold—you'd be afraid to break it
 embracing it!
The plum flower blooms, its red is still wet;
The cherry flower falls like a spot of face powder, but
 its color is still white.
One day tied us each to each like the male and
 female phoenix;
In morning wind, on nights of the moon, we give up
 our love.

But Trinh Trung Ngo was basically a businessman, and he really didn't understand poetry. The young woman had

[1] Fingers.
[2] The Chinese philosopher Chuang-tzu (see pp. 124, 132–133).

to explain to him line by line what the poems meant. Trinh told her how good her work was.

"Your talent," he said, "is up there with Di-an's.[1] You should become a famous poetess."

Nhi-Khanh laughed and said, "What matters, in life, is to fulfill your desires, isn't it? Literature—in the end, literature is a cup of yellow earth. Miss Ts'ai, Miss Pan,[2] look what they were, and where are they now? Isn't it better to look at the country in spring and enjoy the moment you have here? Isn't that the way to live?"

At dawn she left him.

After that Nhi-Khanh came back to Trinh every evening.

More than a month went by. Among Trinh's business associates, there was one man who knew what was going on. He said to Trinh: "Look, you're on the road. You've got to be careful and not start people talking. You shouldn't be chasing girls like this. You met this woman without a marriage broker, you don't know where she lives now, or where she comes from. If she's not somebody's mistress living in an apartment decorated with embroidered silk, she must be some rich man's daughter that lives in red chambers. You're going to wake up one morning and find that her father, or her man, knows about you. Then you'll be in trouble, and you won't have any relatives to help you out. You—look, be smart. Get the girl's address and find out about her. Then you can either dump her, or get her for your own and take her away with you. That's what you *ought* to do."

Trinh knew his friend was right. So one day he said to Nhi-Khanh, "I'm not from this part of the country. It was just luck I met you at all. But, as they say, 'Though I live close by the goddess, I don't know where her home is,' and it makes me feel strange."

Nhi-Khanh said, "Actually, I don't live too far from here. But we've met in secret. I'm only afraid that people's

[1] Di-an: in Chinese Yi-an, for Li Yi-an, better known as Li Ch'ing-chao (*ca.* 1083–*ca.* 1151), whom some call "China's greatest poetess." For a complete translation of her poetry, see Lenore Mayhew and William McNaughton, *As Though Dreaming, the Tz'u of Pure Jade by Li Ch'ing-chao* (Mushinsha/Serendipity, 1977).

[2] Ts'ai Yen (flourished A.D. 206) and Pan Chieh-yü (first century B.C.), two famous Chinese poetesses.

ears and eyes might be suspicious of me. That's why . . . I like to wait until the stars are out to come see you, and why I like to go back with the moon."

Trinh, however, was not dissuaded. So she laughed and said to him, "My house is, well, it's poor. I'll be embarrassed. But if you want to come with me, come."

And so that night, at midnight, under a cloudy night sky, they went to East Village.

The place was run around by a bamboo hedge. Here and there grew clumps of dry reeds. At the center was a small thatched hut, not very well built. On every side creepers ran up the walls.

The lady pointed to it and said, "Here it is. Where I 'keep my needle and thread' and take my rest. Open the door and wait till I light the lamp."

Trinh ducked his head to go in. He stopped in the door. A puff of wind came, died, came again . . . and every time it came, it brought a fetid odor that frightened Trinh. Suddenly a light came up inside. Trinh looked in and saw, on his left, a little osier bed. On the bed was set a red coffin, over which was draped a strip of red silk. On the strip of silk Trinh could read, in silver letters, the words, "Coffin of Nhi-Khanh." On the ground beside the coffin was a little terra-cotta statue of a servant woman carrying a violin. Trinh felt his blood go cold and his hair stand up. He stepped back and turned to run. He saw the woman standing in his path. She said, "You've come this far, why go back now? Didn't I tell you, in my poem the other day, that I'd slept with Death? Please, follow me as soon as you can, so we can be buried in the same grave. We swore we would! I sleep here by myself. I won't let you go! You can't!"

She took hold of his coat. But luckily the tail was old, and Trinh was able to rip free and get away. When he got back to the Lieu-khe Bridge, he could hardly speak.

Next morning Trinh Trung Ngo went to East Village to find out what he could. In fact there had been a granddaughter of a certain Mr. Hoi, twenty years old. She had died six months before. She was buried just outside the village.

Soon Trinh was seriously ill. And the young lady came to see him still. Sometimes she shouted to him from the parapet, sometimes she came and whispered at the windows of his junk. When these things happened Trinh wanted to get up and go with her. The men in the crew had to hold him down, and he swore at them, and said: "Where my wife lives, it's beautiful. They live in a palace perfumed with orchids and musk. I want to go. Why should I stay in this cage of dust? What's it matter to you? Why are you keeping me here?"

One night, everybody on the junk was sound asleep. Somebody woke up and noticed Trinh was gone. It looked as though he'd been gone for some time. They ran to shore looking for him. They found him outside the village, his arms around the coffin of Nhi-Khanh. He was dead.

They buried Trinh Trung Ngo there with Nhi-Khanh.

At this time people began, on dark nights, to see Trinh and Nhi-Khanh walking hand in hand, sometimes singing, sometimes crying. If they met anyone out at night, they always asked him to pray for them and to offer sacrifices. If they weren't satisfied, there would be calamities.

Finally, the village people couldn't stand it anymore. They took Trinh's and Nhi-Khanh's bones from the tomb and threw them into the river. On the riverbank at that place there is a pagoda, and by the pagoda there was an old kapok tree. People said the tree was more than a hundred years old. The unappeased spirits of the two lovers took the tree for their instrument and became demons. When anyone tried to cut down the tree, his saw would shatter, his ax would break. So nobody was ever able to cut down the old kapok tree.

In the Canh-ngo year of the Khai-huu reign-period of the Tran Dynasty (1330), a Taoist monk spent the night in the old pagoda there.

The river was cold, the moon was pale. Everything was quiet. The monk sat looking out at the dark. Suddenly he saw a man and a woman outside, both completely naked, laughing and fooling around. After a while they walked up and knocked at the pagoda door. The monk supposed it was a couple of lewd young lovers, letting themselves go to amorous frolics in the moonlight. He thought the way they behaved was pretty poor, and so he slammed the door on them without speaking.

Next morning the monk went and told one of the village elders what had happened. He told the old man how disgusted he was, the way morals had gone to pieces in the modern world.

"Oh," said the old man. "What you saw were demons. Demons have taken that old tree as their instrument. Happened several years ago. Wish you had a magic sword or something, could kill these evil spirits. Would do the people around here a lot of good."

The Taoist monk thought about this for a while. Finally, he said: "Well, I have taken it on myself to help people. This thing of yours, now that I've seen it with my own eyes—if I didn't use my magical powers, it would be as if I'd let somebody drown without even trying to save them."

So the Taoist got the villagers together. He set up an altar for an offering. The monk wrote three magic formulae, one of which he stuck up on the tree. The second he threw in the river, and the third he burned, watching the breeze whip its smoke around.

Then the monk shouted in a terrible voice: "Immoral demons have done their evil here for too long now! Celestial armies! I pray you destroy this evil breed! Nothing can stop the magic. It works fast as fire."

An instant later black clouds gathered, and it got so dark you couldn't see anything more than a few feet away. Great waves rose on the river. Their roar filled heaven and earth.

Suddenly the wind dropped. Gradually the sky cleared up. Then they saw that the old tree had been knocked down, and its branches and trunk had been split and shattered into little pieces like hempen threads. They heard in the air the sounds of a bastinade mixed with weeping. The crowd of villagers looked up and saw six or seven hundred soldiers with buffalo heads; the soldiers had the two demons tied up and were taking them away.

The people of the village tried to give the Taoist monk money and many gifts, grateful as they were, but he pulled up the skirts of his robe and wouldn't take anything from them.

He went off into the mountains, and they didn't see him again.

William McNaughton

Chapter 12
VIETNAMESE POETRY

Initially, Vietnamese literature was written in classical Chinese, using the Chinese characters. But, no later than the fourteenth century, the Vietnamese, moved by the natural desire to use their own language for literary purposes, worked out a way to write it down.

As a result there were two literatures in Vietnam: one in *Han* (classical Chinese), and one in *nom* (Vietnamese). Many talented writers worked in both *Han* and *nom*, and the Vietnamese themselves feel that their own national literary genius was tutored and nourished by the Chinese influence.

Many Chinese forms, literary attitudes, conventions, rhetorical tricks, and topics of invention can be found in Vietnamese literature. There are hundreds of examples of the Quatrain form and of short poems like the Chinese *chüeh-chü.* The Vietnamese also wrote, in imitation of the Chinese, prose songs or *fu* (*phu* in Vietnamese). The eight-line poem, carefully rhymed and rigidly balanced in its sequences of linguistic tones, is also used, and it is a direct counterpart of the Chinese *lü-shih.*

In the seventeenth or eighteenth century there developed what some students call the most remarkable genre in Vietnamese literature, the long narrative poem; in effect, a novel-in-verse, generally written in the meter of folk poetry, six-eight verse. Many of these poems were written, and they were particularly popular between 1700 and 1858. The *Kim Van Kieu* of Nguyen Du (1765–1820, not to be confused with his earlier namesake) is such a work, and it is generally considered to be *the* masterpiece of Vietnamese literature. Nguyen Du wrote much of his poetry in classical Chinese, but he moved to *nom* for the *Kim Van Kieu.* The Vietnamese themselves give credit to Nguyen Du's long apprenticeship in Chinese poetry for the great skill with which *Kieu* is written. The poem also probably has a direct literary source in a Chinese novel, *The Tale of Chin, Yun and Ch'iao,* by Hsu Wei (sixteenth century). *Kim Van Kieu* is praised in Hanoi today because it defends the individual's right to choose his own spouse, rather than to have the choice made for him by his family; because it has the woman taking initiatives to rejoin her lover; because it speaks of physical love without descending to vulgarity, and because, in spite of the puritanism of its age, it defends the right of widows to love again in their lives.[1]

Ngo Chan Lu'u
(959–1011)

Good-bye to Ambassador Ly Giac[2]

Under spreading light
　　　　the wind tugs your brocade sail:
Good-bye, Ambassador!
　　　　Going back to the Celestial Emperor
You will cross mountains
　　　　and cross blue waves.
The road home runs off
　　　　and vanishes in the distant horizon.
Heart tight,
　　　　I drink: good-bye.
I lean back against the carriage.
　　Saying good-bye is hard.
　　　　You were good,
And when you see
　　the Emperor again,
　　　　I hope you'll say,
We here in the south,
　　　　we know where the borders are . . .

William McNaughton

[1] Nguyen Khac Vien, *op. cit.,* Vol. II, p. 22.
[2] Ly Giac has just finished his service as Chinese ambassador to Vietnam.

Dieu Nhan
(1072–1143)

Dieu Nhan is known as Vietnam's first woman poet. A daughter of the royal family, she entered a Buddhist order after her husband's death and headed a community of "bonzesses" (female priests). The following is her "death verse."

Birth, Old Age, Disease, Death

Birth, old age, disease, death,
—That's what it is, what it's always been
And you want to be free of it?
Untie the knots; the knots retie themselves.
Blind, men go to Buddha;
troubled, men go to Dhyana.[1]
Forget Buddha.
Forget Dhyana.
And keep your mouth shut.
Words have nothing to do with it.

William McNaughton

Khong Lo
(d. 1119)

What I Believe

The mountains twist away like dragons
And snakes: my hut is in the right place.
All day long I enjoy
this simple life out in the country.
Sometimes I climb a lonely peak
And whoop a long whoop
That freezes the universe . . .

William McNaughton

[1] Dhyana: see p. 413.

Tran Minh Tong
(1300–1357)

Bach Dang River[1]

The mountains,
Like swords held toward the sky, pierce the clouds.
The water dragon, sucking up the tide, raises
billows of snow.
The spring rain has quit.
The ground is covered with flowers
Like gold buckles. The evening wind
Blows cool, the pines make a sound
Like flutes shaking the sky. Look at this—
A countryside of unchangeable rivers and
unchangeable
Hills . . .

I lean on the balcony
and think of defeats
And victories of the Viets and the Ho.[2]
On the wide waters the setting sun's rays
Turn red: I think
Of the continual flowing of invaders' blood.

William McNaughton

[1] The Bach Dang River was the site of great Vietnamese victories over Chinese imperial forces (A.D. 938) and over Mongol invaders (A.D. 1288).

[2] Ho: the Mongols.

Nguyen Huc
(fifteenth century)

After the War

I saw the fields: wasteland.
    Heart murdered, I go back
    the way I had come.
The invader came through there.
    Exuberant grass and trees are gone,
    Only wild scrub shows, this spring.
Ten years of war have wiped out all life.
I think of my little retreat
    ten thousand miles away . . .
In the mountains, a little rice
    fried with celery—enough to live on.
At Hi Bi Bridge, who would put back
    into my hands *The Problems of Strategy?*
I turn toward the capital lost in the distance.
    Miles of space
Lie beyond miles,
    And I can find no site for my house.

William McNaughton

Le Thanh Tong
(1442–1497)

Le Thanh Tong was king from 1460–1497, the golden age of the Later Le dynasty. He established a poets' academy called "The Altar of Poetry." His reign was one of peace and prosperity.

Che Village

Westward the sun sets behind the hills,
    And here I am already at Tam Che.
The waters of the big river are tinged with blue.

The higher peaks are colored by the moon.
Day in day out the river-market is crowded,
        And boats and sampans in a thousand shapes
            Lie on the bank.
Could you find anything more magnificent anywhere?
And why? The people have seen taxes go down.
They have seen land-rents reduced.

William McNaughton

Nguyen Binh Khiem
(1491–1585)

The Rats[1]

The people all want it
        and why not?
            —a little to eat,
A refuge from the cold,
And we pay our respects
        to those intelligent men
Who taught men how to grow five grains
—Grow them and support their parents
        with the respect they deserve,
And feed their wives and children
According to the love they have for them.
But these goddamn rats
        —*big* rats—without pity
Deceive and steal.
What's left in the fields?
        A few shriveled grains of rice.
What's left in the granaries? Air.
The farmer's bent shoulders:
        fatigue. He sighs.
His wife is skin and bones:
                she cries.
A nation's people are its most sacred thing,

[1] "The Rats" is an imitation of an old Chinese song (see p. 99).

And what do you
        (you rats)
                do for their lives?
Get in the way, without pity get in the way.
You hide yourselves in citadel walls
Hide yourselves even underneath the altar
Of the Earth god; that way
It's easier to get away with your crimes.
Men hate you, gods
Hate you:
You who do this evil in the world,
The world will dispose
        of you
            someday, of this be sure.
Your bodies will be thrown out in the markets and
  yards.
Your flesh will be torn by vultures and crows,
And the common people,
        crushed now by poverty,
One day,
        in happiness,
                in peace,
Themselves will enjoy the fruits of their work.

William McNaughton

Ho Xuan Huong
(eighteenth century)

An always-popular woman poet, Ho is now much praised in Vietnam for her defense of women and her denial of masculine superiority; and because—surprising to find in a government most of whose international counterparts are rather puritanical—she "speaks directly of sexual love and brings out, without embarrassment and yet without crudeness, the secrets of a woman's body. . . . Her poetry is evocative and shivers with sensuality."[1]

[1] Nguyen Khac Vien, *op. cit.,* Vol II, p. 170.

The Swing[1]

Hurrah for whoever put in the good poles!
Some climb up to swing and others watch.
He arches his knees and bends,
Bends his back;
She curves her back and strains; strains her thighs.
Four fringes of red pantaloons
snap in the breeze.
Two pairs of legs
stretch out two by two.
Do they understand
these games of spring they play?

The poles are gone,
The places where they were fixed are empty now.

William McNaughton

Confession of a "Little Wife"[2]

You want to know what it's like? Piss!
One of us sleeps under quilts,
The other freezes.
If you're lucky he gives you a touch
Once or twice
a month (Three times? Never!)—
You watch and wait to catch a bowlful,
And the rice is badly cooked!

You step and fetch like a servant,
only,
You never get paid.
Oh, if I had known
What it was like,

[1] Like much of Ho's poetry, "The Swing," in order to be understood, must be read with an active sense of possible sexual *double entendres,* puns, and allusions.

[2] "Little wife": a concubine, a second wife.

I would have gone on living
alone like I was living before.

William McNaughton

Dirty Old Bonze[1]

A life of self-denial—heavy like a load
of stones:
I mean, a nothing is enough,
an absolute nothing.
The boat of compassion would have reached the
Western shores,
but a contrary wind
Tangled ropes and sails.[2]

William McNaughton

Nguyen Du
(1765–1820)

Kim Van Kieu: Chapter Four[3]

One day
a young traveler came by the blue house.
He was named Ky-tam, family Thuc,

[1] Bonze: a Buddhist priest.

[2] The Western shores: Buddhist paradise. Compassion: the cardinal virtue. Ropes and sails: *lôn lèo*. *Lèo lôn* means to make love. "Wind," as in China, may mean "sexual desire": *cf.* Mayhew and McNaughton, *A Gold Orchid*, p. 31n.

[3] The main character in *Kim Van Kieu* is the young woman Kieu. In order to save her father's life she agrees to a "marriage"—only to find that she has, in fact, been sold into a life of prostitution. In the section given here, her life as a prostitute—her life in "the blue houses"—already has begun. Though the section ends happily, Kieu has many more troubles to face later in the poem.

and he came from a line of mandarins.
His first home had been in Tich county,
Thuong province, and he had come
with his father to Lam-chung to start a business.
Ky-tam was attracted by the reputation
"Queen of Flowers" that attached to Kieu,
and he sent his red card into the perfumed rooms.
Soon, behind the fringed curtains
he found himself face
to face with the peach flower.
All of her expressions
he found delicious, all of
her ways he found delightful,
"Camellia flower on a young stem."
The more the spring wind and rain caressed her,
caressed her, the more beautiful she became.
Moon and flowers,
flowers and moon—
bitter metaphors! What heart
can hold itself in
against the beauty of spring nights?

. . . .

They gave each other peaches in the morning,
gave each other plums in the evening.

. . . .

Then unexpectedly Ky-tam's father
had to go home, and so Ky-tam
lost his head ten times more
than he had before.
In these spring days they got chance after chance
to "meet the spring"[1] . . . took the air on the terrace . . .
watched the moon from the yard . . .
got drunk from "the Immortal's gourd" . . .
took turns making up impromptu poems.
They burned sandalwood at dawn
and tasted tea at noon.
They kept track
of who won at chess
and played duets on the guitar.

[1] "Meet the spring"; that is, make love.

Headlong they threw themselves into these delights,
And the better Ky-tam got to know Kieu
And Kieu to know Ky-tam,
the more lost in love they were.
In the small room of gauze, one lazy day,
Kieu let down the red curtains and took a bath
in water boiled in orchids.

What form! This temple of love
the gods built, stood up
in ivory and white,
in smoothness of jade,
And Ky-tam could not look away.
In the grass script,
in classical style,
he wrote a poem about his love of her.

. . . .

Kieu said: "I'm grateful to you,
"But this idea you have—get married—
"Could you really do it? Could I do it?"

. . . .

Kieu's face darkened. She saw more clearly than ever
what it really meant
"to be a woman with a broken womb." She said:

. . . .

"On the terrace of cinnamon trees, in the palace
"of the moon,
"beautiful Hong-nga already rules.[1]
"Your destiny and hers
"were tied together long ago
with the silk cords of marriage.

. . . .

I would
break like a flower
"in the she-lion's mouth.

. . . .

"And you still have your father over you.
He's a kind man,

[1] "Beautiful Hong-nga": Western readers may not understand this unless they realize that in Vietnam, as in China, a man might have two (or more) wives living in the same house with him. However only one of them, the first, really had any status. *Cf.* Ho Xuan Huong's poem, p. 311.

"but will he see his way to be kind to me?
"What value will he see in the willow on the path,
"in the flower on the wall?
"Having come from the blue houses, I'll be sent back
to the blue houses and to their kind."

. . . .

Ky-tam said: "What are you afraid of?
"Doesn't your heart know my heart?

. . . .

"Trust me. I'll work out the difficulties.
"I'll take care of the problems. Trust me."

. . . .

And so they said a thousand things
to each other
and called the rivers and oceans to witness
their oaths: sweet conversation without end.
The night was too short.
Already, outside, the mountains in the west
cut into the moon's silver disk.

In the yard, the plane trees, their leaves
were dotted with yellow. In the autumn hedges
the balls of chrysanthemums had begun to form.
Ky-tam's father, in his thick-padded saddle,
returned from his trip. Like clouds, like lightning
the old man's anger exploded.
His mind boiled with one thought: how to separate
the lovers. He decided not to fool around:
he ordered that Kieu, "the woman with painted
cheeks," go back
to the blue houses. Ky-tam got his courage together and
went to soften the old man. He appealed to
his heart. He said, "I know I have done many
"wrong things. If I am beaten by rain, blasted
"by lightning, cut by the ax, struck by
"the hammer, how can I complain? But now
"I've put my hand in indigo. I was
"stupid, but it's too late now to be wise and if
"she and I had been together only a day, well, the
guitar
"you've held in your arms, how can you break
"its strings? Father, if you can't change
your heart about this,

"—I don't want to go against you
"—but—what does life mean to me then?"
When Ky-tam said this, words like granite or
iron, the old man felt his liver blaze inside him.
He went and knelt at the local court to
file a complaint. The peaceful plain shuddered
suddenly under wild waves. The judge issued a summons
on red paper. Kieu and Ky-tam went together
with the process servers, and together knelt in the yard
of many flowers.
Kneeling, they looked up.
A hard and dark face, as if
to make them humble and afraid, began speaking in a
harsh voice.
"This young man has been led astray;
as for the girl,
well,
"She's a common whore. Flowers on the flowing
water,
"decay of cheap perfume—
"this is she and her kind. She uses rouge
"And lipstick to lead astray our young.
"According to the evidence here presented by
the plaintiff
"examine the case from whatever side, a wrong
has been done.
"There are two possible actions we can take under
the law,
"and I leave you your choice:
"one, the punishment prescribed by the law;
"two, that this girl
simply go back to the blue house."
Kieu said:

....

"I'm a weak thing, but let justice
"strike." The judge said:
"Let the sentence be
"carried out." The three pieces of criminals' wood[1]
were locked around the peony branch: ready to
take what

[1] "Criminals' wood": that is, they are locking Kieu into the cangue (a sort of portable pillory).

came, Kieu did not cry,
"Injustice!" Her cheeks like fruit were
spotted with tears; her willow-leaf
eyebrows were arched with grief.

. . . .

And pitiful young Thuc!
He watched from a distance, and his heart twisted
in pain. He began to cry and shout:
"It's all my fault!
"She didn't do anything wrong!
"If I'd done what she said in the beginning,
"they wouldn't be doing this to her now!
"I'm a fool! I didn't know
"what would happen. Whose fault is it,
"if the moon is humiliated,
"and the flower destroyed?"
The judge heard these remarks,
and moved by them, he put some questions to
Ky-tam.
His voice breaking and trembling,
Ky-tam retold everything he and Kieu
had said, that day of the marriage proposal.
"She said it would end like this!
"A long time ago she knew this would happen
"to her today. It's me! I'm to blame!
"I wanted to do it my way!
"What's happened to her now is my fault!"
These words touched the judge. He softened a little
and thought he saw a way to get them
out of it. "If she is really like this,"
the judge said, "she has some sense."
And Ky-tam answered, "The life she's in,
"like floating duckweed,
"like froth on the moving water,
"she's still learned to use the brush and ink a little."
The judge laughed. "Well then, fine!
"She can show her talent. Let her improvise a poem
in the cangue."
Kieu obeyed his order.
Her brush was quick, and the flowered
paper was soon taken and laid
on the mandarin's desk for him to judge.
"Why," he said, "it's good . . . it's better

"than the best poetry of the T'ang dynasty![1]

. . . .

"Should we add discord to discord?
"Pile evil on evil?
"Mess up the measure?
"Untune this duet of fine guitars?
"When a case comes before the court,
"the court is obliged to judge it,
"on the surface, strictly according to the law;
"but in the last analysis, by the light of our hearts.
"Let son and daughter-in-law
pick up
"their family life again.
Well then! Calm down,
"and let this case be closed."
Immediately he ordered that the official ceremony
should be prepared.
The flowery palanquin flew on wings of wind,
red torches cut into the night of stars.

Formations of flute and tambourine,
in joyful concert, conducted the couple
to the room of red roses.

Old Thuc began to love her for her virtue,
to admire her for her
talent,
and so he suppressed any angry words.
The house smelled of lilies and of orchids,
and the bitter taste Ky-tam and Kieu
had tasted, made sweeter now love's sweet taste.

William McNaughton

[1] The T'ang dynasty: the greatest age of Chinese poetry.

Cao Ba Quat
(1809–1853)

Chinese Opera

Wooden frames, an elevated stage,
blazing lights—
Boom! a shout,
an icy wind: enter the hero,
Heavy beard, military strut,
coat of mail, and a soldier
With terrible eyes, showing off
on his horse. And are there
No real men today, that people
Amuse themselves
with these old-time costumes?
What about this opium business?[1]
Have you heard of that?

They worry me,
these people sitting here nose in the air
Watching the play!

William McNaughton

Nguyen Khuyen
(1835–1909)

Women

Women, tea, and wine—
My three eternal curses.
I have to give them up.
All right, tea maybe.
And maybe even wine.

Bill Faber

[1] This poem was written around the time of the first Anglo-Chinese Opium War (1840).

Ho Chi Minh
(1890–1969)

Ho Chi Minh went to France as a young man and lived there as a manual laborer for many years. In 1925 he founded the Young Revolutionaries of Vietnam and in 1930 the Indochinese Communist Party. He was elected President of (North) Vietnam in 1945. Many Vietnamese admire him for his literary as well as his political accomplishments.

Water Ration

Half a basin each.
Take a bath, make tea.
Tea and no bath,
Or a bath and no tea?

Bill Faber

Country Prison

Only a pale green when I came,
Now the rice is cut and stored.
Farmers laugh. I hear them,
Here, across the rice fields.

Bill Faber

Exercise Time—Permission to Walk in the Prison Yard

I reel,
My legs are like cotton.

The guard shouts,
"You—back! That's enough horsing around!"

Bill Faber

Le Duc Tho
(b. 1911)

Active in Communist organizations since 1929, Le is now a member of the Political Office of the Central Committee of the Vietnamese Workers' Party.

A Night on the Hill

for Comrade Phan Say

The thatched hut bows down its narrow roof.
A wood fire,
A soft light
In the room welcome the evening's visitors.
Tomorrow we start again the wearying march
Across jungles, across rivers.

Coming from every side,
Wind and mist,
Through the cracks in the woven wall,
Fill the little hut
With damp and chill.
But we feel better now:
An unfamiliar visitor has come.

I've never seen you, my brother, before today,
But I love you with a fierce love.
With your rice bowl and dry fish
You warm yourself at the fire with me.

"How many times have you crossed
"Ba rên and Dôc But?"
On his thin face,

Yellow and pale with the fevers of the jungle,
Comes a smile of real happiness.

"Where are your wife and children?"

"I haven't seen them for a long time.
"You know what the enemy is like: search-and-destroy,
"Search-and-destroy. I wonder if they're still alive."

And you look thoughtfully
Into the fire. The fire
Cracks in the round log.
You laugh—a good laugh—
And say,
"What about your people?"

"My mother is an old old lady.
"She's gone back to the countryside.
"Her love, the memory of her . . .
"Nothing now, not even a word."

It's a long road running south.
So many rivers, so much jungle to cross!
But my heart is happy
And will take the danger as it comes.

Waters flowing on, where to?
May a stranger on the road
Tell you how homesick
He feels?
Mist hangs in the top of the trees.
The birds in the woods stop singing,
And night tosses a grayish veil
Across the last shadows of evening.

The rice in the fireplace is done.
It will fill our bellies and warm our hearts.
Tomorrow everybody will go his way,
And you? Will you remember that we stopped here
  tonight?
Remember this evening at Dôc But?
This new friendship of ours?

Will you remember our shared hate of the common
enemy
And our hearts filled with shared love?

Dôc But, January 15, 1949

William McNaughton

Xuan Thuy
(b. 1912)

Between 1938 and 1943 Thuy was in jail for anti-colonial activities and finally was deported. He is now a member of the Central Committee of the Workers' Party in North Vietnam, and Minister of Foreign Affairs.

For Today's Happiness and the Happiness to Come

Dance, hands! Bloom, mouths!
Brothers and sisters, the fighting North has come
through the fire.
Today the Yankee has given up.

....

Rockets and bombs, did they really think that these
would bring our people to their knees?

....

People and army, water and fish, love deeper than the
seas.
Let our flesh remain marked with rain and sun,
evils we have beaten.

....

From Paris I tell you how happy I am,

....

On the quais in Paris, the tender ivy reaches toward
the Seine.
I hear a voice I know, singing
"Au milieu de l'automne est entré le printemps.

"Bien aimé, ma pensée viendra-t-elle jusqu'à toi?"
And here we are, halfway down the road.

The other half of the long road,
Dew and fog, stretches in front of you.
But today I know *that day* will come . . .
Happy and warm the Vietnamese sun will shine on
  the whole country
When that day comes, and Vietnam
Is united again.

William McNaughton

Huy Can
(b. 1919)

Huy Can is one of the major poets of modern Vietnam. In 1945 he was elected to the National Committee for National Liberation. He has been in the central government since 1945, most recently as vice-minister of culture.

Arhats of the Tay-phuong Pagoda[1]

Arhats of the Tay-phuong Pagoda,
I can't get you off my mind.
There you are in Buddha's land,
And yet your faces are images of grief.

There you are, bones like life in your limbs.
What fire in your emaciated bodies,
What infinite anguish, has sunk your eyes?
There you are after so long
Bent over with an unspoken grief.

[1] Arhats: see p. 37. The poem refers to a number of statues sculpted by anonymous artists of the eighteenth century.

There you are, eyes wide open with tragedy,
Eyebrows angled and knit.
Your forehead rises in the wave of transmigrations
of the soul,
Your lips go slack with bitter things,
Your soul dries out, and your nerves;
Your hands twist, and beats in them an ancient blood.

There you are bending back your arms and legs
As if you wanted to return to your mother's womb,
And your ears that hang to your knees
Hear still the lamentations of life.

. . . .

Do you really tremble on the path of your discipline
A last time with human fever
Trying to take off the coat of human happiness
That you suffer like ordinary beings?

Oh, Old Master, sculptor, where are you now?
Come back and solve this puzzle for me—
Sculpting so many lives in misery,
What were you telling us about Buddha's land?

Or maybe these things, at the center of winds and
storms
Like a confidence in the life lived—
Maybe they are our fathers, their bones, their
blood . . .
Our tormented fathers, and their daily lives.

Our fathers, backs bent with the burdens of those
days,
Fathers who lived in the age of Nguyen Du,
Hearts and souls in the fire, foreheads burned—
Compassionate . . . and impotent.

Fathers, how it hurts in your bowels!
Life then "mark time," marched!
And every hope born in your hearts
Turned brown like buds without sun.

A secular twilight wiped out our fathers' steps
Who were looking for a way out and a solution.

Over your faces, you statues,
I feel come up again mists of the past.

Arhats of the Tay-phuong Pagoda,
Your grandchildren are setting out for happiness.
I look at you again, the hands of your statues
Disappear in fogs, shadows, mists . . .

Oh, fathers that we love—
Your suffering in life is close to us,
Your steps are lost in the wood fibers,
You step across the ages,
You come with us down the road this spring.

William McNaughton

To Huu
(b. 1920)

The Three Sounds

In three sounds "the meaning of life":
The motor growls without rest,
The bell reverberates without remorse,
The gong booms without pity.
Each speaks out its tonality,
Its language, its truth.

The motor roars, Start working
Sweat weep oil water
You're beat So work
Your whole life no matter what
Work then work then work again
Rest never And don't make trouble.

The bell whispers, In prayer
Take your misery as it is
Eternal happiness
Is earned by humility

Resentment be damned
The wind carry it away.

The gong stirs him up,   Go to jail!
Stand up there   Bend your back
Get a look   at chains   at whips
Cangues   rifles   blades
What do you mean "the right to live"
Fine   Turn you over to the executioner.

The gong booms without pity,
The motor growls without rest,
The bell reverberates without remorse:

"Life's meaning" in three sounds.

William McNaughton

PART FIVE: INDIA

Chapter 13
INDIAN TALES

In India the story has a very long and distinguished history as a literary form, and Indian animal fables were known and admired around the world even in ancient times. Some scholars, perhaps overstating the case slightly, say that "all the animal fables of the world can ultimately be traced" to the two ancient Indian masterpieces in this genre, the *Panchatantra* (see pp. 332–335) and the *Hitopadesa*.[1]

Also very ancient in Indian literature are the *Jataka*, or birth stories (that is, stories of Gautama Buddha in previous incarnations as the *Bodhisattva*, before his final incarnation as Gautama Buddha). The *Jataka* are attached to the *Tripitaka* ("Three Baskets"), or canon of Theravada Buddhism, as commentaries on a collection of verses in that canon. Their ultimate origin is probably in popular legends and fables.

Between 1063 and 1081, the *Ocean of Story* (*Kathasaritsgara*) was composed. This vast, versified compendium of stories is in Sanskrit, but it is supposed to be based (with many liberties taken by the composer) on a very early work, perhaps third century, in the Paisachi dialect. The Paisachi original was considered an "inspired work": its author presumably overheard the god Shiva tell the stories to his wife. The work is a *katha;* that is, one of the heroes tells his own story. In telling it, he also tells stories told to him by others who, in the course of their narrations, may tell stories told to them by still others, and so on.

The story is one of the most dynamic literary forms in modern India, and the number and quality available made it difficult to make a selection for this anthology. The Tagore story originally was done in Bengali; the other two were originally composed in English. Thus they illustrate

[1] Alex Preminger *et al., op. cit.*, p. 387.

one of the most interesting features of modern Indian literature—its Indo-Anglican component. One of them, "Karma," also presents, beautifully and poignantly, the dilemma of some modern Anglo-Indians.

"Bidpai"

The author of the collection of Sanskrit "beast fables," called *Panchatantra,* is usually identified as "Bidpai"—which may just mean "Wise man." The *Panchatantra* was probably compiled before A.D. 500 and it was introduced into European literature via an Arabic version. It is supposed to derive from Buddhist sources and to have been used as a manual for the education of the sons of royalty. It is written mainly in prose, with interspersed aphoristic verses.

THE PANCHATANTRA

Story 5: Heron and Crab

In a certain region there was a lake that was full of all kinds of fish. And a certain heron, who had come to old age and was unable to kill fish, made his home there. So he went to the edge of the lake and made himself appear dejected, and waited. There was a crab there, who was surrounded by many fish; and he said: "Uncle, why are you not trying to get food today as you used to?" The heron said: "I am an eater of fish; so I will speak to you without guile. Heretofore I have sustained my life by getting hold of you. At present, my means of livelihood is this day destroyed; that is why I am downcast." Said he: "Uncle, how is that?" The heron said:

"Today some fishermen passed near this lake and said: 'This lake has plenty of fish; we will throw the net into it tomorrow.' Then one of them said: 'There are other lakes near the town which we have not yet visited; we will visit them and then come back here.' So, my friend, you are all as good as done for, and I also am ruined, because my source of livelihood will be cut off. And that is why I am so grieved that I am abstaining from food today." Then the crab told this to the fish. Thereupon all the fish came together and said to the heron: "From the very source whence danger is traditionally said to come, a means of escape may also come. So be so good as to save us!" The heron said: "I am a bird and cannot cope with men. However, I will convey you one at a time from this lake to another pond, that is not shallow." Thereupon, because they were so frightened they trusted in him and said to him: "Little father! Brother! Uncle! Take me! Me first!" So that villain took the fish one after another and threw them down on a flat rock not far away, and ate them one at a time, and enjoyed himself vastly. But the crab was in deadly fear of losing his life, and repeatedly implored him: "Uncle, pray be good enough to save me, too, from the jaws of death." But that wretched creature thought: I am tired of this monotonous fish-meat; I will taste the delicious meat of this (crab), which I have never had before. Then he picked up the crab and flew through the air, not going near a single pool of water, until he was about to throw him down on that rock on which he did the killing, when the crab caught sight of the pile of bones of the fish that had been eaten already. And at that he thought: This villain has tricked and eaten the fish. So what would be a timely thing to do now? At any rate:

When a wise man is attacked and sees no escape for himself, then he dies fighting along with his foe.

So the foolish heron, who knew nothing about the grip of the crab's pincers, got his head cut off by the crab. But the crab took the heron's neck, like a lotus stem, and very slowly crawled back to that same lake where the fish were. And they said to him: "Brother, where is our uncle yonder?" Then he said: "He is dead. Here is the villain's head. By his trickery he ate many of your companions; but he met his death through me."

Story 6: Lion and Hare

In a certain forest region there was a lion named Haughty. And he kept up a continuous slaughter of the beasts. Then all the beasts came together and humbly addressed the king of beasts: "Sire, what profit is there in this pitiless and purposeless slaughtering of all the beasts, which endangers your lordship's prospects in the next world? It is evident that we are utterly undone (by it), and you also will fail of sustenance, so that it is fatal to both parties. So grant us this favor. We ourselves will send to your lordship for your food one wild creature every day, from each tribe in turn." The lion said: "Agreed." From that time on they sent him a single beast each day, and he continually ate the same. Now once upon a time as the lot passed from tribe to tribe it came the turn of a hare. But he, when all the beasts sent him forth, reflected: This means the end of me; I am entering the jaws of death. What now would be a timely thing for me to do? Yet after all, is anything impossible for the clever? So I will kill the lion by craft. Thereupon he proceeded very slowly, so that he arrived too late for dinner time. But the lion, his throat lean with hunger, was filled with rage and said to him furiously: "No matter how angry one is, killing is the worst thing one can do! You are a dead creature this day. Tell me, why this delay on your part?" Then the hare bowed and said courteously: "My lord, it is not my fault. As I was coming along another lion stopped me on the road and was going to eat me. And I said: 'I am going to our lord the lion Haughty, to serve as his dinner.' Then he said: 'That Haughty is a thief. So go and call him and return quickly, that whichever of us two shall prove himself king by his prowess may eat all of these beasts.' So I have come to report this to my lord." Hearing this the lion said angrily: "How can there be another lion here in this wood ruled by my right arm! Go and show me the scoundrel quickly!" The hare said: "In that case come, my lord, and I will show him to you." But he, the hare, took him and showed him a deep well full of clear water, saying: "Look there! There he is!" Then that fool of a lion saw his own image in the water, and thought: This is that rival of mine, and was furiously angry. And he roared his lion's roar. Thereupon a roar of redoubled strength came back out of the well, because of the echo from it. And when the lion heard this roar, he thought: He must be exceedingly strong! And he hurled himself upon him and perished. But the hare, being overjoyed himself and having brought joy to all the beasts, received their grateful thanks and dwelt in that wood in peace.

Franklin Egerton

Rabindranath Tagore
(1861–1941)

Son of a very wealthy Bengali family, Tagore wrote plays, poems, novels, short stories, essays, and works on philosophy; and he set his own poems to music. His philosophical work was well received by Indian intellectuals, his plays and poems were loved by the common people. He wrote in Bengali but translated many of his works into English himself. Tagore won the Nobel Prize in 1913.

MASHI AND OTHER STORIES

Subha

When the girl was given the name of Subhashini,[1] who could have guessed that she would prove dumb? Her two elder sisters were Sukeshini[2] and Suhasni,[3] and for the sake of uniformity her father named his youngest girl Subhashini. She was called Subha for short.

Her two elder sisters had been married with the usual cost and difficulty, and now the youngest daughter lay like a silent weight upon the heart of her parents. All the world seemed to think that, because she did not speak, therefore she did not feel; it discussed her future and its own anxiety

[1] Sweetly speaking.
[2] Lovely locked.
[3] Sweetly smiling.

freely in her presence. She had understood from her earliest childhood that God had sent her like a curse to her father's house, so she withdrew herself from ordinary people, and tried to live apart. If only they would all forget her she felt she could endure it. But who can forget pain? Night and day her parents' minds were aching on her account. Especially her mother looked upon her as a deformity in herself. To a mother, a daughter is a more closely intimate part of herself than a son can be, and a fault in her is a source of personal shame. Banikantha, Subha's father, loved her rather better than his other daughters; her mother regarded her with aversion as a stain upon her own body.

If Subha lacked speech, she did not lack a pair of large dark eyes, shaded with long lashes; and her lips trembled like a leaf in response to any thought that rose in her mind.

When we express our thought in words, the medium is not found easily. There must be a process of translation, which is often inexact, and then we fall into error. But black eyes need no translating; the mind itself throws a shadow upon them. In them thought opens or shuts, shines forth, or goes out in darkness, hangs steadfast like the setting moon, or, like the swift and restless lightning, illumines all quarters of the sky. They who from birth have had no other speech than the trembling of their lips learn a language of the eyes, endless in expression, deep as the sea, clear as the heavens, wherein play dawn and sunset, light and shadow. The dumb have a lonely grandeur like Nature's own. Wherefore the other children almost dreaded Subha, and never played with her. She was silent and companionless as noontide.

The hamlet where she lived was Chandipur. Its river, small for a river of Bengal, kept to its narrow bounds like a daughter of the middle class. This busy streak of water never overflowed its banks, but went about its duties as though it were a member of every family in the villages beside it. On either side were houses and banks shaded with trees. So stepping from her queenly throne, the river goddess became a garden deity of each home, and forgetful of herself, performed her task of endless benediction with swift and cheerful foot.

Banikantha's house looked upon the stream. Here Nature fulfilled her want of speech, and spoke for her. The murmur of the brook, the voice of the village folk, the songs of the boatmen, the crying of the birds, and rustle of trees mingled, and were one with the trembling of her heart. They became one vast wave of sound, which beat upon her restless soul. This murmur and movement of Nature were the dumb girl's language; that speech of the dark eyes, which the long lashes shaded, was the language of the world about her. From the trees, where the cicadas chirped, to the quiet stars there was nothing but signs and gestures, weeping and sighing. And in the deep midnoon, when the boatmen and fisherfolk had gone to their dinner, when the villagers slept, and birds were still, when the ferry-boats were idle, when the great busy world paused in its toil, and became suddenly a lonely, awful giant, then beneath the vast impressive heavens there were only dumb Nature and a dumb girl, sitting very silent—one under the spreading sunlight, the other where a small tree cast its shadow.

But Subha was not altogether without friends. In the stall were two cows, Sarbbashi and Panguli. They had never heard their names from her lips, but they knew her footfall. Though she had no words, she murmured lovingly and they understood her gentle murmuring better than all speech. When she fondled them or scolded or coaxed them, they understood her better than men could do. Subha would come to the shed, and throw her arms around Sarbbashi's neck; she would rub her cheek against her friends, and Panguli would turn her great kind eyes and lick her face. Whenever she heard any words that hurt her, she would come to these dumb friends out of due time. It was as though they guessed her anguish of spirit from her quiet look of sadness. Coming close to her, they would rub their horns softly against her arms, and in dumb, puzzled fashion try to comfort her. Besides these two, there were goats and a kitten; but Subha had not the same equality of friendship with them, though they showed the same attachment. Every time it got a chance, night or day, the kitten would jump into her lap, and settle down to slumber, and show its appreciation of an aid to sleep as Subha drew her soft fingers over its neck and back.

Subha had a comrade also among the higher animals, and it is hard to say what were the girl's relations with him, for he could speak, and his gift of speech left them without any common language. He was the youngest boy of the Gosains, Pratap by name, an idle fellow. After long effort, his parents had abandoned the hope that he would ever make his living. Now wastrels have this advantage, that, though their own folk disapprove of them, they are generally popular with everyone else. Having no work to chain them, they become public property. Just as every town needs an open space where all may breathe, so a village needs two or three gentlemen of leisure, who can give time to all; so that, if we are lazy and want a companion, one is to hand.

Pratap's chief ambition was to catch fish. He managed to waste a lot of time this way, and might be seen almost any afternoon so employed. It was thus most often that he met Subha. Whatever he was about, he liked a companion: and, when one is catching fish, a silent companion is best of all. Pratap respected Subha for her taciturnity, and, as everyone called her Subha, he showed his affection by calling her Su. Subha used to sit beneath a tamarind, and Pratap, a little distance off, would cast his line. Pratap took with him a small allowance of betel, and Subha prepared it for him. And I think that, sitting and gazing a long while, she desired ardently to bring some great help to Pratap, to be of real aid, to prove by any means that she was not a useless burden to the world. But there was nothing to do. Then she turned to the Creator in prayer for some rare power, that by an astonishing miracle she might startle Pratap into exclaiming: "My! I never dreamed our Su could have done this!"

Only think! If Subha had been a water nymph, she might have risen slowly from the river, bringing the gem of a snake's crown to the landing place. Then Pratap, leaving his paltry fishing, might dive into the lower world, and see there, on a golden bed in a palace of silver, whom else but dumb little Su, Banikantha's child! Yes, our Su, the only daughter of the king of that shining city of jewels! But that might not be, it was impossible. Not that anything is really impossible, but Su had been born, not into the royal house of Patalpur,[1] but into Banikantha's family, and she knew no means of astonishing the Gosains' boy.

[1] The Lower World

Gradually she grew up. Gradually she began to find herself. A new inexpressible consciousness like a tide from the central places of the sea, when the moon is full, swept through her. She saw herself, questioned herself, but no answer came that she could understand.

Once upon a time, late on a night of full moon, she slowly opened her door, and peeped out timidly. Nature, herself at full moon, like lonely Subha, was looking down on the sleeping earth. Her strong young life beat within her; joy and sadness filled her being to its brim; she reached the limits even of her own illimitable loneliness, nay, passed beyond them. Her heart was heavy, and she could not speak! At the skirts of this silent, troubled Mother stood a silent, troubled girl.

The thought of her marriage filled her parents with an anxious care. People blamed them, and even talked of making them outcasts. Banikantha was well off; they had fish curry twice daily; and consequently he did not lack enemies. Then the women interfered, and Bani went away for a few days. Presently he returned, and said: "We must go to Calcutta."

They got ready to go to this strange country. Subha's heart was heavy with tears, like a mist-wrapped dawn. With a vague fear that had been gathering for days, she dogged her father and mother like a dumb animal. With her large eyes wide open, she scanned their faces as though she wished to learn something. But not a word did they vouchsafe. One afternoon in the midst of all this, as Pratap was fishing, he laughed: "So then, Su, they have caught your bridegroom and you are going to be married! Mind you don't forget me altogether!" Then he turned his mind again to his fish. As a stricken doe looks in the hunter's face, asking in silent agony: "What have I done to you?" so Subha looked at Pratap. That day she sat no longer beneath her tree. Banikantha, having finished his nap, was smoking in his bedroom when Subha dropped down at his feet and burst out weeping as she gazed toward him. Banikantha tried to comfort her, and his cheek grew wet with tears.

It was settled that on the morrow they should go to Calcutta. Subha went to the cow shed to bid farewell to her childhood's comrades. She fed them with her hand; she clasped their necks; she looked into their faces; and tears fell fast from the eyes that spoke for her. That night was the tenth of the moon. Subha left her room, and flung herself down on her grassy couch beside her dear river. It was as if she were throwing her arms about Earth, her strong, silent mother, and trying to say: "Do not let me leave you, Mother. Put your arms about me, as I have put mine about you, and hold me fast."

One day in a house in Calcutta, Subha's mother dressed her up with great care. She imprisoned her hair, knotting it up in laces; she hung her about with ornaments and did her best to kill her natural beauty. Subha's eyes filled with tears. Her mother, fearing they would grow swollen with weeping, scolded her harshly, but the tears disregarded the scolding. The bridegroom came with a friend to inspect the bride. Her parents were dizzy with anxiety and fear when they saw the god arrive to select the beast for his sacrifice. Behind the stage, the mother called her instructions aloud, and increased her daughter's weeping twofold, before she sent her into the examiner's presence. The great man, after scanning her a long time, observed: "Not so bad."

He took special note of her tears, and thought she must have a tender heart. He put it to her credit in the account, arguing that the heart, which today was distressed at leaving her parents, would presently prove a useful possession. Like the oyster's pearls, the child's tears only increased her value, and he made no other comment.

The almanac was consulted, and the marriage took place on an auspicious day. Having delivered over their dumb girl into another's hands, Subha's parents returned home. Thank God! Their caste in this and their safety in the next world were assured! The bridegroom's work lay in the west, and shortly after their marriage he took his wife thither.

In less than ten days everyone knew that the bride was dumb! At least, if anyone did not, it was not her fault, for she deceived no one. Her eyes told them everything, though no one understood her. She looked on every hand; she found no speech; she missed the faces, familiar from birth, of those who had understood a dumb girl's language. In her silent heart there sounded an endless, voiceless weeping, which only the Searcher of Hearts could hear.

Using both eyes and ears *this* time, her lord made another careful examination, using his ears this time as well as his eyes, and married a second wife who could speak.

Translated from the original Bengali by various writers.

Mulk Raj Anand
(b. 1905)

THE BARBER'S TRADE UNION
(To John Lehmann)

Among the makers of modern India, Chandu, the barber boy of our village, has a place which will be denied him unless I press for the recognition of his contribution to history. Chandu's peculiar claim to recognition rested, to tell the truth, on an exploit of which he did not know the full significance. But then, unlike most great men of India today, he had no very exaggerated notion of his own importance, though he shared with them a certain naïve egotism that was sometimes disconcerting and sometimes rather charming.

I knew Chandu ever since the days when he wore a piece of rag in the middle of his naked, distended-bellied body, and when we wallowed together in the mire of the village lanes, playing at soldiering, shopkeeping, or clerking, and other little games which we invented for the delectation of our two selves and of our mothers, who alone of all the elders condescended to notice us.

Chandu was my senior by about six months, and he always took the lead in all matters. And I willingly followed, because truly he was a genius at catching wasps, and at pressing the poison out of their tails, at tying their tiny legs to cotton thread and flying them, while I always got stung on the cheeks if I dared to go anywhere near the platform of the village well where these insects settled on the puddles to drink water.

When we grew up he still seemed to me the embodiment of perfection, because he could make and fly paper kites of such intricate design and of such balance as I could never achieve.

To be sure, he was not so good at doing sums at school as I was, perhaps because his father apprenticed him early to the hereditary profession of the barber's caste and sent him out haircutting in the village. He had no time for the home tasks that our schoolmaster gave us. But he was better than I at reciting poetry, any day, for not only did he remember by rote the verses in the textbook, but he could repeat the endless pages of prose in that book so that they seemed like poetry.

My mother resented the fact that Chandu won a scholarship at school while I had to pay fees to be taught. And she constantly dissuaded me from playing with him, saying that Chandu was a low-caste barber's son and that I ought to keep up the status of my caste and class. But whatever innate ideas I had inherited from my forefathers, I certainly hadn't inherited any sense of superiority. Indeed, I was always rather ashamed of the red caste mark that my mother put on my forehead every morning, and of the formalized pattern of the *uchkin,* the tight cotton trousers, the gold-worked shoes, and the silk turban in which I dressed; and I longed for the right to wear all the spectacular conglomeration of clothes that Chandu wore—a pair of khaki shorts that the retired Subedar had given him, a frayed black velvet waistcoat, decorated all over with shell buttons, and a round felt cap that had once belonged to Lalla Hukam Chand, the lawyer of our village.

And I envied Chandu the freedom of movement he enjoyed after his father died of plague. For then he would do the round of shaving and haircutting at the houses of the high-caste notables in the morning, bathe and dress, and then steal a ride to town, six miles away, on the footrest of the closed carriage in which Lalla Hukam Chand traveled to town.

But Chandu was kind to me. He knew that I was seldom taken to town, and that I had to trudge three weary miles to a secondary school in the big village of Joadiala with the fear of God in my heart, while he had been completely absolved from the ordeal of being flogged by cruel masters as he had left school after his father's death. So he always brought me some gift or other from the town—a paint brush, or gold ink, or white chalk, or a double-edged penknife to sharpen pencils with; and he would entertain me with long merry descriptions of the variety of things he saw in the bazaars of civilization.

He was particularly detailed in his description of the wonderful English styles in clothes that he saw the Sahibs and the lawyers, the *chaprasis* and the policemen wearing at the District Court, where he had to wait for the journey home at the back of Lalla Hukam Chand's phaeton. And, once or twice, he expressed to me a secret wish he had to steal some money from the pitcher where his mother kept the emoluments of his professional skill, to buy himself a rig-out like that of Kalan Khan, the dentist, who, he said, performed miracles in the town, fitting people with rows of teeth and even new eyes. He described to me the appearance of Kalan Khan, a young man with hair parted on one side, and dressed in a starched shirt, with an ivory collar and bow tie, a black coat and striped trousers, and a wonderful rubber overcoat and pumps. And he recounted to me the skill with which this magician unpacked an Angrezi leather handbag and flourished his shining steel instruments.

Then he asked my advice on the question of whether, as a barber educated to the fifth primary class, he would not look more dignified if he, too, wore a dress in the style of Dr. Kalan Khan, "for though I am not a highly educated doctor," he said, "I learned how to treat pimples, boils, and cuts on people's bodies from my father, who learned them from his father before him."

I agreed with his project and encouraged him with the enthusiasm I felt for everything my hero thought or did.

One day I was thrilled to find Chandu at the door of my house in the morning. He was dressed up in a white turban, a white rubber coat (a little too big for him, but nevertheless very splendid), a pair of pumps in which I could see my face reflected in clear silhouette, and he had a leather bag in his hand. He was setting off on his round and had come to show me how grand he looked in his new rig-out.

"Marvelous!" I said. "Marvelous!"

And he rushed off toward the house of the landlord, whom he shaved every morning, myself following admiringly behind.

There were not many people in the street at this time. So

I alone witnessed the glory of Chandu, dressed up as a doctor, except, of course, that he himself seemed rather self-conscious as he strutted up the street, carefully avoiding the taint of cow-dung cakes, which the village women stuck to the walls, and the dirty water that flowed through the drains. But as we entered the home of the landlord we met Devi, the landlord's little son, who clapped his hands with joy and shouted to announce the coming of Chandu, the barber, in a beautiful heroic dress like that of the Padre Sahib of the Mission School.

"Ram! Ram! Ram!" said Bijay Chand, the burly landlord, touching the sacred thread that hung over his ear, since he had just been to the lavatory. "The son of a pig! He is bringing a leather bag of cowhide into our house and a coat of the marrow of, I don't know, some other animal, and those evil black Angrezi shoes. Get out! Get out! You son of a devil! You will defile my religion. I suppose you have no fear of anyone now that your father is dead!"

"But I am wearing the clothes of a doctor, Jagirdar Sahib," said Chandu.

"Go away, you swine, go away and wear clothes befitting your low status as a barber, and don't let me see you practicing any of your newfangled notions, or else I will have you flogged!"

"But Rai Bijay Chand Sahib!" Chandu appealed.

"Get away! Get away! You useless one!" the landlord shouted. "Don't come any nearer, or we will have to treat the whole house with the sacred cow dung to purify it."

Chandu returned. His face was flushed. He was completely taken aback. He did not look at me because of the shame he felt at being insulted before me whose hero he knew he was. And he rushed toward the shop of Thanu Ram, the Sahukar of the village, who kept a grocer's store at the corner of the lane.

"Go to Pandit Parmanand!" I shouted after him. "And tell him that these garments you are wearing are not unclean."

"Ho, so you are in league with him," said Pandit Parmanand, emerging from the landlord's home, where he had been apparently summoned to discuss this unholy emergency. "You boys have been spoiled by the school education that you have got. It may be all right for you to wear those things because you are going to be a learned man, but what right has that low-caste boy to such apparel? He has got to touch our beards, our heads, and our hands. He is defiled enough by God. Why does he want to become more defiled? You are a high-caste boy. And he is a low-caste devil! He is a rogue!"

Chandu had heard this. He did not look back and ran in a flurry, as if he were set on some purpose that occupied him more than the abuse which had been the cause of his flight.

Chandu whistled for me that afternoon in the usual code whistle we had arranged to evade the reproaches of interfering elders that our association often provoked.

"Come for a walk to the bazaar," he said. "I want to talk to you." And hardly had I joined him when he began: "Do you know, I earned a rupee shaving and haircutting near the court this morning. If I hadn't had to come back on the back bar of Hukam Chand's carriage early in the afternoon, I should have earned more. But I am going to teach these orthodox idiots a lesson. I am going on strike. I shall not go to their houses to attend to them. I am going to buy a Japanese bicycle from the gambling son of Lalla Hukam Chand for five rupees, and I shall learn to ride it and I will go to town on it every day. Won't I look grand, riding on a bicycle, with my overcoat, my black leather shoes, and a white turban on my head, specially as there is a peg in front of the two-wheeled carriage for hanging my tool bag?"

"Yes," I agreed, greatly thrilled, not because I imagined the glory of Chandu seated on a bicycle, but because I felt myself nearer the goal of my own ambition; since I felt that if Chandu acquired a bicycle he would at least let me ride to town on the elongated bolt at the back wheel or on the front bar, if he didn't let me learn to ride myself and lend me the machine every now and then.

Chandu negotiated the deal about the bicycle with an assurance that seemed to me a revelation of his capacity for business such as I had never suspected in him, from the reckless way he spent his money. And then he said to me in a confidential voice: "You wait for another day or two. I shall show you something that will make you laugh as you have never laughed before."

"Tell me now," I insisted, with an impatience sharpened by the rhythm of the excitement with which the spirit of his adventure filled my being.

"No, you wait," he said. "I can only give you a hint at the moment. It is a secret that only a barber can know. Now let me get on with the job of learning to handle this machine. You hold it while I get on it, and I think it will be all right."

"But," I said, "this is not the way to learn to ride a bicycle. My father learned to ride from the peg at the back, and my brother learned to ride by first trying to balance on the pedal."

"Your father is a top-heavy baboon!" said Chandu. "And your brother is a long-legged spider.

"I," he continued, "was born, my mother tells me, upside down."

"All right," I said. And I held the bicycle for him. But while my gaze concentrated with admiration on the brilliant sheen of the polished bars, I lost my grip and Chandu fell on the other side with a thud, along with the machine.

There were peals of laughter from the shop of the Sahukar, where several peasants congregated round the figure of the landlord. And then the Sahukar could be heard shouting: "Serves you right, you rascally son of the iron age! Break your bones and die, you upstart! You won't come to your senses otherwise!"

Chandu hung his head with shame, and muttered an oath at me: "You fool, you are no good!" though I had thought that he would grip me by the neck and give me a good thrashing for being the cause of his discomfiture. Then he looked at me, smiled embarrassedly, and said: "We will see who has the last laugh, I or they."

"I will hold the machine tightly this time," I said earnestly, and I picked it up from where it lay.

"Yes, break your bones, you swine," came the landlord's call.

"Don't you care!" Chandu said to me. "I will show them." And he mounted the bicycle as I exerted all my strength to hold it tight. Then he said: "Let go!"

I released my grip.

He had pressed the pedal with a downward pressure of his right foot, hard, and as the wheels revolved, he swayed dangerously to one side. But he had pushed the other pedal now. The machine balanced, inclining to the right a little, so that I saw Chandu lift his rump from the saddle in the most frightening manner. He hung precariously for a moment. His handles wobbled dangerously. He was tottering. At this juncture a mixed noise of laughter and sarcasm arose from the congregation at the shop and I thought that Chandu would come to grief with this confusion, if not on account of his utter incapacity. By a curious miracle, however, Chandu's feet had got into the right rhythm for pedaling and his handle had adjusted itself to his stiff hands, and he rode off with me running behind him, bursting myself with enthusiastic "Shabashes."

A half-mile run and he repeated the trick.

Though I was very eager to share the joy of his newly acquired skill, I didn't see Chandu the next day, as I was being taken to see my aunts in Verka, straight from school.

But on the third day he called for me and said that he would show me the joke he had talked of the other day. I followed quickly, asking the while: "Tell me, what is it all about?"

"Look," he said, hiding behind the oven of the village potter. "Do you see the congregation of men in the Sahukar's shop? Try and see who's there."

I explored the various faces, and for a moment I was quite baffled.

"Only the peasants sitting round waiting for the landlord," I said.

"Look again, idiot," he said, "and see. The landlord is there, his long-jawed face dirtied by the white scum of his unshaved beard."

"Ha! Ha!" I shouted hilariously, struck by the contradiction of the big thick moustache (which I knew the landlord dyed) with the prickly white bush on his jowls. "Ha! Ha!" I roared. "A sick lion! He looks seedy!"

"Shh!" warned Chandu. "Don't make a row! But look at the Sahukar. He looks like a leper with the brown tinge of tobacco on his walrus moustache, which I once used to trim. Now you run past the shop and call 'Beavers, beavers!' They can't say anything to you!"

I was too impetuous a disciple of the impish Chandu to wait to deliberate.

"Beavers! Beavers! Beavers!" I shouted as I ran past the shop to the edge of the platform by the banyan tree.

The peasants who were gathered round the shop burst out laughing, as they had apparently been itching to, for they had noticed the strong growths on the elders' faces, though they had not dared to say anything.

"Catch him, catch him, the little rogue!" shouted the Sahukar. "He is in league with that barber boy, Chandu!"

But of course I had climbed up the banyan tree, from which I jumped on to the wall of the temple and shouted my slogan at the priest.

The rumor about the barber boy's strike spread, and jokes about the unkempt beards of the elders of the village became current in every home. Even those who were of high castes, even the members of the families of the elders, began to giggle with laughter at the shabby appearance of the great ones and made rude remarks about their persons. And it was said that at least the landlord's wife threatened to run away with somebody, because, being younger than her husband by twenty years, she had borne with him as long as he kept himself in trim, but was now disgusted with him beyond the limits of reconciliation.

Chandu did good business in town during these days and saved money, even though he bought new clothes and new tools for himself and gave me various presents.

The village elders threatened to have him sent to prison for his offenses, and ordered his mother to force him to obey before they committed him to the police for a breach of the peace.

But Chandu's mother had for the first time in her life touched the edge of prosperity, and she told them all what she thought of them in a language even plainer than that in which she had always addressed them.

Then they thought of getting the barber of Verka to come and attend them, and offered him an anna instead of the two pice they had usually paid to Chandu.

Chandu, however, had conceived a new notion this time, newer than those he had ever thought of before. Having seen the shop of Nringan Das, the barber of the town, he had applied his brain to the scheme of opening a shop on the wayside at the head of the bazaar, in partnership with his cousin, the barber of Verka, and with Dhunoo and the other barbers within a range of seven miles from his village. He proposed his new idea to his cousin and Dhunoo and all the other barbers at a special meeting of his craft, and, by that gift of the gab he had, besides his other qualities of head and heart, he convinced them all that it was time the elders of the village came to them to be shaved rather than that they should dance attendance upon their lords and masters.

Rajkot District Barber Brothers' Hairdressing and Shaving Saloon has been followed by many other active trade unions of working men in our parts.

Khushwant Singh

(b. 1915)

KARMA

Sir Mohan Lal looked at himself in the mirror of a first-class waiting room at the railway station. The mirror was obviously made in India. The red oxide at its back had come off at several places and long lines of translucent glass cut across its surface. Sir Mohan smiled at the mirror with an air of pity and patronage.

"You are so very much like everything else in this country, inefficient, dirty, indifferent," he murmured.

The mirror smiled back at Sir Mohan.

"You are a bit of all right, old chap," it said. "Distinguished, efficient—even handsome. That neatly trimmed moustache, the suit from Saville Row with the carnation in the buttonhole, the aroma of eau de cologne, talcum powder, and scented soap all about you! Yes, old fellow, you are a bit of all right."

Sir Mohan threw out his chest, smoothed his Balliol tie for the umpteenth time, and waved a good-bye to the mirror.

He glanced at his watch. There was still time for a quick one.

"Koi Hai?"

A bearer in white livery appeared through a wire gauze door.

"Ek Chota," ordered Sir Mohan, and sank into a large cane chair to drink and ruminate.

Outside the waiting room Sir Mohan Lal's luggage lay

piled along the wall. On a small gray steel trunk Lachmi, Lady Mohan Lal, sat chewing a betel leaf and fanning herself with a newspaper. She was short and fat and in her middle forties. She wore a dirty white sari with a red border. On one side of her nose glistened a diamond nose ring, and she had several gold bangles on her arms. She had been talking to the bearer until Sir Mohan had summoned him inside. As soon as he had gone, she hailed a passing railway coolie.

"Where does the zenana stop?"

"Right at the end of the platform."

The coolie flattened his turban to make a cushion, hoisted the steel trunk on his head, and moved down the platform. Lady Lal picked up her brass tiffin carrier and ambled along behind him. On the way she stopped by a hawker's stall to replenish her silver betel-leaf case, and then joined the coolie. She sat down on her steel trunk (which the coolie had put down) and started talking to him.

"Are the trains very crowded on these lines?"

"These days all trains are crowded, but you'll find room in the zenana."

"Then I might as well get over the bother of eating."

Lady Lal opened the brass carrier and took out a bundle of cramped *chapatties* and some mango pickle. While she ate, the coolie sat opposite her on his haunches, drawing lines in the gravel with his finger.

"Are you traveling alone, sister?"

"No, I am with my master, brother. He is in the waiting room. He travels first class. He is a vizier and a barrister, and meets so many officers and Englishmen in the trains—and I am only a native woman. I can't understand English and don't know their ways, so I keep to my zenana interclass."

Lachmi chatted away merrily. She was fond of a little gossip and had no one to talk to at home. Her husband never had any time to spare for her. She lived in the upper story of the house and he on the ground floor. He did not like her poor illiterate relatives hanging about his bungalow, so they never came. He came up to her once in a while at night and stayed for a few minutes. He just ordered her about in anglicized Hindustani, and she obeyed passively. These nocturnal visits had, however, borne no fruit.

The signal came down and the clanging of the bell announced the approaching train. Lady Lal hurriedly finished off her meal. She got up, still licking the stone of the pickled mango. She emitted a long, loud belch as she went to the public tap to rinse her mouth and wash her hands. After washing, she dried her mouth and hands with the loose end of her sari, and walked back to her steel trunk, belching and thanking the gods for the favor of a filling meal.

The train steamed in. Lachmi found herself facing an almost empty inter-class zenana compartment next to the guard's van, at the tail end of the train. The rest of the train was packed. She heaved her squat, bulky frame through the door and found a seat by the window. She produced a two-anna bit from a knot in her sari and dismissed the coolie. She then opened her betel case and made herself two betel leaves filled with a red-and-white paste, minced betel nuts and cardamoms. These she thrust into her mouth till her cheeks bulged on both sides. Then she rested her chin on her hands and sat gazing idly at the jostling crowd on the platform.

The arrival of the train did not disturb Sir Mohan Lal's sangfroid. He continued to sip his Scotch and ordered the bearer to tell him when he had moved the luggage to a first-class compartment. Excitement, bustle, and hurry were exhibitions of bad breeding, and Sir Mohan was eminently well bred. He wanted everything "tickety-boo" and orderly. In his five years abroad, Sir Mohan had acquired the manners and attitudes of the upper classes. He rarely spoke Hindustani. When he did, it was like an Englishman's—only the very necessary words and properly anglicized. But he fancied his English, finished and refined at no less a place than the University of Oxford. He was fond of conversation, and like a cultured Englishman he could talk on almost any subject: books, politics, people. How frequently had he heard English people say that he spoke like an Englishman!

Sir Mohan wondered if he would be traveling alone. It was a cantonment and some English officers might be on the train. His heart warmed at the prospect of an impressive conversation. He never showed any sign of eagerness to talk to the English as most Indians did. Nor was he loud, aggressive, and opinionated like them. He went about his business with an expressionless matter-of-factness. He would retire to his corner by the window and get out a copy of *The Times.* He would fold it in a way in which the name of the paper was visible to others while he did the crossword puzzle. *The Times* always attracted attention. Someone would like to borrow it when he put it aside with a gesture signifying "I've finished with it." Perhaps someone would recognize his Balliol tie, which he always wore while traveling. That would open a vista leading to a fairyland of Oxford colleges, masters, dons, tutors, boat races, and rugger matches. If both *The Times* and the tie failed, Sir Mohan would *"Koi Hai"* his bearer to get the Scotch out. Whisky never failed with Englishmen. Then followed Sir Mohan's handsome gold cigarette case filled with English cigarettes. English cigarettes in India? How on earth did he get them? Sure he didn't mind? And Sir Mohan's understanding smile—of course he didn't. But could he use the Englishman as a medium to commune with his dear old England? Those five years of gray bags and gowns, of sports blazers and mixed doubles, of dinners at the Inns of Court and nights with Piccadilly prostitutes. Five years of a crowded glorious life. Worth far more than the forty-five in India with his dirty, vulgar countrymen, with sordid details of the road to success, of nocturnal visits to the upper story and all-too-brief sexual acts with obese old Lachmi, smelling of sweat and raw onions.

Sir Mohan's thoughts were disturbed by the bearer announcing the installation of the Sahib's luggage in a first-class coupé next to the engine. Sir Mohan walked to his coupé with a studied gait. He was dismayed. The compartment was empty. With a sigh he sat down in a corner and opened the copy of *The Times* he had read several times before.

Sir Mohan looked out of the window down the crowded platform. His face lit up as he saw two English soldiers trudging along, looking in all the compartments for room. They had their haversacks slung behind their backs and walked unsteadily. Sir Mohan decided to welcome them, even though they were entitled to travel only second class. He would speak to the guard.

One of the soldiers came up to the last compartment and

stuck his face through the window. He surveyed the compartment and noticed the unoccupied berth.

" 'Ere, Bill," he shouted, "one 'ere."

His companion came up, also looked in, and looked at Sir Mohan.

"Get the nigger out," he muttered to his companion.

They opened the door, and turned to the half-smiling, half-protesting Sir Mohan.

"Reserved!" yelled Bill.

"*Janta*—Reserved. Army—*Fauj*," exclaimed Jim, pointing to his khaki shirt.

"*Ek dum jao*—get out!"

"I say, I say, surely . . ." protested Sir Mohan in his Oxford accent.

The soldiers paused. It almost sounded like English, but they knew better than to trust their inebriated ears. The engine whistled and the guard waved his green flag.

They picked up Sir Mohan's suitcase and flung it onto the platform. Then followed his Thermos flask, suitcase, bedding, and *The Times*. Sir Mohan was livid with rage.

"Preposterous, preposterous," he shouted, hoarse with anger, "I'll have you arrested—guard, guard!"

Bill and Jim paused again. It did sound like English, but it was too much of the King's for them.

"Keep yer ruddy mouth shut!" And Jim struck Sir Mohan flat on the face.

The engine gave another short whistle and the train began to move. The soldiers caught Sir Mohan by the arms and flung him out of the train. He reeled backward, tripped on his bedding, and landed on the suitcase.

"Toodle-oo!"

Sir Mohan's feet were glued to the earth and he lost his speech. He stared at the lighted windows of the train going past him in quickening tempo. The tail end of the train appeared with a red light and the guard standing in the open doorway with the flags in his hands.

In the inter-class zenana compartment was Lachmi, fair and fat, on whose nose the diamond nose ring glistened against the station lights. Her mouth was bloated with betel saliva which she had been storing up to spit as soon as the train had cleared the station. As the train sped past the lighted part of the platform, Lady Lal spat and sent a jet of red dribble flying across like a dart.

Chapter 14
THE INDIAN NOVEL

The material in the present chapter has been chosen from a masterpiece of modern Indian, or, more accurately, Bengali, literature, *Pather Panchali.* "Pather" means of the road, and "panchali" means a long narrative poem. Panchalis form a large part of medieval Bengali literature and include the colloquial Bengali versions of the two great Indian epics (see pp. 372–375 and 401–403). Should Pather Panchali be translated "Epic of the Road"? "Saga of the Road"? Some authorities prefer "Song of the Road."

Pather Panchali became an important part of modern world culture a few years ago when a generation of Western filmgoers saw Satyajit Ray's film based on the novel, and knew at once they were seeing a masterpiece. The book is the story of life in a Bengali village. Modern Bengali writers have often taken the village as a theme or subject—or at least countersubject—rather than as a setting. Saratchandra Chatterji writes about the village realistically, almost sarcastically; Rabindranath Tagore idealizes it, perhaps sentimentalizes it. Bibhutibhushan Banerji, author of *Pather Panchali,* shows it to us, firmly and unvaryingly, through the eyes of a young boy and a young girl.

We learn from Banerji's diaries that the novel is quite autobiographical. Like the boy's (Opu's) father, his father was talented, intelligent, and (economically, at least) unsuccessful; like Opu's mother, his mother struggled all her life against grinding poverty. There was even an aged female relative in Banerji's house, as in Opu's.

Banerji was born in a village north of Calcutta. Although handicapped by his poverty, he nevertheless got a college education. He worked as a teacher; as an inspector for the Society for the Protection of Cattle; as a clerk; and as a teacher again. His fifty or so published works are mostly fiction, but they also include a Bengali grammar, a translation of *Ivanhoe*, and some works on astrology and on the occult.

Bibhutibhushan Banerji
(1899–1950)

PATHER PANCHALI

Chapter 13

Proshonno was the village schoolmaster. He ran a grocery shop as well as the school, and the school and grocery store were in adjoining rooms. There was no partition.

The classroom did not have any of the usual paraphernalia, except for a cane. Parents and schoolmaster alike believed the cane was the secret of education, and the schoolmaster had from parents the authority to use it as much as he liked so long as he didn't bend a boy's limb with it, or knock out his eye. Proshonno knew nothing about educational methods, and he did not have the proper equipment, but he was very good with the cane. None of his students was ever killed by it, or even blinded or lamed, and considering the way he laid about with the cane, that may be considered a miracle.

It was early January. This particular morning, Opu lay in his bed and waited for the sun to come up. The air was cold, and Opu lay wrapped in a quilt.

"Opu, get up! Hurry!" His mother came in.

"Today you're going to school. Daddy will take you. Aren't you happy? You'll have books and a slate. Now get up and go wash your face."

In the bed opened two very sleepy eyes. School! Opu stared at his mother, and the eyes got very big and round. Weren't only bad boys sent to school? He wasn't a boy who disobeyed his mother or fought with brothers and sisters. Why should he go to school?

After a while Shorbojoya came in.

"Opu, get up!" she said. "Go wash your face! I'm wrapping up some baked rice for you to take. You can eat it in school. Up, dear!"

Opu stuck out his tongue. He didn't believe what she said, and he wasn't going to do what she told him. He closed his eyes again. There was a funny little expression on his face. He did not move.

Then his father came in. That was the end of it. Opu got up. So he was going to have to go to school! It was his mother's fault. He knew it. He was not very nice to her. When she gave him the wrapped rice, he said, "You'll see! I won't come home!" He tried to sob.

"Oh, my!" his mother said. "You won't come home? Don't be silly! Enough of that!"

She smiled, put her hand under his chin, and kissed him.

"You'll learn a lot of things at school. You work hard, and when you grow up you can get a good job, and you'll earn a lot of money. No doubt about that!"

She turned to his father and said, "Tell the teacher to be easy on him."

He went to school with his father. Before his father left Opu there, he said, "Opu, I'll pick you up when school's out. Do your work, and listen to the teacher. And be good!"

Horihor turned and started walking home. Opu stood and watched him, watched him until his image disappeared around a curve in the road. Opu was alone. He felt as if he was in the middle of an ocean.

Opu sat and looked at the floor. When finally he looked up, he saw that Proshonno was weighing some salt for a customer. There were other boys sitting around Opu. The other boys sat on grass mats. They were reading something in an irritating sing-song voice. Opu did not like the metallic sound of their voices, and he didn't like the way their bodies moved forward and backward, forward and backward as they read. For some reason it made him feel scared.

There was only one other boy as small as Opu. This other boy sat by himself, leaning back against a pillar. The boy had brought a palm leaf to school to write on, but now he was chewing it.

There was a big boy with a mole on his cheek. He sat

and stared at something under the bench in the grocery store.

Two other boys sat in front of Opu; they had a slate and were playing "house" on it. "This is my cross," one of them whispered.

"This is my circle," said the other boy. And so they played the game, and the house got bigger.

Proshonno was still waiting on people buying groceries. The two boys watched him out of the corners of their eyes. Opu began to write letters on his slate. He wrote them very large.

Some time passed, Opu didn't know how much time. He was startled as he heard Proshonno call, "Phoni! What are you drawing on your slate?"

The two boys in front of Opu put their forearms over their slates. The teacher, however, had a sharp eye.

"Shotish," he said to the boy with the mole, "bring Phoni's slate here." The big boy fell on the two like a hawk, caught the slate, and carried it to Proshonno at the bench in the store.

"So! This is what you're doing! Shotish, bring them here. By their ears."

Shotish swooped again. And as he led the two boys to Proshonno, Opu saw the scared expression on their faces, and he began to giggle. He suppressed it, and then began to giggle again.

"Who's laughing?" the teacher said. "What do you think is funny, boy? Do you think this is a theater? A theater, boy? Is that what you think?"

A theater? What was a theater? Opu thought. He felt his face get cold with fear.

"Shotish," said the teacher, "get me a brick. There are some over there. Under the tamarind tree. Get a big one. I'll make him hold it on his head."

Now Opu was really scared. His throat was dry. But the brick, he found out when it came, was for the other boys. Because he was new, or because he was so young, the teacher was letting him off.

Eight other students attended the school in the afternoon. There were girls and boys. Everyone except Opu brought a mat to sit on. His mother had given him a worn old rug. There were no walls to the classroom. It was open on all four sides, and there was a fence to cut off the view.

Inside were students, sitting in rows; outside, there was only the jungle.

On the west, behind the house, there was an orchard. Proshonno had inherited it from his ancestors.

The sun was bright and warm that afternoon. Its warmth and brightness drifted into the schoolroom through the orchard, through the pomelo, mangosteen, guava, and mango trees. The sun lit up the room's bamboo pillars. You could not see any other house from there, only the orchard, the jungle, and the narrow path that led to the school.

The children were memorizing their lessons. This they did by reading aloud. The children's voices chanted in different keys, and the children leaned in and out while they chanted, as if this helped. Occasionally Proshonno's voice rose above the noise.

"Kebola! Why are you looking at his slate? Do you want your ears twisted? . . . Nutu, are you going to spend all your time wetting your eraser? One more time and I'll . . ."

Proshonno usually sat on a palm-leaf mat and leaned back against a pillar. He put oil on his hair, and behind his head on the pillar was a dark round spot.

Sometimes in the late afternoon, Dinu Palit and Raju Ray would walk over from the village. Opu liked to listen while they talked to Proshonno. It was a lot more interesting than his lesson.

Once Raju Ray said that when he was young he heard a proverb: "The goddess of wealth lives in business houses." So he opened a little tobacco shop in the Asharku market. (Opu listened intently.) Raju Ray opened the little shop's matting door and sat slicing up tobacco with a knife. At night he would go down to the river, wash, and eat fish soup from a little bowl. Sometimes he would light a clay lamp and sit and read the *Mahabhart* or his father's copy of Dashu Ray's ballad. At night during monsoon it got very dark outside. No one went or came these rainy nights; frogs croaked—in the pond behind his house. Beautiful! Opu decided that when he grew up he would open a little tobacco shop.

Sometimes Rajkrishna Shanyal would come over. He lived at the far end of the village and when he came, he told stories that seemed to Opu more moving and more imaginative. No matter what he talked about, even a very ordinary thing, Opu could see it and feel it. Shanyal liked to go here and there to see new things. He had been to Dvarka, to the Savitri hills, to Chandranath. And he didn't go alone, he took his wife and family with him. They stayed until Shanyal had spent all his money, and then they came home. Yet Shanyal loved home, too. At least it seemed so. You often saw him sitting in his room, smoking a flat-bottomed water pipe. Whether Shanyal loved home or not, these days, even in an old-fashioned village, you didn't see many people who would spend so much time at home. And from time to time people would see that Shanyal's door was locked, and nobody was around the compound. And people would say they had probably gone to the Vindhya hills, or to Chandranath again. And nobody would see Shanyal or his family for a while. Then one day, around noon, some neighbor might look out at an unexpected noise, and there Shanyal would be with his family and two loaded bullock carts: back from their travels. Soon Shanyal would be asking people to help him cut down the weeds and creepers in his yard—they might be three feet high by now—so he could get into his house.

When Opu saw him coming to the school, Shanyal always had a thick stick in his hand. "Proshonno!" Shanyal would say. "Here we are! How are you? Got that good web out again, unh? Catching many flies?"

This time, when Shanyal came, Opu was working on multiplication tables. He smiled happily, and edged toward where Shanyal had sat down on a palm-leaf mat. Opu got his books together and set them and his slate aside, as if school were over. There wouldn't be any more class today. Opu sat with his eyes open wide. He listened with a concentration as intense and definite as a hungry beggar's.

"You know where the indigo factory is?" said Shanyal. "On the road that goes up there, there's a place called Naltakuri's Jol. A long time ago, there was a villager named Chondor Hajra. Mati Hajra's brother. Well, Chondor Hajra went out beyond, to cut trees in the jungle. It was the monsoon season, and there were a lot of places where the rain had loosened up the earth, and there had been earth slides. Chondor saw something sticking up in one of the slides; looked like the top of a brass jar. He went over, and that's what it was, so he dug the jar up and took it home. What do you think was in it? It was full of old coins. That's why Chondor Hajra lived so long like a nobleman." Shanyal said that with his own eyes he had seen proof of these things.

Sometimes Shanyal told stories about his trips on the railroad. He told everybody where the Savitri hills were. Climbing them, his wife had found it pretty hard going. And once, when he was trying to give an offering at the Nabhigaya shrine, he had had a fight with the attendants. One place there they had some really good, well, *candies* to eat. Shanyal had mentioned their name, and to Opu it sounded like "pyranas." Opu laughed: funny word. But he remembered it. When he was grown up, he would have "pyranas" to eat.

And one day Shanyal told a story about some place (Opu couldn't remember its name) where lots of people used to live. Shanyal said that he and his friends, when it was getting pretty dark, were going through a tamarind forest. They were going to see "the Chika mosque" (Opu didn't know what that was; as he listened, it seemed to be an old deserted house). About dark, Shanyal and his friends came to "the Chika mosque" and went in. A swarm of little bats beat the air and flew past them. Opu could see it: the dark world, the jungle, nobody around, the broken door, the bats rushing by, the dark inside, dark as the west room in Ronu's house.

And the time Shanyal met a fakir who lived under a banyan tree. If you offered the fakir the pipe of opium to smoke, he got very happy, and asked you what kind of fruit you liked. You told him whatever it was, and the fakir said, "Go over to that tree, you'll find it." And you did, and the tree would be—if you'd said mangoes—a mango tree, but if you'd said something else, like "pomegranates," it would be a pomegranate tree; or a guava tree; or, if you had said bananas, hanging from it would be a bunch of bananas.

Raju Ray said, "Must have been some kind of magic. One time my uncle . . ."

Dinu Palit cut him off: "Magic? I know a real story about *magic*. It's not a hokey story. The thing really happened. I was there.

"You know Buddho, the carter? Works out of Beledanga. Maybe you don't know him, Raju, but Rajkrishra—you must have seen him around. He wore mules, wooden ones, tied to his feet. He was an old man the time I'm talking about, but you could see him at Nite the blacksmith's getting his plowshare sharpened. When he died he was a hundred. That was twenty-five years ago. Hands and wrists, ump! He was so strong *then* he could grip out any of us young men.

"Well, long time ago . . . I was about nineteen or twenty, I guess. We had bathed in the Ganges and were coming back from Chakda by cart. There was my aunt, and Ram—you know, Ononto Mukherji's nephew—and me. Ram lives at Khulna now.

"So there we were, near Kanashana in the open country. It was about sunset. Rajkrishna! You know what it's like there. Very isolated and scary place. Besides, we had a woman with us, and a lot of money. We were nervous, I'll tell you. There's a village there now, but at the time I'm talking about, nothing. You can guess what happened.

"Four men ran out at us, two from the left, two from the right. Big, strong, dark men. They grabbed the bamboo pole at the back of the cart. I tell you we were scared. We sat frozen. But the cart never stopped, just kept rolling, rolling, and the four men couldn't let go of the pole, they kept coming, coming along with us. Buddho turned his eye on them from time to time, I saw him do it. He gave us a sign not to say anything and not to be afraid.

"After a while we could see Nawabganj bazaar ahead, as the cart rolled slowly along, and then we could see the police station. The four toughs started shouting to Buddho.

" 'Sir, forgive us! We didn't know . . . please let us go . . .'

" 'Let you go?' said Buddho. 'Why should I let you go? Criminals! We're going to the station and you're going to get locked up.'

"The men continued to whine and wheedle, however, and finally Buddho said to them: 'Okay. I'll let you go if you swear not to do this again.'

"Suddenly the men could let go of the pole. They bent down and took the dust from Buddho's feet, and then they turned and ran away. I saw all this myself. What was it? I don't know. Buddho had some magic. When the four men took hold of the cart, they couldn't let go. They had to come on with the cart. Looked like they were nailed to it. So when it comes to magic . . ."

The stories went on. It got late. The sun was now low in the sky; long red rays lay between the trees around the school. Tailorbirds, heads thrown back, sat swinging on the vines that hung from jackfruit and *jagadumar* trees. Inside the air was heavy with smells. You could smell rush mats and old books and earth of the floor; you could smell the heavy odor of tobacco that had been sliced with Proshonno's big knife, and the wind carried other smells in from the trees and bushes.

One day something very strange and beautiful happened at school. In the afternoon, no one having come to visit with Proshonno (so that there could be no lazy talk and stories), the teacher gave a class instead. Opu was reading his primer when Proshonno said, "Get your slates. We're going to have dictation."

Proshonno began to dictate, although he spoke without a book. But Opu knew the words were not Proshonno's words: Proshonno was reciting, from his head, as from his head Opu could recite lines of Dashu Ray's ballad. Opu listened. He had never heard before so many beautiful words put together. He didn't understand it all. Too many long words he didn't know. But he could hear the words fall and rise like a melody, and though he did not understand it, he could feel syllables light and heavy come and go in rhythm, and the slow words, fast words, heavy words, light words, made him see a picture, beautiful but hazy, like something seen in a mist.

Mount Prasravan
rises high in the heart of Janasthan;
above its summit the sky
lies like a blue shining crown;
clouds, driven down by unstopping winds
from the upper air,
fall like a cape from its shoulders,
down its sides run the tall "forest-kings,"
cool, sweet-smelling, beautiful,
and the Godavari flows
a line of crystal around its feet.

Opu knew, but did not know how he knew, that the path he looked down now was the path, running through open country and vanishing, that he had seen two years before, on the Sarasvati festival, when he and his father had gone to see the blue-throated jay near the indigo factory. On either side of the path were many birds, and many trees, and many bushes he had never seen. That day Opu had stared a long time down the path. He had asked himself, Where does it go? He could not imagine any answer. His father said it was the Shonadanga road, that it went by Madhobpur and Dasghara to the ferry at Dhalrite. Opu did not believe it. It was not just a plain old road to the ferry at Dhalrite. It ran farther than that, it ran to the land of the *Ramayan* and the *Mahabharat*: the land that came into his mind whenever he looked at the top of the banyan tree.

Now, with Proshonno's dictation, Opu understood that path better. It ran on and on to Mount Prasravan in the heart of Janasthan. The trees and bushes, smelling sweet; the evening light, were part of his dreamland; but he did not know the words to describe his dreamland as a whole. How far away was Mount Prasravan with clouds, driven down by unstopping winds from the upper air, falling like a cape from its shoulders?

Opu did not know. But when he was big, he would go see it.

In fact the mountain, its sides thick with bushes and trees; the Godavari full of sandbanks; that dark place where men lived; the weird ragged peak circled by blue clouds—these things are not in any country described in Valmiki's *Ramayan*. Valmiki did not make them, nor the poet Bhavabhuti. At evening a bird from the past sang, and a badly educated village boy made them in his amazed mind. They were so real. He knew them so well.

Mount Prasravan, you can't find it in any world atlas; but a child who knew no geography dreamed it, its blue peaks hidden behind ever-moving clouds, and the mount took its place in his mind, where it would stay forever.

Chapter 18

There was one thing Opu hadn't told anybody yet. He hadn't even told his sister.

Once about noon he had opened a wooden chest of his father's. He was very quiet, and no one saw him do it. The chest was full of books, and in one of them Opu found this amazing bit of information.

He had known it was noon because the bamboo clump didn't throw a long shadow across the yard, east to west (on the wide Shonodanga plain, villagers tell time by the shadows of the big banyan tree).

That day Opu's father was not at home. Opu went into the room, shut the door, and opened the chest. Nobody came . . . Opu was very excited. He opened this book, opened that book, turned over the pages, turning to find pictures, or a good story.

On the cover of one book was the title, *An Anthology of Ancient Philosophical Works.* Opu did not know what the title meant, or what the book might be about. The cover was faded and stained, like a piece of marble. He opened it, and a band of silverfish ran over the page and disappeared. Opu lifted the book to his nose. It smelled funny: old. The pages were thick, dust-colored. Opu liked the smell of them. It made him think of his father, it always did. He did not know why.

Opu liked that book best, with its broken board cover that looked like marble. He put the other books, one by one, back into the box, but that one he hid under his bolster. And when he was alone, he would read it.

One day he read the wildest thing in it. If anybody had told him, he wouldn't have believed it. Nobody would have believed it. But this wasn't something somebody told him. It was written down in a book. In the book, they were talking about mercury. The book said if you put some mercury in a vulture's egg and leave the egg for a few days in the sun, then if you hold the egg in your mouth, you can fly around in the sky.

Fly around in the sky! Opu couldn't believe it. He read it over and over.

At this point Opu put the book in his own broken box and went outside to think. The more he thought, the wilder it seemed.

He went and found his sister. "Didi," he said, "where do vultures build their nests? Do you know?"

She didn't know. Opu went to the village and asked the boys; asked Shotu, Nilu, Kinu, Patal, Nera. He asked them all.

"They don't build 'em around here," one boy said. "They build 'em in the open country. Way up in the trees."

When he got back his mother was mad. "Where have you been in this heat?"

Opu went to his room and pretended to rest. He opened the book again. There it was! Wild! You could fly around in the sky *that easy*, and nobody knew about it! Maybe nobody but his father had this book . . . or maybe just nobody had ever read this part of it before. . . .

He smelled the book again. Smelled the same. You could fly! It was written in the book. It had to be true.

He knew where to get the mercury. Mercury is quicksilver, and quicksilver is on the backs of mirrors. He knew that. They had a broken mirror in their house. No problem about the mercury. But where do you get vultures' eggs?

One day after lunch Durga called Opu, "Opu, come 'ere. Come see the fun."

Durga stood by the bamboo near the back door. She had saved a handful of rice from lunch. She stood there calling, "Bhulo—o—o." Once, and then she was silent. She looked at Opu and smiled. The smile seemed to say: the gates of a magic city are about to open!

A dog trotted up.

"See," said Durga. "He came! Did you see where he came from?"

Durga giggled. Opu decided she had done this before. Maybe she did it every day. She seemed to be very happy about it. "You call," she said to herself. "Nobody's around. Everything is quiet . . ."

She put the handful of rice on the ground and stood with her eyes closed. She seemed very excited as if she had hoped the dog might come and had feared he would not. She talked to herself about it: "I guess Bhulo won't come today. I'll watch where he comes from. Maybe he didn't hear me . . ."

And then, a noise in the bushes, and out came Bhulo, panting and tearing leaves and creepers!

Durga's body shivered with excitement. Her eyes burned. To herself she said, "He heard me. Where does he come from? Tomorrow I won't call loudly. I'll see if he still comes."

Her mother scolded her, but Durga saved a little food from lunch every day to feed the dog. Durga really enjoyed it.

Calling a dog, Opu thought. What's so great about that? That was Durga's game. A girl's game. Opu wasn't interested. Watch the hungry dog eat his food! Very exciting, Opu thought. He wasn't interested in dogs. He was interested in vultures' eggs.

Finally Opu got a lead. The young cowherds tied their cattle to the jackfruit tree, Hiru the barber's jackfruit tree, and went into the village for oil and tobacco. Opu knew one young cowherd, a guy who lived in their end of the village. One day Opu spoke to him:

"You go all over, do you ever see any, unh, vultures' nests? If you get me some vultures' eggs I'll pay you two *pice* for them."

A few days later, the cowherd came by Opu's house and called to him. Opu went out. From a bag at his waist the cowherd took out two little black eggs.

"Look what I've got for you, sir," he said, as all people of lower caste say "sir" to the Brahmins.

Opu reached out and took them. He turned them over and over in his hand. He was very excited. "Vultures' eggs," he said. And then to the cowherd: "They're real vultures' eggs, aren't they?"

"Oh, sure," the cowherd said. "I got them from the very top of a really big tree. They've got to be vultures' eggs. It was pretty dangerous, I tell you." Opu felt he had to believe it. It was so convincing.

"But," the cowherd added, "you'll have to give me two *annas* for them."

Opu's face fell. Two *annas* was a lot of money!

"I'll give you two *pice*," Opu said, "and all my cowries. You can have the tin box they're in, too. There are a lot of gold-colored ones. Want to see them?"

The cowherd seemed to know more about deals than Opu. He didn't want to sell except for cash. They haggled and argued, and finally the cowherd said he'd sell for four *pice*.

Opu got two *pice* from his sister (it wasn't easy), and he and the cowherd closed the deal. Opu got the eggs, but finally had to give the cowherd some cowries, too. The cowries were very important to Opu. Normally he wouldn't have traded the cowries for anything. But what was playing with cowries? He was going to fly around in the sky!

Opu held the eggs in his hand. His mind was light like a

balloon in wind. Then a shadow, a doubt, fell across his mind. Up till now he'd known it would work. But now . . . now with the eggs in his hand, he wasn't so sure. He didn't *doubt* it . . . but he wasn't sure, either.

Opu went back to Nera's orchard that evening before dark. He sat on a branch that had been lopped from a rose-apple tree. His mind was busy. Should I fly now? Where should I fly to? Uncle's house? Where Daddy's gone? Fly across the river? Or fly where the stars come up, like the sparrows and mynah birds? Should I fly today or tomorrow?

Later that evening Durga wanted an old piece of cloth for a wick. She was rummaging in the pots and pans, where there was a bundle of torn rags. Something rolled off the shelf and fell to the floor. It was dark inside, and Durga could not see what had fallen, so she picked it up and took it outside.

"Oh, Mom!" she cried. "Look at the eggs! Two of them! They fell and broke. Some bird must have flown into the house and laid them."

Let's not go into what happened later. For a whole day Opu wouldn't eat. He cried and made scenes. Shorbojoya went to the pond for her bath, and she was talking about it.

"Do you know what Opu says, Shejbou? He's really being bad. It's awful. He says, if you have vultures' eggs, you can fly. The cowherd is a thief. He sold Opu some crows' eggs, told him they were vultures' eggs. Opu gave him four *pice* for them! Sometimes Opu doesn't seem very smart. Shejbou, I don't know what to do about him."

But what did Shorbojoya know? Not everybody had read *Anthology of Ancient Philosophical Works,* and they didn't know about mercury, either.

Good thing, too. Otherwise everybody would be able to fly around in the sky.

Adapted and translated by William McNaughton

Chapter 15
INDIAN POEMS

"Indian poetry"—it's almost like saying "the poetry of the Western world." The poetry of India runs back some four thousand years; it had two classical traditions, the Sanskrit and the Tamil, each of which extends over a longer span of years than the Christian Era. In addition, India has about seventeen literary languages with written literatures and tradition. The following few words, then, can be expected only to give the reader a rough "sense of direction" in this vast poetic world. I believe the reader also will find it helpful to know the material in the introductions to Chapters 16 and 17 on Hinduism and on Indian Buddhism.

The Indians have a special word for the highest poetry, a word perhaps close to—in our own tradition—Longinus's sublime, or sublime poetry. The word is *kavya.* Didactic poetry, poetry dealing with ritual and philosophy, or versified works on such subjects as astronomy and medicine are not *kavya.* Narrative verse usually is not *kavya. Kavya* depends on mood, on suggestion; *kavya* delights us and holds our interest not by story or plot, but (as nearly as I can make out) by poetic means that, to borrow Longinus's words, "with a bold stroke of the imagination, transport the soul and scatter all before them."

SANSKRIT

The Sanskrit literary tradition dates back some four thousand years. The term Sanskrit originally meant perfected, refined, and Classical Sanskrit usually means the language the great grammarians Panini (? fourth century B.C.) and Patanjali (second century B.C.) regularized from the spoken language of North India.

The Sanskrit tradition begins with the *Rigveda*. Vedic poems form the foundation of Indian literature and of Indian philosophy and religion. The poets of the *Rigveda* sing in praise of their gods, and their gods are often the forces and energies of Nature: light, fire, sun, the dawn, wind, etc. The meters of classical Sanskrit develop directly from the Veda. (Because of their religious importance, I have put selections from the *Rigveda* in Chapter 16.)

Historically, after the vedas come the two great epics of ancient India: Valmiki's *Ramayana* and Vyasa's *Mahabharata*. These two works have molded people's ideals and modified their religious vision over all of India. Some scholars estimate that all five hundred million Indians know these stories in one form or another. From Sanskrit the *Ramayana* has been translated into the major literary languages of India—Hindi, Bengali, Assamese, Oriya, Tamil, Kannada, Kashmiri, Telegu, Malayalam—and in some of them the translation has become as well-known, as revered, and as influential as the original.

The selection given here continues this tradition, based as it is on the eleventh-century Tamil version by Kamban. The *Ramayana* is about the great love of Rama and Sita; about Sita's suffering; about Rama's battle with the "evil antagonist" Ravana; about friendship, brotherly love, and (especially) love of father for son.

The *Mahabharata* tells the story of the feud and war between two cousins, Kauravas and Pandavas. One of its great dialogues between Lord Krishna and Arjuna on the eve of battle, the *Bhagavad-Gita*, has become famous around the world as a religious classic. (Some selections appear here in Chapter 16.)

If we consider the *Mahabharata* as a true epic and the *Ramayana* as an artificial one, the Sanskrit tradition contains a third kind, the great *kavya*, or court epic. The court epics rely more on description than on narration, and they were written to a strict set of conventions. These conventions, though learned and artificial, can be derived in good measure from the two earlier epic masterpieces, especially from the *Ramayana*. As this set of conventions, according to one scholar, "contains the basic repertory of Sanskrit poetry,"[1] it might be wise briefly to consider it here.

[1] Daniel Ingalls, *An Anthology of Sanskrit Court Poetry* (Cambridge: Harvard University Press, 1965), pp. 33–34.

A great *kavya* has a moral dimension: it should further the four ends of man (wealth, love and pleasure, virtue, and salvation or release from further transmigration). It should take its plot from myth or history. It should tell of the sorrow of separated lovers and should describe a wedding and the birth of a son. It should include a king's council, an embassy, an army marching out, a battle, and the hero's victory. There should be, in any great *kavya,* descriptions of cities, seas, and mountains, and of moonrise and sunrise. Ornamentally, there should be incidents of garden parties, bathing parties, drinking parties, and love-making.

TAMIL

Tamil is the other classic language of Indian literature. It belongs to the Dravidian family—a completely different language family from that of Sanskrit—and a form of it is spoken today in Madras, in southeastern India. Classical Tamil literature, sometimes called Sangam literature, should probably be dated between the seventh century B.C. and A.D. 300.

From a very early period, Tamil students of their own literature have divided all poetry into *akam* and *puram. Puram,* roughly, is non-love poetry, and it includes three of the four essential aims of life: wealth, virtue, and salvation. War, politics, social relations, gifts, and solicitations all fall into *puram* poetry.

Akam, or love poetry, has a set of conventions as complex as the rules of courtly love that influenced the European troubadour poetry and which were codified by Andreas Capellanus. These conventions will bear a brief look, as some knowledge of them can increase our delight and enhance our understanding of Indian (especially Tamil) love poetry.

According to these conventions, there are seven phases of love, only five of which are considered worthy of treatment in the highest poetry. Each of these seven phases is, by convention, associated with a geographical region, with various flowers or trees, and with times of day.

In summary, they are:

1) lovers' first meeting and (in due time) union; a mountain flower called *kurinji*; mountains; the cold season;

2) lovers' separation from each other (or, sometimes, lovers' separation from their kin and friends after an elopement); the *palai* tree (an evergreen hardy in droughts); "wasteland," either mountain or forest; summer;

3) heroine weeping because of her separation from the hero; a water-flower; the seashore under the wind god;

4) husband's unfaithfulness, wife's chagrin and resentment; a tree with red flowers growing near the water; pastoral country;

5) wife waiting patiently for her husband to return from business; jasmine; forests; the rainy season.

The other two phases of love, unsuitable as a subject for the highest poetry, are forced, loveless love—love for duty's sake, or for the sake of convenience, or lust; and "base relationship"—one-sided love, unrequited love, and love imposed on an immature girl. The author of the grammar *Tolkappiyam* (?pre-seventh century B.C.), our main source of information about the Sangam literary traditions and these conventions of love poetry, cynically calls forced, loveless love "the most common type."[1]

From here, and from the conventions and ideals of Sanskrit poetry given above, Indian poetry develops through the centuries to modern poetry. Modern Indian literatures, as distinct from the classical Sanskrit tradition, have been evolving for about a thousand years. After Kalidasa (?*ca.* A.D. 400), who is in the classical Sanskrit tradition, poets like Kabir (1399–1518), Vidyapati (fl.? A.D. 1400), and Tukharam (1608–1649) sang—as the poets of no other culture have sung better—of mystic union with God, or of man's union with woman.

[1] For an excellent discussion of this material, see A. K. Ramanujan, *The Interior Landscape* (Bloomington: Indiana University Press, 1967), pp. 97–115.

Valmiki

(? third century B.C.)

The attribution of *The Ramayana* to "Valmiki" is traditional.

THE RAMAYANA

Rama and Ravana in Battle

The gods in heaven noticed Ravana's determined move and felt that Rama would need all the support they could muster. They requested Indra to send down his special chariot for Rama's use. When the chariot appeared at his camp, Rama was deeply impressed with the magnitude and brilliance of the vehicle. "How has this come to be here?" he asked.

"Sir," the charioteer answered, "my name is Matali. I have the honor of being the charioteer of Indra. Brahma, the four-faced god and the creator of the Universe, and Shiva, whose power has emboldened Ravana now to challenge you, have commanded me to bring it here for your use." . . .

There followed an aerial pursuit at dizzying speed across the dome of the sky and rim of the earth. Ravana's arrows came down like rain; he was bent upon destroying everything in the world. But Rama's arrows diverted, broke, or neutralized Ravana's. Terror-stricken, the gods watched this pursuit. Presently Ravana's arrows struck Rama's horses and pierced the heart of Matali himself. The charioteer fell. Rama paused for a while in grief, undecided as to his next step. Then he recovered and resumed his offensive. At that moment the divine eagle Garuda was seen perched on Rama's flagpost, and the gods who were watching felt that this could be an auspicious sign.

After circling the globe several times, the dueling chariots returned, and the fight continued over Lanka. It was impossible to be very clear about the location of the battleground as the fight occurred here, there, and everywhere.

Rama's arrows pierced Ravana's armor and made him wince. . . .

Now Ravana said to himself, "These are all petty weapons. I should really get down to proper business." And he invoked the one called "Maya," a weapon that created illusions and confused the enemy.

With proper incantations and worship, he sent off this weapon and it created an illusion of reviving all the armies and its leaders—Kumbakarna, Indrajit, and the others—and bringing them back to the battlefield. Presently Rama found all those who, he thought, were no more, coming on with battle cries and surrounding him. Every man in the enemy's army was again up in arms. They seemed to fall on Rama with victorious cries. This was very confusing, and Rama asked Matali, whom he had by now revived, "What is happening now? How are all these coming back? They were dead." Matali explained, "In your original identity you are the creator of illusions in this universe. Please know that Ravana has created phantoms to confuse you. If you make up your mind, you can dispel them immediately." Matali's explanation was a great help. Rama at once invoked a weapon called "Gnana," which means "wisdom" or "perception." This was a very rare weapon, and he sent it forth. And all the terrifying armies that seemed to have come on in such a great mass suddenly evaporated into thin air.

Ravana then shot an asthra called "Thama," whose nature was to create total darkness in all the worlds. The arrows came with heads exposing frightening eyes and fangs, and fiery tongues. End to end the earth was enveloped in total darkness and the whole of creation was paralyzed. This asthra also created a deluge of rain on one side, a rain of stones on the other, a hailstorm showering down intermittently, and a tornado sweeping the earth. Ravana was sure that this would arrest Rama's enterprise. But Rama was able to meet it with what was named "Shivasthra." He understood the nature of the phenomenon and the cause of it and chose the appropriate asthra for counteracting it.

Ravana now shot off what he considered his deadliest weapon—a trident endowed with extraordinary destructive power, once gifted to Ravana by the gods. When it started on its journey there was real panic all around. It came on flaming toward Rama, its speed or course unaffected by the arrows he flung at it.

When Rama noticed his arrows falling down ineffectively while the trident sailed toward him, for a moment he lost heart. When it came quite near, he uttered a certain mantra from the depth of his being, and while he was breathing out that incantation, an esoteric syllable in perfect timing, the trident collapsed. . . .

Now Rama had to pause to consider what final measure he should take to bring this campaign to an end. After much thought, he decided to use "Brahmasthra," a weapon specially designed by the Creator Brahma on a former occasion, when he had to provide one for Shiva to destroy Tripura, the old monster who assumed the forms of flying mountains and settled down on habitations and cities, seeking to destroy the world. The Brahmasthra was a special gift to be used only when all other means had failed. Now Rama, with prayers and worship, invoked its fullest power and sent it in Ravana's direction, aiming at his heart rather than his head; Ravana being vulnerable at heart. While he had prayed for indestructibility of his several heads and arms, he had forgotten to strengthen his heart, where the Brahmasthra entered and ended his career.

Rama watched him fall headlong from his chariot, face down onto the earth, and that was the end of the great campaign. Now one noticed Ravana's face aglow with a new quality. Rama's arrows had burned off the layers of dross, the anger, conceit, cruelty, lust, and egotism that had encrusted his real self, and now his personality came through in its pristine form—of one who was devout and capable of tremendous attainments. His constant meditation on Rama, although as an adversary, now seemed to bear fruit, as his face shone with serenity and peace. Rama noticed it from his chariot above and commanded Matali, "Set me down on the ground." When the chariot descended and came to rest on its wheels, Rama got down and commanded Matali, "I am grateful for your services to me. You may now take the chariot back to Indra."

Surrounded by his brother Lakshmana and Hanuman and all his other war chiefs, Rama approached Ravana's body and stood gazing on it. He noted his crowns and jewelry scattered piecemeal on the ground. The decorations and the extraordinary workmanship of the armor on his chest were blood-covered. Rama sighed as if to say, "What might he not have achieved but for the evil stirring within him!" . . .

Vibishana, Ravana's brother, came forward. "What you have achieved is unique. I say so although it meant the death of my brother." . . .

Rama said, "Honor him and cherish his memory so that his spirit may go to heaven, where he has his place. And now I will leave you to attend to his funeral arrangements befitting his grandeur."

From the shortened modern prose version by R. K. Narayan (suggested by the Tamil version of Kamban)

TAMIL POEMS FROM THE SANGAM AGE

(? second century B.C.–second century A.D.)

Devakulathar

(dates unknown)

My lover is lord of hill country
Where on steep slopes
    the black-branched trees
Shoot up,
        and the wild honey bee
Gathers rich honey,

And my love for him
    is wider than the world
    is higher than the sky
    is deeper
        than the deep sea.

Lenore Mayhew

Mangudi Marudhanar
(dates unknown)

The big conch shells are silent.
At the shops in the bazaar
The awning poles are all down:
Every shop is closed.
The elegant young women,
          wearing their marriage jewels,
                    have gone to bed.
Thin jelly cakes streaked like honeycombs,
Round sweet cakes hot and made with candy
   and spices,
Rice flour cakes mixed with fruit jam—
These cakes are untended,
          the vendors are dozing;
The festival dancers,
          the hired actors
                    are dozing;
And all who stretch on beds
          have fallen into a deep sleep
Like the cool and noisy sea
                    at rest.

Lenore Mayhew

Kathayan Kannanar
(dates unknown)

A tangle of *kalli*
Where *koogai* scream
          even in daylight
And where ghosts
          with uneven teeth
Move in the air:
The smoke-filled burial ground
Where tears of lovers
Soak the white ash
          of newly-burned bones,

This place of terror
never dies,
Lives on, gathering in the dead.

Lenore Mayhew

Poigayar
(dates unknown)

When the great war-javelin
Enters the body of the elephant,
Stunned and unsteady
he kneels,
And his ears lie close to the ground

As if he listens
to the secret truths
Of the earth goddess . . .

Lenore Mayhew

Anonymous

The great and famous city of Mathurai
Is like the lotus flower of God Vishnu:
Its streets are the petals of the flower,
God Shiva's temple is the center,
The citizens are the plentiful pollen,
The poor, the crowding beetles.
And in Mathurai
we wake to the chanting of the four Vedas,
Sacred scriptures from the tongue of Brahma,
born of the lotus flower.
We do not wake to the tame cock's crowing
As all do
in Urayur and Vanchi.

Lenore Mayhew

Asiriyan Nallanthuvanar

(dates unknown)

Kanthal buds like closed fists,
Kanthal flowers like angry, hooded cobras,
Bent waterlilies like opened umbrellas
from bushes, from trees, from distant ponds
Sweep along together;
They crowd into the long underground sluices,
The full water rises up
and pours over
The well-guarded walls of the rich
Like the water mixed with petals
That spurts from the raised trunks
of mighty elephants.

Lenore Mayhew

Kadiyalur Uruthirankannanar

(dates unknown)

The gate to the great kitchen
has double doors
Engraved with tigers,
The Goddess of Wealth
is painted on the walls.
The charity of this kitchen
gives glory in this world
And dharma in the next.
Rivers of gruel flow out,
and the oxen fight to drink;
The crowded road gets muddy,
and passing chariots splatter the mire.
Clouds of dirt
settle on the brilliant sculpture
and on the fine paintings of the palaces,
Making them look like large dusty elephants.

Lenore Mayhew

Irayanar
(dates unknown)

Loveliest of winged beetles,
You who live
by finding honey in flowers,
Now without flattery
tell me:
Among the flowers that you know,
are there any
that smell sweeter
Than the curled hair
of my wife,
She of even teeth
and the proud beauty
of peacocks?

Lenore Mayhew

Palai Padia Perungadungo
(dates unknown)

Can I eat?
Can I live?
I will be
as a palmyra-leaf cup
discarded when water has
appeased the thirsty;
I will be
as a populous village
suddenly left empty;
I will be
as the *vengai* flower
worn like a jewel in the hair
until faded and thrown away.

Lenore Mayhew

TAMIL POEMS FROM THE ANTHOLOGY KURUNTOKAI
(first three centuries A.D.)

Anilatu Munrilar
(dates unknown)

When my lover is by my side
I am happy
as a city
in the rapture of a carnival,

and when he is gone
I grieve like a deserted house
in a little hamlet
of the wastelands

where the squirrel plays
in the front yard.

A. K. Ramanujan

Catti Natanar
(dates unknown)

As a little white snake
with lovely stripes on its young body
troubles the jungle elephant
this slip of a girl
her teeth like sprouts of new rice
her wrists stacked with bangles
troubles me.

A. K. Ramanujan

POEMS FROM THE MIDDLE CLASSICAL PERIOD OF SANSKRIT (A.D. *700–1050*)*, FROM VIDYAKARA* (*latter half of eleventh century,* A.D.)*, COMPILER, THE TREASURY OF WELL-TURNED VERSE*

Bhasa[1]

(pre-seventh century)

Moon rays—
the cat has mistaken them for milk
and laps his empty dish;
where they weave among the branches,
the elephant sees lotus stems,
a young girl
after making love
reaches out for them
thinking she has found her dress.
So the arrogant moon
in the power of her light
deceives us all.

Lenore Mayhew

Vidduka

(dates unknown)

The dark drinks up the sun,
The dry-voiced crow
is quiet in his nest,
And the owl in the hollow tree
Fixes his eye on the night.
He shrinks his head into his shoulders
Until he looks like a small hand-drum.

Lenore Mayhew

[1] The ascription of this poem to Bhāsa is doubtful.

Vikatanitamba
(dates unknown)

As he came to bed, the knot fell open of itself,
The dress held only somehow to my hips
By the strands of the loosened girdle.
So much I know, my dear;
But when within his arms, I can't remember who he
was,
Or who I was, or what we did or how.

Daniel H. H. Ingalls

Yogesvara
(fl. *ca.* 800–900)

The heron, hunting fish, sets his foot cautiously
In the clear water of the stream,
His eyes turning this way and that.
Holding one foot up, from time to time
He cocks his neck and glances hopefully
At the trembling of a leaf.

Daniel H. H. Ingalls

Rajasekhara
(fl. *ca.* 900)

First Poem

The red sun loses its heat
and falls to the western hills.
It neatly wraps and carries off
the life of day.
Under the persistent touch
of evening
the world grows somber

like an old painting
darkened by smoke.

Lenore Mayhew

Second Poem[1]

Night begins.
The moon comes out
Red,
Then amber,
Then the pale gold
of a girl's cheek
As she waits for her lover;
At last,
driving back the dark,
It turns white
and radiant
as the lotus flower.

Lenore Mayhew

Konka[2]

(dates unknown)

Grown bold
with love and laughter,
The girl
tries the man's part.
Her legs and arms
are tender as young vines,
and in the middle of the play
She appeals to him with her eyes,

[1] The ascription of this poem to Rajasekhara is doubtful. It may have been written by Chittapa.

[2] The ascription of this poem to Konka is doubtful.

then embarrassed
looks away.

Lenore Mayhew

Manovinoda

(fl. bet. 900 and 1100)

When night stains the world
As dark a color as the cuckoo's throat,
We guess at mountaintops
by gathered light;
At creatures by voices;
At trees
by the perfume of flowers;
And at palaces
By patterned lamplight
spread across the grass.

Lenore Mayhew

(End of poems from the "Treasury of Well-turned Verse.")

Vidyapati

(? fl. *ca.* 1400)

Two Poems

1.

As the mirror to my hand,
the flowers to my hair,
kohl to my eyes,
tāmbul to my mouth,
musk to my breast,
necklace to my throat,
ecstasy to my flesh,
heart to my home—

as wing to bird,
water to fish,
life to the living—
so you to me.
But tell me,
Mādhava, beloved,
who are you?
Who are you really?

Vidyāpati says, they are one another.

Edward C. Dimock, Jr., and Denise Levertov

2.

Her cloud of hair eclipses the luster of her face,
like Rahu greedy for the moon;
the garland glitters in her unbound hair, a wave of
the Ganges in the waters of the Yamuna.
How beautiful the deliberate, sensuous union of the
two; the girl playing this time the active
role,
riding her lover's outstretched body in delight;
her smiling lips shine with drops of sweat; the god
of love offering pearls to the moon.
She of beautiful face hotly kisses the mouth of her
beloved; the moon, with face bent down,
drinks of the lotus.
The garland hanging on her heavy breasts seems like
a stream of milk from golden jars.
The tinkling bells which decorate her hips sound the
triumphal music of the god of love.

Edward C. Dimock, Jr., and Denise Levertov

Kabir
(1399–1518)

One day—most authorities are agreed on this—Kabir had an overpowering vision of the Divine (whom Kabir calls "Ram"). From then on his energies were devoted to writing in praise of the subject of his vision and to traveling to talk and worship with other "holy men." He believed every man should experience God for himself, and he attacked asceticism and the paraphernalia of organized churches and religious schools. He was persecuted by the Hindus and condemned to death by the Muslim emperor Sikander Lodi, although he fortunately escaped. His poetry was enormously popular even in his lifetime. Kabir wrote in Hindi.

What Good Is Litany?

What good is litany, penitence,
fasting, ceremony
If the heart is divided?
O bigot! You must fix your mind on Mādhava,[1]
You will not find God with tricks!

Give up cupidity
and the ways of the world.
Give up sensuality, anger, pride.

Religious practice
glues men to their vanity,
And they gather to worship stones!

Kabir says this:
I have found it in love.
Only simple hearts come to Raghourai.[2]

Lenore Mayhew

[1] Madhava: a name of Krishna. Kabir uses it to mean Ram (God).
[2] Raghourai: Prince of the Raghu. Another of Kabir's names for God.

The Earth Passes Away

The earth passes away
The sky passes away
And in each body
the soul's light is snuffed out.

O Lord Ram
The multitudes pass away
They appear
and disappear
The four Vedas pass away
Tradition
and the Koran pass away
And Shiva will pass away
and the meditation of Yoga.

But Kabir's God
Lives on
Unchanged
In all the beings
of the world.

Lenore Mayhew

O Lily, Why Do You Wither?

O lily, why do you wither?
Even your stem is full of water:

You were born in the water,
you live in the water,
Your only home is water.

You feel no burning at your roots,
in your head there is no fire:
Where can you fix your desire?

Kabir says this:
Those who rest in the water of Ram
will not die.
Of this I am sure.

Lenore Mayhew

There's a Moon in My Body

There's a moon in my body, but I can't see it!
A moon and a sun.
A drum never touched by hands, beating,
and I can't hear it!

As long as a human being worries about when he
will die,
and what he has that is his,
all of his works are zero.
When affection for the I-creature and what it owns is
dead, then the work of the Teacher is over.

The purpose of labor is to learn;
when you know it, the labor is over.
The apple blossom exists to create fruit; when that
comes,
the petals fall.

The musk is inside the deer, but the deer does not
look for it:
it wanders around looking for grass.

Robert Bly

Tukharam
(1608–1649)

Tukharam was an illiterate poet, the descendant of peasants, son of a village shopkeeper, and himself a village shopkeeper. He belonged to the Sudra, the lowest of India's four great caste divisions. Inspired by a religious vision, he gave up his practical pursuits for religious pilgrimage.

I've Opened a Shop

I've opened a shop:
I charge according to your desire.

I keep the cash-register of God:
I pay and receive according to your need.

I've gone over your account,
I know its debits and credits.

According to what you pay, says Tukha,
I give you good quality or bad.

William McNaughton

The Child Who Aims at His Own True Good

The child who aims
at his own true Good
—what happiness
for the father
and the mother!

In the family
where the children
grow up in holiness,
God himself
takes delight:

where they love
to hear the Gita read,
where they put
their heart
on Vithaba.

If I had
children like that to serve me,
says Tukha,
I wouldn't ask
for any higher destiny.

William McNaughton

Rabindranath Tagore
(1861–1941)

Tagore's Nobel Prize was awarded primarily on the basis of his book of poems *Gitanjali,* selections from which appear below. The translations are also by Tagore.

My Song Has Put Off Her Adornments

My song has put off her adornments. She has no pride of dress and decoration. Ornaments would mar our union; they would come between thee and me; their jingling would drown thy whispers.

My poet's vanity dies in shame before thy sight. O master poet, I have sat down at thy feet. Only let me make my life simple and straight, like a flute of reed for thee to fill with music.

Leave This Chanting and Singing

Leave this chanting and singing and telling of beads! Who dost thou worship in this lonely dark corner of a temple with doors all shut? Open thine eyes and see thy God is not before thee!

He is there where the tiller is tilling the hard ground and where the pathmaker is breaking stones. He is with them in sun and in shower, and his garment is covered with dust. Put off thy holy mantle and even like him come down on the dusty soil!

Deliverance? Where is this deliverance to be found? Our master himself has joyfully taken upon him the bonds of creation; he is bound with us all for ever.

Come out of thy meditations and leave aside thy flowers and incense! What harm is there if thy clothes become tattered and stained? Meet him and stand by him in toil and in sweat of thy brow.

The Day Is No More

The day is no more, the shadow is upon the earth. It is time that I go to the stream to fill up my pitcher.

The evening air is eager with the sad music of the water. Ah, it calls me out into the dusk. In the lonely lane there is no passerby, the wind is up, the ripples are rampant in the river.

I know not if I shall come back home. I know not whom I shall chance to meet. There at the fording in the little boat the unknown man plays upon his lute.

Ageya

(Sachchidananda Vatsyayan—b. 1911)

Jet Flight

Not through heaven but unformed light.
Wing-balanced and cut loose
From gravity,
We glide.
New-combed cloud fleece
Is spread below us, dream of white
And impossibly delicate cloth.
Here I think I dream my own solidity.

And there
Through the torn floor of cumulus,
Is it earth I really see?
Those lines, trailing through green or shade or light,
The city shapes, and laboring spires,
Memorialize this creature who creates.

Or angling, crossing, curving, driving straight?
Then, like a jewel, cresting man's own crown,
Losing pure altitude,
We burrow under smog,
That drab and dirty tissue in which works
A suffocating womb of mobbed plenitude.
At bottom,

Now, we touch
The hard earth
Where blood grows weighty
In the veins and this most urgent ring,
Just behind the eardrums, sings
The desolate dumbness of our being.

Descend a further step,
Breathe deep;
Close up the silver dream,
Our casket-chariot behind;
Step down, then stroll,
And there before you stands,
Unpredictable, your image:
Man, from whose eyes, his own Unbounded Self's
Unblinking grief stares out.

L. E. Nathan

Kedar Nath Agrawal
(b. 1912)

Storm

Like a stallion
I raced cantering over the heads of the forest.
Like a young bird
The biggest tree was startled and shrieked aloud.
Violently trembling, the feathery leaves were ripped off.
Broken, as if the wild bulls of the plateau
Had been set out to feed upon the dark green twigs
Of the silent night.

H. M. Guy

Shamsher Bahadur Singh
(b. 1911)

Morning

The rock
That was crouched
On a shelf
Awoke
And automatically
Stretched
Itself.

James Mauch

Ajit Kumar
(b. 1933)

You Are Alone

. . . But the accursed twilight came,
Brought with it the bad spirits of past memories
And a shabby dusk.

All of a sudden, as if wet fuel started smoking,
As if that sort of smoke rose up from the houses
In a spiral, with a dark hazy line behind it,
Mind and eyes burned with bitter tears.

This twilight, with somewhere a patch of light
But mostly darkness prevailing,
Increases, as if building a fence of giant size
For a giant with no heart.
I feel that my life is in a cage,
And outside, tigers, bears, wild dogs—
Memories, hurts, fears—
Surround me,

My life inextricably set
In the accursed twilight.

Josephine Miles

Khirti Chaudhari
(b. 1935)

A Star Quivered

A star quivered in a corner of the sky.
I thought, yes
Everything sometime or other will shine out like this.

A pebble stirred
The water of the drowsy waves.
I knew
At least for once inertia will be shaken.

Blossoms flowered
In the deeps of forests,
Their fragrance spoke out, yes
Once at least I scatter and bestow.

What more to ask
Than images of my aspiration—
But belief nods no
A dream is better,
What can an image do but shine or scatter,
What will it offer?

Josephine Miles

Chapter 16

HINDU RELIGIOUS AND PHILOSOPHICAL WRITINGS

The religion of 75 percent of the people of India today is some form of Hinduism, either the Higher Hinduism or a Popular or Sectarian Hinduism, which includes worship of various animals, trees, stones, even diseases. And all Hinduism can be seen as a development of the older religion, Brahmanism. Strictly speaking, Brahmanism finds its literary expression in the Vedas and in the *Upanishads;* Hinduism finds its in the *Bhagavad Gita,* the *Kama Sutra,* and in tantras and other later texts. The Hindus, however, recognize as the source of ultimate religious truth the Veda, which they call *shruti* (revelation). Later scriptures are called *smriti* (tradition; i.e., of men).

Archaeological evidence indicates that the earliest religious beliefs in the Indus River valley included fertility cults, symbolized by figurines of pregnant females (which may be evidence of an Earth goddess cult) and by stone phalluses and worship of a deity very much like the later god Shiva (who is associated with the bull and is sometimes symbolized by the phallus). The early Indians seem also to have attached religious significance to various real animals—tigers, crocodiles, buffalos, elephants—as well as to fantastic animals.

About 1500 B.C. Aryans from the northwest invaded India and brought with them new religious beliefs associated with gods representing or personifying natural forces. The Aryans' rituals involved sacrifices and fire: they drank an exhilarating distillation or brew called *soma.* In personifying or deifying natural forces, the Aryans' beliefs were like those of other Indo-European traditions, especially those of Iran, Greece, and Rome. The Veda, of which we have already spoken, is the written record—in hymns, ritual texts, and philosophical treatises—of their beliefs. (The earliest Veda is the set of hymns called the *Rigveda*, which probably was composed between 1500 B.C. and 900 B.C.)

Aryan mythology describes the god Inra killing a demon-snake, Vritra, thereby establishing a cosmic order (*rita*) and bringing into being the conditions necessary for life. The god Varuna administered the cosmic order thus created. Under the order, other gods and men had specific responsibilities or functions (*vrata*) to perform, and neglect in their performance led to a bad afterlife.

To protect the cosmic order, a ritual developed involving, among other things, a fire-sacrifice. The fire itself was personified as the god Agni, who in time came to be seen as a god of three forms; on earth, fire; in the air, lightning; in the sky, the sun. Sacrificial prayers called *brahman* were composed, and the priest responsible for reciting them was called *brahaman*. Here lies the origin of the "brahman" caste in India, and the origin of the name of the religion Brahmanism. The religious texts, the Upanishads, most of which were composed between 900 B.C. and 500 B.C., interpret the Vedic ritual and its relation to man and the universe.

Hinduism contains a large number of sects, bound together in a single belief by certain important characteristics: the caste system; the religious authority of the Vedas, and, in early Hindu texts, the three ends of man—*dharma* (virtue, duty, righteousness), wealth, and love (or pleasure). Later, a fourth end of man became important: the renunciation of duty, wealth, and love in order to seek spiritual perfection.

In Hinduism the soul is eternal; but it is bound to the material world by the law of *karma*, according to which the soul is born and born again into the material world until, finally, it may achieve release (*moksha*) from these transmigrations and rebirths. The *Bhagavad Gita* identifies three paths toward *moksha*: knowledge, selfless action, and devotion (to God).

The Hindus believe that all reality is one and spiritual, and that each individual soul is identical with this reality and shares its characteristics: pure being, intelligence, and bliss. Everything that seems to divide the soul from this reality ("the Brahman") is *maya,* illusion; and the path of knowledge develops awareness of these truths.[1]

The path of devotion means belief in a supreme personal god who is creator, preserver, destroyer of the universe. "Salvation," in other words, involves some degree of nearness to, of communion with, God. The major division in Hinduism is between devotees of Vishnu and devotees of Shiva. The Hindu's "devotion" to his god usually takes place as *puja*—a ritual of worship and service. An idol of the god is bathed, offered food and flowers, and entertained with dances and music.

Puja alters the Brahmanistic tradition, of which the characteristic was sacrifice; and alters the Upanishad tradition, of which the characteristic was renunciation. There are various other shifts of emphasis, subtle and less subtle, between Hinduism and Brahmanism. Vishnu and Shiva were very minor figures in the early Vedas, for example. The Brahmanistic *rita* (cosmic order) became Hindu *dharma,* and Hinduism itself is sometimes called Sanatana Dharma, the Eternal Dharma. The word *dharma* comes from a root *dhr* meaning to sustain, and its basic meaning is something like moral law.

THE RIGVEDA

To the Storm Gods

What now, storm gods?—will you take us by both
hands,
As a dead father takes his son after the offering of
kusha grass?

[1] The similarity of some Hindu ideas to certain Buddhist ideas will be apparent (see pp. 411–412). This similarity is not surprising, since Gautama Buddha lived in India. In fact, in Buddhism rebirth takes place under laws of karma that are essentially the same as those of Hinduism, though they are explained differently.

Where now, storm gods? What do you seek in the sky
that you cannot find on earth?
Where are your cows grazing?

Who receives your latest favors, storm gods?
Your blessings and your delights?

Listen to me, storm gods!
If you were mortal, and I a god,

None would spurn me, as a deer spurned in pasture
grass,
Nor would I walk the road to death.

You are terrible and powerful, O storm gods:
You bring everlasting rain in the desert.

Dark rainclouds shroud the sky,
Turning day into night, drenching the earth.

And when the storm gods shout, the earth trembles,
Men reel and shudder.

On strong-hoofed, untiring horses, the storm gods
pursue
Other glittering clouds pregnant with rain.

Hold the reins tight!
May your fillies be strong, your horses swift!

Let us praise Agni, our shining friend.
Agni, lord of prayer, receive my song!

The song is in my mouth!
It opens like a cloud!
It is a song of praise!

It praises the storm gods!
They are beautiful and terrible!
Their glory is everlasting!

To Agni

They are born to die: skin
flows into skin, flows
out of skin.
He lies in the lap of his mother:
He looks about.

He sees their sacrifice:
They invoke him with unwinking eyes,
They know the secret of his strength.

P. Lal

THE UPANISHADS

The Lord (Eesha-Upanishad)

That is perfect. This is perfect. Perfect comes from perfect. Take perfect from perfect, the remainder is perfect.

May peace and peace and peace be everywhere.

Whatever lives is full of the Lord. Claim nothing; enjoy, do not covet His property.

Then hope for a hundred years of life doing your duty. No other way can prevent deeds from clinging, proud as you are of your human life.

They that deny the Self, return after death to a godless birth, blind, enveloped in darkness.

The Self is one. Unmoving, it moves faster than the mind. The senses lag, but Self runs ahead. Unmoving, it outruns pursuit. Out of Self comes the breath that is the life of all things.

Unmoving, it moves; is far away, yet near; within all, outside all.

Of a certainty the man who can see all creatures in himself, himself in all creatures, knows no sorrow.

How can a wise man, knowing the unity of life, seeing all creatures in himself, be deluded or sorrowful?

The Self is everywhere, without a body, without a shape, whole, pure, wise, all-knowing, far-shining, self-depending, all-transcending; in the eternal procession assigning to every period its proper duty. . . .

They have put a golden stopper into the neck of the bottle. Pull it, Lord! Let out reality. I am full of longing.

At the Feet of the Monk (Mundaka Upanishad)

Book II

1

"This is the truth: the sparks, though of one nature with the fire, leap from it; uncounted beings leap from the Everlasting, but these, my son, merge into It again. . . .

2

"Shining, yet hidden, Spirit lives in the cavern. Everything that sways, breathes, opens, closes, lives in Spirit; beyond learning, beyond everything, better than anything; living, unliving.

"It is undying blazing Spirit, that seed of all seeds, wherein lay hidden the world and all its creatures. It is life, speech, mind, reality, immortality. It is there to be struck. Strike it, my son! . . .

"He that knows Him as the shaped and the shapeless, cuts through the knot of his heart, solves every doubt, exhausts every action.

"In a beautiful golden scabbard hides the stainless, indivisible, luminous Spirit.

"Neither sun, moon, star, neither fire nor lightning, lights Him. When He shines, everything begins to shine. Everything in the world reflects His light.

"Spirit is everywhere, upon the right, upon the left, above, below, behind, in front. What is the world but Spirit?"

Shree Purohit Swami and William Butler Yeats

Vyasa
(dates unknown)

According to more recent views, ascription of the *Mahabharata* to the ancient sage Vyasa is legendary. These views hold that the *Mahabharata* was composed between 200 B.C. and A.D. 200 by a number of bards and that priests later revised it, at the same time interpolating long passages on theology, morals and statecraft. The *Bhagavad-Gita* is extracted from the *Mahabharata*. It is, in the main, Krishna the Charioteer's sermon before the climactic battle of the *Mahabharata*.[1]

THE BHAGAVAD-GITA

Chapter 12: The Yoga of Divine Love

Arjuna says: Who knows yoga better?
Those who worship you in this unchanging way?
Or those who worship the Imperishable and
  Unmanifest?

Shri Krishna says: He whose mind holds to me,
Who worships me in this unchanging way—
He is perfect in yoga.

He who worships the Imperishable, the Undefinable,
The Unmanifest, the Omnipresent, the
  Incomprehensible,
The Immutable, the Unchanging, the Eternal;

Who controls his senses always;
Who always keeps a level mind no matter what;
Who works for the welfare of all living things:
He attains Me only and no other.

He who holds his mind to the Unmanifest
Has harder work: for creatures with bodies

[1] See also Chapter Fifteen.

To attain the Unmanifest is difficult indeed.

. . . .

To know is better than to do,
To meditate than to know,
And to renounce action's ends is better than to
meditate.
Peace comes straight from such renunciation.

Chapter 15: The Way to the Supreme Self

Shri Krishna says: The scriptures say
There is an undying Asvattha Tree,
Root above,
branch below,
Its leaves are the Vedas and
He who knows the Tree knows the Vedas.

Its branches stretch
Above and below,
Its branches are nourished
By energy, by inertia, by their balance,
Its buds are what the senses know;
Its roots thrust downward
In the world of men, and men move
To action . . .

None here understands its true form,
None understands its end, or its origin,
None understands its existence even.
Take the ax of detachment, cut down
This Asvattha with its strong roots, and pray:

"I rest in the Primal Being from whom comes
"Unending activity." You should seek the Goal.
They who reach the Goal never come back.

. . . .

The light in the sun
That shines through the universe, the light in the
moon

That shines in the fire: know that
That light is Mine.

I flow into
The earth, and all beings stand
With My energy; I become sap and soma,
I nourish the various grasses,

I come into the bodies
Of all living things,
As the five Vaishvanara
I mix with the breaths upward
And downward,
I digest the four foods.

I sit in the hearts of all.
From Me come Memory
And Knowledge, from Me the loss
Of Memory and Knowledge,
It is I
That am known through the Vedas,
I who wrote Vedanta,
And I who know the Vedas.

William McNaughton

Vatsyayana
(*ca.* A.D. 400)

We know virtually nothing of Vatsyayana; even his dates are much in dispute. It is thought that he wrote the *Kama Sutra* from a number of earlier sources.

In the U.S. there is a widespread belief that the *Kama Sutra* is a technical manual on sexual pleasure. The work does contain some practical—even imaginative—advice on sexual technique, but it is far from a sexual recipe book. Furthermore, if the ancient Indian writers on sexual pleasure talk of "the yawning position," "the position of the wife of Indra," "the twining position," and "the mare's position," they are at least equaled in these areas by such ancient Chinese writers as the author of *Master Tung Hsuan's Art of the Bedroom.* "Master Tung Hsuan," whose book was also much honored in Japan, writes of "Silk-reeling," "Pair-eyed Fish," "Hovering Butterflies," "Reversed Flying Ducks," "Two Tall Pines by the Altar," etc.

In my opinion, the importance of the *Kama Sutra* lies in its reverent approach to its subject. Kama, after all, is for Indians one of the three (or four) *purusarthas,* or goals of human life. The *Upanishads* also recognize this holiness of the sexual relation:

> Woman is fire,
> O Gautama
> Her hips are the fuel, her body's hair
> the smoke, her sexual part
> the flame,
> Love-making the glowing coals,
> And climax is the flying sparks.
> The gods offer seed in this fire;
> From their offering springs man.
> He lives as long as he lives.
>
> (*Brhadaranyaka Upanishad* VI, 2.1)

An indubitable balance, a special grace distinguishes the *Kama Sutra.* As its French translator says:

> The specifically erotic instruction in the *Kama Sutra* is part of a religion of life. Above all, what distinguishes it, on this level, from European erotic works written by men with masculine pleasure in mind, is that the *Kama Sutra* gives woman her place. She is not just a sexual object, she is an intelligent and sensitive creature, man's partner and equal, and man must earn her "favors" and must give her the satisfactions which she wants.[1]

[1] *Le Kama Soutra de Vatsyayana, Manuel d'Érotique Hindoue* (Paris: Club Géant—Presses de la Renaissance, 1968), "Introduction," p. 21.

THE KAMA SUTRA

Part I: Society and Social Concepts

Chapter 2

On the Acquisition of Dharma, Artha, and Kama

Man, the period of whose life is one hundred years, should practice Dharma, Artha, and Kama at different times and in such a manner that they may harmonize, and not clash in any way. He should acquire learning in his childhood; in his youth and middle age he should attend to Artha and Kama; and in his old age he should perform Dharma, and thus seek to gain Moksha, that is, release from further transmigration. Or, because of the uncertainty of life, he may practice them at times when they are enjoined to be practiced. But one thing is to be noted; he should lead the life of a religious student until he finishes his education.

Dharma is obedience to the command of the Shastra, or Holy Writ, of the Hindus to do certain things, such as the performance of sacrifices, which are not generally done because they do not belong to this world, and produce no visible effect; and not do other things, such as eating meat, which is often done because it belongs to this world, and has visible effects.

Dharma should be learned from the Shruti (Holy Writ), and from those conversant with it.

Artha is the acquisition of arts, land, gold, cattle, wealth, equipages, and friends. It is also the protection of what is acquired, and the increase of what is protected.

Artha should be learned from the king's officers, and from merchants who may be versed in the ways of commerce.

Kama is the enjoyment of appropriate objects by the five senses of hearing, feeling, seeing, tasting, and smelling, assisted by the mind together with the soul. The ingredient in this is a peculiar contact between the organ of sense and its object, and the consciousness of pleasure that arises from that contact is called Kama.

Kama is to be learned from the *Kama Sutra* (aphorisms on love) and the practice of citizens.

When all three, Dharma, Artha, and Kama, come together, the former is better than the one which follows it; that is, Dharma is better than Artha, and Artha is better than Kama. . . .

Chapter 5

On the Kinds of Women Resorted to by the Citizen . . .

When Kama is practiced by men of the four classes, according to the rules of the Holy Writ (that is, by lawful marriage), with virgins of their own caste, it then becomes a means of acquiring lawful progeny and good fame, and it is not opposed to the customs of the world. On the contrary, the practice of Kama with women of the higher castes, and with those previously enjoyed by others, even though they be of the same caste, is prohibited. But the practice of Kama with women of the lower castes, with women excommunicated from their own caste, with public women and with women twice married, is neither enjoined nor prohibited. The object of practicing Kama with such women is pleasure only. . . .

Part II: On Sexual Union

Chapter 6

On the Various Ways of Lying Down, and the Different Kinds of Congress

. . . The Deer Woman has the following three ways of lying down:

The widely opened position
The yawning position
The position of the wife of Indra. . . .

There are also the "clasping position" and the "low congress," and in the "lowest congress," together with the "pressing position," are the "twining position" and the "mare's position." . . . There are . . . two verses on the subjects, as follows:

> An ingenious person should multiply the kinds of congress after the fashion of the different kinds of beasts and of birds. For these different kinds of congress, performed according to the usage of each country, and the liking of each individual, generate love, friendship, and respect in the hearts of women.

Chapter 8

On Women Acting the Part of a Man; and on the Work of a Man

When a woman sees that her lover is fatigued by constant congress, without having his desire satisfied, she should, with his permission, lay him down upon his back, and give him assistance by acting his part. She may also do this to satisfy the curiosity of her lover, or her own desire of novelty.

There are two ways of doing this: the first is when during congress she turns around, and gets on top of her lover, in such a manner as to continue the congress, without obstructing the pleasure of it; and the other is when she acts the man's part from the beginning. At such a time, with flowers in her hair hanging loose, and her smiles broken by hard breathings, she should press upon her lover's bosom with her own breasts; and, lowering her head frequently, she should do in return the same actions which he used to do before, returning his blows and chaffing him. She should say, "I was laid down by you, and fatigued with hard congress; I shall now therefore lay you down in return." She should then again manifest her own bashfulness, her fatigue, and her desire of stopping the congress. In this way she would do the work of a man, which we shall presently relate.

Whatever is done by a man for giving pleasure to a woman is called the work of a man. . . .

The acts to be done by the man are:

Moving forward
Friction or churning
Piercing
Rubbing
Pressing
Giving a blow
The blow of a boar
The blow of a bull
The sporting of a sparrow. . . .

When a woman acts the part of a man, she has the following things to do in addition to the nine given above:

The pair of tongs
The top
The swing

When the woman is tired, she should place her forehead on that of her lover and should thus take rest without disturbing the union . . . and when the woman has rested herself the man should turn around and begin the congress again.

There are also some verses on the subject, as follows:

> Though a woman is reserved, and keeps her feelings concealed, yet when she gets on top of a man, she then shows all her love and desire. A man should gather from the actions of the woman of what disposition she is, and in what way she likes to be enjoyed.

Chapter 10

How to Begin and How to End the Congress . . .

In the pleasure room, decorated with flowers, and fragrant with perfumes, attended by his friends and servants, the citizen should receive the woman, who will come bathed and dressed, and will invite her to take refreshment and to drink freely. He should then seat her on his left side, and holding her hair, and touching also the end of the knot of her garment, he should gently embrace her with his right arm. They should then carry on an amusing conversation on various subjects, and may also talk suggestively of things which would be considered as coarse, or not to be mentioned generally in society. They may then sing, either with or without gesticulations, and play on musical instruments, talk about the arts, and persuade each other to drink. At last, when the woman is overcome with love and desire, the citizen should dismiss the people that may be with him, giving them flowers, ointments and betel leaves; and then when the two are left alone, they should proceed as has been already described in the previous chapters.

Such is the beginning of sexual union. At the end of the congress, the lovers, with modesty, and not looking at each other, should go separately to the washing room. After this, sitting in their own places, they should eat some betel leaves and the citizen should apply with his own hand to the body of the woman some pure sandalwood ointment, or ointment of some other kind. He should then embrace her with his left arm, and with agreeable words should cause her to drink from a cup held in his own hand, or he may give her water to drink. They can then eat sweetmeats, or anything else, according to their liking, and may drink fresh juice, soup, gruel, extracts of meat, sherbet, the juice of the mango fruits, the extract of the juice of the citron tree mixed with sugar, or anything that may be liked in different countries, and known to be sweet, soft, and pure. The lovers may also sit on the terrace of the palace or house, and enjoy the moonlight, and carry on an agreeable conversation. At this time, too, while the woman lies in his lap, with her face toward the moon, the citizen should show her the different planets, the morning star, the polar star, and the seven Rishis, or Great Bear.

This is the end of sexual union.

Part III: About the Acquisition of a Wife[1]

Chapter 2
On Creating Confidence in the Girl

For the first three days after marriage, the girl and her husband should sleep on the floor, abstain from sexual

[1] The divisions of the *Kama Sutra* continue: Part IV: About a Wife; Part V: About the Wives of Other Men; Part VI: About Courtesans; and Part VII: On the Means of Attracting Others to Yourself.

pleasures, and eat their food without seasoning it either with alkali or salt. For the next seven days they should bathe amidst the sounds of auspicious musical instruments, should decorate themselves, dine together, and pay attention to their relatives as well as to those who may have come to witness their marriage. This is applicable to persons of all castes. On the night of the tenth day the man should begin in a lonely place with soft words, and thus create confidence in the girl. Some authors say that for the purpose of winning her over he should not speak to her for three days; but the followers of Babhravya are of the opinion that if the man does not speak with her for three days, the girl may be discouraged by seeing him spiritless, like a pillar, and, becoming dejected, she may begin to despise him as a eunuch. . . . Women being of a tender nature, want tender beginnings. . . . If the girl is grown up, or if the man has known her for some time, he may embrace her by the light of a lamp; but if he is not well acquainted with her, or if she is a young girl, he should then embrace her in darkness.

When the girl accepts the embrace, the man should put a "tambula," or screw of betel nut and betel leaves, in her mouth, and if she will not take it, he should induce her to do so by conciliatory words, entreaties, oaths, and kneeling at her feet, for it is a universal rule that however bashful or angry a woman may be, she never disregards a man's kneeling at her feet. At this time of giving this tambula, he should kiss her mouth softly and gracefully, without making any sound. . . .

There are, moreover, some verses on the subject as follows:

> A man acting according to the inclinations of a girl should try to gain her over so that she may love him and place her confidence in him. A man does not succeed either by implicitly following the inclination of a girl or by wholly opposing her, and he should therefore adopt a middle course. He who knows how to make himself beloved by women, as well as to increase their honor and create confidence in them, becomes an object of their love.

Sir Richard F. Burton

Chapter 17
INDIAN BUDDHIST WRITINGS

The word "Buddha" means "enlightened, awakened." Under the patronage of the emperor Ashoka (*ca.* 273–237 B.C.), Buddhism achieved great success; it had its heyday in India between 200 B.C. and A.D. 200. Thereafter, it began to lose ground to the older religion, Hinduism. At the time of the Muslim conquest, about A.D. 1192, Buddhism disappeared as an organized religious force in India, although it continued to thrive in Tibet, Ceylon, Southeast Asia, China, Japan, and other areas.

Siddhartha Gautama, or Gautama Sakyamuni, who was the founder of Buddhism and whose dates are usually given as *ca.* 563–483 B.C., was a chief's son in the hill tribe of the Shakyas. After an unsuccessful search for enlightenment and religious peace in the sects and religious practices of his day, Siddhartha Gautama is supposed to have attained enlightenment one night while sitting under a fig tree; that is, he had a vision, which came to be elaborated as Buddhism. Later, at Benares, he met five ascetics with whom he had previously sought the religious light. There, in the Deer Park, he preached to them his first great sermon: The Four Noble Truths and The Eightfold Path. With this first sermon, Buddha "set in motion the Wheel of the Law"; i.e., he began the conquest of the world by the Kingdom of Dharma, the Doctrine. Buddha's doctrine offered a "middle way" between asceticism and worldly life, and at his death he left a band of yellow-robed *bhikkus* (literally, "beggars," but usually translated as "monks") to transmit it.

The main development in Buddhist doctrine took place around the second century A.D., when an entirely new kind of Buddhism, called Mahayana Buddhism, developed. The earlier Buddhism is called by its adherents "Theravada," or "The Teaching of the Elders"; and by Mahayana Buddhists, "Hinayana," or "The Lesser Vehicle" ("Mahayana" means "Greater Vehicle"). Theravada survives now in Ceylon, Burma, Thailand, Cambodia, and Laos, but everywhere else the Mahayana has prevailed.

The two main schools in Mahayana Buddhism are the Doctrine of the Middle Position and the Doctrine of Consciousness, or Way of Yoga.

The Middle Position school was founded by Nagarjuna (first to second centuries A.D.), whose doctrine is, basically, that only emptiness, or nothingness, exists. All the "reality" we see is illusion, as a nearsighted monk might imagine he saw flies in his begging bowl. One upshot of this view is that every rational theory about the world is a theory about unreality, worked out by an unreal mind with unreal thoughts. Nevertheless, adherents of this school believe that reality—emptiness—can be experienced, in meditation, with directness and certainty, and they believe that all beings are already Buddha, if they would only realize it. Nagarjuna's doctrine found ready acceptance in China and Japan, especially among those who understood the Taoist vision of things. Its relation to Chinese Ch'an and Japanese Zen Buddhism is obvious.

The other main Mahayana school, The Doctrine of Consciousness, or Way of Yoga, holds that salvation can be achieved by exhausting the store of consciousness, producer of illusions, until one becomes pure being itself. Yogic practices are an important means to this: the adept is taught to conjure up visions until finally he becomes convinced that all phenomena are totally subjective.

The most important work in the Mahayana canon is *The Lotus Sutra,* which purports to present all the major doctrines of Mahayana Buddhism. It has had an enormous popularity in China and Japan, and one Japanese sect—the Nichiren—takes *The Lotus Sutra* as its only canonic text.

THE SERMON AT DEER PARK

At the Deer Park, Buddha said
To the Five Monks: Two things
The wanderer should not do—
One, he should not choose desire or desire's end,
pleasure.

If he choose them, he will be degraded
And coarsened, he will move
Toward rebirth and squalor
To no purpose. Two, he should not choose
Hardship and pain, either.
If he choose them, he will find,
To no purpose, squalor and grief.
This is The Middle Way.

The Middle Way does not swerve to that side
Or this side.
It puts light in the mind,
Clears out the eyes, and sharpens the intelligence.
The Middle Way leads to peace,
Understanding, enlightenment,
And Nirvana.

What is
The Middle Way? It is the Eightfold Path:
Have right views,
Right intent,
Right speech,
Right actions,
Right trade or profession,
Right effort, right mindfulness,
And right *dhyana*.[1]
This is the Middle Way. . . .

[1] *Dhyana* is a word that simply does not translate. *Dhyana* has two aspects: the active aspect of concentration, and the passive aspect of realization, of rapture. Having come through the seventh fold of the Eightfold Path, the believer should sit quietly with his mind empty and tranquil, but attentive and concentrated, fixed on its pure essence. If vagrant thoughts force their way in, the believer should force them back out, patiently, and begin again. In this, gentle, deliberate, regular breathing plays an important part. The believer is advised to think of his breathing as a loop always moving in the same direction, then to forget breathing and think of the loop as moving more and more slowly, as becoming smaller and smaller, until it comes to rest at a point between the eyes. At first, the believer should perhaps hold some simple thought in his mind, count the outgoing breaths, repeat Buddha's name, or hold in the mind some koan puzzle that can only be solved intuitively. But he should not think *about* these things; he should keep the mind fixed on its pure essence. (This note on *dhyana* is condensed and adapted from Dwight Goddard, *A Buddhist Bible*, pp. 652–53.)

And this
Is the Truth on Sorrow:
To be born is sorrow, to age is sorrow,
To get sick is sorrow, to die is sorrow,
To meet the unpleasant is sorrow, to lose the
  pleasant is sorrow,
An unfulfilled wish is sorrow;
The five parts of identity are all sorrow.

And this
Is the Truth on Sorrow's
Beginning: sorrow begins from hankering,
Hankering brings rebirth, rebirth leads to delight
  and desire,
And the reborn chases pleasure now here now
  there—
Craves sex, craves life, craves power.

And this is the Truth
On stopping sorrow: stop the hankering
So that no passion remains—get away from it,
Be free of it, make it let go, leave it no room.

And by this Truth
You may find the way that leads
To the stopping of sorrow—
By the Eightfold Path:
Do right when you see, when you decide,
Talk, act, earn your living
    work, remember, and when you practice *dhyana*.

William McNaughton

MAJJHIMA-NIKAYA

Malunkyaputta was perplexed
    with metaphysical questions,
And so he asked the Buddha
    to untie his doubts.
"When you joined the community,"
    said Buddha, "I may have

Said to you,
'Malunkyaputta, come
And study with me.
I will teach you
Whether the world will last forever,
whether it is limited
Or illimitable, whether the life-force is identical
to the body, or distinct from it,
whether the Perfect One
survives after death, or not.' "
"No, my teacher," replied Malunkyaputta,
"You did not say these things to me."
Then the Buddha said,
"A man
Gets hit with a poisoned arrow.
His friends and relatives call in
A famous doctor.
Now suppose
The wounded man
started talking like this:
'Nobody can touch this wound
until I find out
who shot the arrow,
And whether he
was a noble or a brahman,
Or was a vaishaya or a shudra.'
Or suppose the wounded man
Said, 'Nobody can touch this wound
until I find out
What the man's name is who shot me,
what family he belongs to,
whether he is a short man or a tall man
or else a man
Of medium height,
and what kind of weapon
He used,
And what it looked like.'
Malunkyaputta, tell me—
What
would happen then?
The man would die of his wound.

. . . .

I don't talk about those 'big problems'
because the knowledge of those things
Won't take you down the road
of health, and none of them
Leads to illumination or to peace of mind.
What lead to illumination and peace of mind
are the things
I have taught you:
The Truths on sorrow,
on sorrow's beginning,
and on stopping sorrow.
So, Malunkyaputta,
what I have not made clear
Will never be clear,
but what I have
Made clear
Is truly clear."[1]

All things felt, conceived, known
Are aggregates, and not pure things,
You cannot cut them apart,
One part from another . . .
or demonstrate the difference by which
A thing seen or felt
is conceived,
or by which
a thing
conceived
is known.[2]

William McNaughton

SAMYUTTA-NIKAYA

All matter
is a bubble of foam,
all sensation a bubble
of water;
consciousness
is

[1] From *Majjhima-Nikaya* I, 426 ff.
[2] From *Majjhima-Nikaya* II, 293.

An illusion,
the human will is like
the trunk of a banana tree.[1]

William McNaughton

UDANA

And Buddha said:
"O monks, there is a place
Where no earth is, and no water, and no fire,
And no air, and no seeing,
nor this world,
nor a next,
Nor sun, nor moon.
I say,
O monks,
in it there is no going,
and no coming,
And no standing still,
no death,
no birth.
It is a thing
That does not hold
and does not
change,
And nothing keeps it up.
It is the end of suffering."[2]

William McNaughton

THE SURANGAMA SUTRA

The name means "The Buddha's Great Crown Sutra." It was composed in Sanskrit about A.D. 100 by an unknown writer and translated into Chinese about A.D. 717 by the master Paramartha.

[1] From *Samyutta-Nikaya* III, 140–142.
[2] From *Udana* VIII, 1.

. . . When the Lord Tathagata[1] had finished this supreme instruction, whose profound and comprehensive thoughts had been expressed in well-chosen words and beautiful style, Ananda and the whole assembly were enlightened, and they praised the Lord Buddha for his sacred teaching.

But Ananda was not yet satisfied. In reverential manner and spirit, he addressed the Lord Buddha, saying—Noble Lord! Though I have listened carefully to my Lord's noble and compassionate teaching about the exclusive unity and oneness of the pure, mysterious, and eternal Essence, I do not yet fully realize its meaning. It seems to teach that, as soon as the six sense organs have become emancipated from their contaminations and attachments, the remaining arbitrary conceptions of the thinking mind will fall away of themselves, leaving only the one intrinsic Essence, and that this process of emancipation will proceed in an orderly and spontaneous fashion. Pray, my Lord, have great forbearance with us less advanced disciples and, for the sake of all future disciples, repeat this instruction in more detail, so that it may purify our minds and the minds of all future disciples.

The Lord Tathagata arranged his garments and, taking a silk handkerchief, proceeded to tie a knot in it and showed it to the assembly, saying, What is this?

With one accord, they replied:—It is a silk handkerchief in which you have tied a knot.

The Lord Tathagata tied another knot in the handkerchief and said:—What is this?

They replied:—It is another knot, Blessed Lord.

Again the Lord tied other knots until there were six. Then, showing the handkerchief to the assembly and indicating the knots one by one, he asked, What is this? And what is This? And to each question Ananda and the other answered as before:—It is a knot.

Then the Lord Buddha said:—Ananda! When I showed you the first knot, you called it a knot, and when I showed you the second and the third and so on, you still insisted they were all knots.

Ananda replied:—Noble Lord! The handkerchief is made of silk threads of different colors and is woven into a

[1] Tathagata: one of the names of Buddha.

single piece, but when it is tied into a knot, it is right to call it a knot, also, and if the Lord were to tie it into a hundred knots, each one would be a knot. However, my Lord has only tied it six times—not seven or five—so there are only six knots. Why does my Lord seem to recognize only the first tying as a knot?

The Lord Buddha replied:—Ananda, you are right in saying that this beautiful handkerchief is one piece and that when I tied it six times there were six knots. Now look at it closely. The silk handkerchief is the same piece of woven silk, the tying has not changed it in the slightest, except in appearance—it is still a handkerchief. Now think, Ananda. When the handkerchief was tied the first time, the first knot appeared; and then later and successively, the second knot and the third to the sixth. If I now take this sixth knot and begin to count them backward, the sixth knot becomes the first, does it not?

Ananda replied:—No, my Lord, when the handkerchief was tied six times, the last tying was the sixth knot; it can by no means be called the first knot. No matter what you say, there is no possibility of confusing the order of the knots—it is and always will be the sixth knot.

The Lord Buddha agreed to this, saying:—So it is, Ananda. The six knots may not all be exactly alike, but when you seek the root of their different forms, they are all arrangements of the single handkerchief. You can not confuse the single handkerchief, you may confuse the knots, their differences and order, but you can not confuse the handkerchief because it is a single whole. The same is true of your six sense organs—they are knots tied in the essential unity of your mind and out of its unity there appears the variety.

The Lord Buddha continued:—Ananda, if you do not like to have knots tied in the handkerchief but prefer its original state, what would you do?

Ananda replied:—Noble Lord! As long as the knots exist in the handkerchief there will be the possibility of a discussion about them—which is first and which is second—but when the knots are all untied, there can be no further discussion about them because they will all have disappeared and only the beautiful handkerchief will remain in its original state of oneness.

The Lord Buddha was pleased with this reply and said:—

That is true, Ananda. The same is true about the relation of the six organs of sense to the Essential Mind. As the six sense organs become freed from their contaminations, the remaining arbitrary conceptions of the discriminating mind will disappear also. It is because your mind, having become diseased and bewildered because of the false sense-conceptions accumulated since beginningless time, has developed many desires, attachments and habits. . . .

Ananda! Let me ask you another question. This handkerchief has six knots tied in it. If I untie them can they all be untied at once?

No, my Lord. The knots were originally tied one by one in a certain order, so when we come to untie them we must follow the reverse order. For although the knots were made in one handkerchief, they were not made at one time and can not be untied at one time.

Again the Lord Buddha was pleased at the reply and said:—It is the same with the disentanglements of the conceptions of the six senses. The first knot of false conceptions that must be untied is the one relating to the false conception of an ego-personality; one must first of all attain a realization of its utter non-reality. When this realization of the unreality of one's own ego-personality is perfectly attained, it becomes enlightening, then the next knot to be untied is the one relating to personal attainments of any kind. This arbitrary conception must be untangled and its unreality fully realized.

Bhikshu Wai-tao and Dwight Goddard

Nagarjuna
(first to second centuries)

The Eightfold Negation

Do things get snuffed out? No. Do things get born? No. Do things remain the same? No. Do things change? No. Are things identical? No. Do things differ? No. Do things proceed? No. Do things recede? No.

The Four Points of Argumentation

Take anything whatever: it does not exist; it does not non-exist; it does not both exist and non-exist; and it does not neither exist nor non-exist.

Nagarjuna said,
"Everything is true,
and everything is false.
Everything is true and false
at the same time.
Everything is false and true at the same time.
This is what the Buddha teaches."[1]

William McNaughton

Author Unknown

THE LOTUS SUTRA

Chapter 3: A Parable

A man has an old house, said Buddha.
The house is large but shakes on its base,
The terraces are decaying, the columns rotting at the bottom.

The windows and balconies are broken,
The wall and its plaster and coverings flake or hang loose.

The coping is ripped and old, the thatch shot through with holes.
Five hundred creatures live in this house. The house has closets and rooms filled with excrement.
The rafters are rotted through,
The walls are crumbling to dust.

[1] See M. Bussagli, *Che Cosa Ha Veramente Detto Buddha* (Rome: Ubaldini, 1968), pp. 61–62.

Vultures by millions settle in,
Doves, owls, and other birds; poisonous snakes and constrictors
Coil in the corners, scorpions and mice
Scuttle across the floors.

Evil things of all kinds live in the house; sometimes you may meet
Inhuman things, and anyplace in the house
May lie piles of excrement and pools of urine.

The house teems with bugs, worms, and fireflies; dogs' and jackals' howls
Resound through the rooms. Hyenas are in the house
That eat human corpses, and the jackals and dogs run through,
Hungry, and looking for corpse-matter.

Those animals,
Weak from eternal hunger, go here and there for their prey;
Prey found, they snarl and snap over it. This is what the house is like.

There are horrible goblins in it, too, that rape or tear human corpses,
And many places crawl with centipedes, big snakes, and vipers.
These creatures creep into the corners and lay down their broods,
And often the goblins come and eat these broods.

. . . .

The house is like that, and the man owns it,
And when he is out, the house bursts into flame, and a mass of fire wraps the house.
The house's beams and rafters take fire, its columns and walls blaze up, devils and ghosts shriek in the flames.
Vultures by hundreds fly out, inhuman things run out with burned faces, blackened animals in hundreds pour out on every side, roaring and bellowing.
Devils flit, burning; burning, they bite and tear, and each spatters each with his blood.

Hyenas die in the fire, and dying eat each other; great
piles of excrement flame, a stench fills the air.
Centipedes try to get out, the monsters eat them; ghosts
float with burning hair,
They shriek with hunger and heat.

From outside the house the owner looks at this scene.
He hears his children playing inside, unaware of the fire
(and fools are like this in their ignorance),
And the owner steps in to save his children.

The children disregard his words and go on
with their play . . .
And the father thinks and says to his children, "There are
carts outside,
Yoked to them are deer, goats, bullocks, why don't you
go out
and play with them?"
And the children run out and reach the open air,
safe. . . .

The children say, "May we have the carts now?" And carts
made of
fine stuff, yoked with bullocks, having benches and rows
of bells,
Hung with umbrellas and flags and decorated with rare
stones
and pearls, embellished with gold and with wreaths,
and covered with cloth and with fine white muslin;
Carts holding silk mattresses and pillows, and rugs
embroidered with cranes and swans;
Carts drawn by strong, well-fed white bullocks—
Carts like these that man gives his children, and they run
laughing to play with them.

Sariputra, I the great Seer am like that man; I protect all
beings,
All creatures abstracted in the pleasures of the triple world,[1]

[1] The triple world: there are supposed to be three planes of existence in the cosmos—things that have desires, things that have material existence without desire, and things that have no material existence.

they are my children.
And this triple world is as evil and as dangerous as that
house.
It is wrapped in a mass of flames of birth, old age, and
disease. . . .

I told my children its evils to save them, and they paid no
attention.
So I tell them of the three vehicles,[1] and with this device
I show them how to avoid the evils of the triple world.
Those children that follow me; those that are strong in
the six faculties and three sciences; the Pratyeka-
Buddhas,
the infallible Bodhisattvas, and those others, my
children too,
With this story I show the Buddha vehicle. Take it, you will
all become Ginas.[2]

William McNaughton

Chapter 5: On Plants[3]

Then the Buddha said to Maha-Kasyapa
And the other old disciples:
"Suppose
in a three-thousand-
great-thousand-fold cosmos,
There are worlds
and mountains
and rivers and streams
and valleys and thickets and forests,
and everywhere
growing things spring up
tiny, various, large, manifold
each

[1] The three vehicles: those that have heard the Buddha's preaching and have become Buddhas, Pratyeka-Buddhas, and Bodhisattvas.
[2] Literally, "winners," *i.e.*, complete attainers of the way to Buddhahood.
[3] The translation is based on the Chinese version by Kumarajiva (fourth to fifth centuries A.D.).

sprouting, lengthening, greening
in its own way.
And suppose
a dense cloud spreads over
shading the three-thousand-great-thousand-fold
and pours down rain.
This rain
waters equally all things
nourishes the roots of all things
strengthens all things
every twig, every trunk, every flower
every fruit,
every curled leaf,
every strong branch.
From this one rain
all things become
according to the nature of their seed.
Know that Tathagata
spreads like this great cloud
over the numberless thousands
of *kotis*[1] of classes of living beings,
Extending the Law.

I am Tathagata, the all-wise,
The teacher, the Buddha,
The honored, the enlightened.
Those who are not saved
I will save,
Those who are not free
I will set free,
Those who are not comforted
I will comfort.
I know the world
and the worlds to come.

Hear the Law,
O gods
men
and asuras."[2]

Lenore Mayhew

[1] *Koti:* a very large number, sometimes said to be ten million.
[2] Asura: in the earliest Hindu scriptures, the Vedas, there are two kinds of nature gods—good ones called devas and bad ones called asuras.

THE BODHISATTVA'S RENUNCIATION

The excerpt below comes from *Instructions of Akshavamati* and *The Vairadhvaja Sutra,* as cited in Shantideva's *Compendium of Doctrine* (seventh century A.D.). The Bodhisattva's virtues are supposed to be generosity, moral conduct, patience, courage or energy, meditation, and wisdom. Sometimes another four virtues are identified: Skill in knowing the right means, determination, strength, and knowledge.

The bodhisattva is lonely, with no . . . companion, and he puts on the armor of supreme wisdom. He acts himself, and leaves nothing to others, working with a will steeled with courage and strength. He is strong in his own strength . . . and he resolves thus:

"Whatever all beings should obtain, I will help them to obtain. . . . The virtue of generosity is not my helper—I am the helper of generosity. Nor do the virtues of morality, patience, courage, meditation, and wisdom help me—it is I who support them. . . . I alone, standing in this round and adamantine world, must subdue Mara, with all his hosts and chariots, and develop supreme enlightenment with the wisdom of instantaneous insight!" . . .

Just as the rising sun, the child of the gods, is not stopped . . . by all the dust rising from the four continents of the earth . . . or by wreaths of smoke . . . or by rugged mountains, so the bodhisattva, the Great Being . . . is not deterred from bringing to fruition the root of good, whether by the malice of others . . . or by their sin or heresy, or by their agitation of mind. . . . He will not lay down his arms of enlightenment because of the corrupt generations of men, nor does he waver in his resolution to save the world because of their wretched quarrels. . . . He does not lose heart on account of their faults. . . .

"All creatures are in pain," he resolves, "all suffer from bad and hindering karma . . . so that they cannot see the Buddhas or hear the Law of Righteousness or know the Order. . . . All that mass of pain and evil karma I take in my own body. . . . I take upon myself the burden of sorrow; I resolve to do so; I endure it all. I do not turn back or run away, I do not tremble . . . I am not afraid . . .

nor do I despair. Assuredly I must bear the burdens of all beings . . . for I have resolved to save them all. I must set them all free; I must save the whole world from the forest of birth, old age, disease, and rebirth, from misfortune and sin, from the round of birth and death, from the toils of heresy. . . . For all beings are caught in the net of craving, encompassed by ignorance, held by the desire for existence; they are doomed to destruction, shut in a cage of pain . . . ; they are ignorant, untrustworthy, full of doubts, always at loggerheads one with another, always prone to see evil; they cannot find a refuge in the ocean of existence; they are all on the edge of the gulf of destruction.

"I work to establish the kingdom of perfect wisdom for all beings. I care not at all for my own deliverance. I must save all beings from the torrent of rebirth with the raft of my omniscient mind. I must pull them back from the great precipice. I must free them from all misfortune, ferry them over the stream of rebirth.

"For I have taken upon myself, by my own will, the whole of the pain of all things living. Thus I dare try every abode of pain, in . . . every part of the universe, for I must not defraud the world of the root of good. I resolve to dwell in each state of misfortune through countless ages . . . for the salvation of all beings . . . for it is better that I alone suffer than that all beings sink to the worlds of misfortune. There I shall give myself into bondage, to redeem all the world from the forest of purgatory, from rebirth as beasts, from the realm of death. I shall bear all grief and pain in my own body, for the good of all things living. I venture to stand surety for all beings, speaking the truth, trustworthy, not breaking my word. I shall not forsake them. . . . I must so bring to fruition the root of goodness that all beings find the utmost joy, unheard of joy, the joy of omniscience. I must be their charioteer, I must be their leader, I must be their torchbearer, I must be their guide to safety. . . . I must not wait for the help of another, nor must I lose my resolution and leave my tasks to another. I must not turn back in my efforts to save all beings nor cease to use my merit for the destruction of all pain. And I must not be satisfied with small successes."

From William Theodore de Bary *et al.*,
Sources of the Indian Tradition